# Table of Contents

Foreword. . . . . . . . . . ix

Preface. . . . . . . . . . xi

1. The Basics. . . . . . . . . . 1
 1.1 Lambda Expressions 2
 1.2 Method References 6
 1.3 Constructor References 10
 1.4 Functional Interfaces 15
 1.5 Default Methods in Interfaces 18
 1.6 Static Methods in Interfaces 21

2. The java.util.function Package. . . . . . . . . . 25
 2.1 Consumers 26
 2.2 Suppliers 28
 2.3 Predicates 31
 2.4 Functions 35

3. Streams. . . . . . . . . . 39
 3.1 Creating Streams 39
 3.2 Boxed Streams 43
 3.3 Reduction Operations Using Reduce 46
 3.4 Check Sorting Using Reduce 55
 3.5 Debugging Streams with peek 57
 3.6 Converting Strings to Streams and Back 60
 3.7 Counting Elements 63
 3.8 Summary Statistics 65
 3.9 Finding the First Element in a Stream 68

3.10 Using anyMatch, allMatch, and noneMatch 73
3.11 Stream flatMap Versus map 75
3.12 Concatenating Streams 79
3.13 Lazy Streams 83

**4. Comparators and Collectors....... 87**
4.1 Sorting Using a Comparator 87
4.2 Converting a Stream into a Collection 91
4.3 Adding a Linear Collection to a Map 94
4.4 Sorting Maps 97
4.5 Partitioning and Grouping 100
4.6 Downstream Collectors 102
4.7 Finding Max and Min Values 104
4.8 Creating Immutable Collections 107
4.9 Implementing the Collector Interface 109

**5. Issues with Streams, Lambdas, and Method References....... 115**
5.1 The java.util.Objects Class 115
5.2 Lambdas and Effectively Final 117
5.3 Streams of Random Numbers 120
5.4 Default Methods in Map 122
5.5 Default Method Conflict 127
5.6 Iterating Over Collections and Maps 130
5.7 Logging with a Supplier 132
5.8 Closure Composition 134
5.9 Using an Extracted Method for Exception Handling 138
5.10 Checked Exceptions and Lambdas 141
5.11 Using a Generic Exception Wrapper 144

**6. The Optional Type....... 147**
6.1 Creating an Optional 148
6.2 Retrieving Values from an Optional 150
6.3 Optional in Getters and Setters 154
6.4 Optional flatMap Versus map 156
6.5 Mapping Optionals 160

**7. File I/O....... 165**
7.1 Process Files 166
7.2 Retrieving Files as a Stream 169
7.3 Walking the Filesystem 170
7.4 Searching the Filesystem 172

PHAC 10/17

# Modern Java Recipes

*Simple Solutions to Difficult Problems in Java 8 and 9*

*Ken Kousen*

Beijing • Boston • Farnham • Sebastopol • Tokyo

**Modern Java Recipes**
by Ken Kousen



Printed in the United States of America.

Published by O'Reilly Media, Inc., 1005 Gravenstein Highway North, Sebastopol, CA 95472.

O'Reilly books may be purchased for educational, business, or sales promotional use. Online editions are also available for most titles (*http://oreilly.com/safari*). For more information, contact our corporate/institutional sales department: 800-998-9938 or *corporate@oreilly.com*.

**Editors:** Brian Foster and Jeff Bleiel
**Production Editor:** Justin Billing
**Copyeditor:** Kim Cofer
**Proofreader:** Jasmine Kwityn
**Indexer:** Ellen Troutman-Zaig
**Interior Designer:** David Futato
**Cover Designer:** Karen Montgomery
**Illustrator:** Rebecca Demarest

August 2017: First Edition

**Revision History for the First Edition**
2017-08-04: First Release

See *http://oreilly.com/catalog/errata.csp?isbn=9781491973172* for release details.



978-1-491-97317-2

[LSI]

*Hey Xander, this one's yours. Surprise!*

**8. The java.time Package. . . . . . . . . . 175**
8.1 Using the Basic Date-Time Classes 176
8.2 Creating Dates and Times from Existing Instances 180
8.3 Adjusters and Queries 185
8.4 Convert from java.util.Date to java.time.LocalDate 190
8.5 Parsing and Formatting 194
8.6 Finding Time Zones with Unusual Offsets 197
8.7 Finding Region Names from Offsets 200
8.8 Time Between Events 202

**9. Parallelism and Concurrency. . . . . . . . . . 205**
9.1 Converting from Sequential to Parallel Streams 206
9.2 When Parallel Helps 209
9.3 Changing the Pool Size 215
9.4 The Future Interface 217
9.5 Completing a CompletableFuture 220
9.6 Coordinating CompletableFutures, Part 1 225
9.7 Coordinating CompletableFutures, Part 2 231

**10. Java 9 Additions. . . . . . . . . . 239**
10.1 Modules in Jigsaw 240
10.2 Private Methods in Interfaces 245
10.3 Creating Immutable Collections 247
10.4 Stream: ofNullable, iterate, takeWhile, and dropWhile 252
10.5 Downstream Collectors: filtering and flatMapping 255
10.6 Optional: stream, or, ifPresentOrElse 259
10.7 Date Ranges 262

**A. Generics and Java 8. . . . . . . . . . 267**

**Index. . . . . . . . . . 287**

# Foreword

There's no doubt that the new features in Java 8, particularly lambda expressions and the Streams API, are a huge step forward for the Java language. I've been using Java 8 and telling developers about the new features at conferences, in workshops, and via blog posts for a several years now. What's clear to me is that although lambdas and streams bring a more functional style of programming to Java (and also allow us to seamlessly make use of parallel processing power), it's not these attributes that make them so appealing to developers once they start using them—it's how much easier it is to solve certain types of problems using these idioms, and how much more productive they make us.

My passion as a developer, presenter, and writer is not just to make other developers aware of the evolution of the Java language, but to show how this evolution helps make our lives as developers easier—how we have options for simpler solutions to problems, or even solve different types of problems. What I love about Ken's work is that he focuses on exactly this—helping you learn something new without having to wade through details you already know or don't need, focusing on the parts of a technology that are valuable to real world developers.

I first came across Ken's work when he presented "Making Java Groovy" at JavaOne. At the time, the team I was working on was struggling with writing readable and useful tests, and one of the solutions we were contemplating was Groovy. As a long-time Java programmer, I was reluctant to learn a whole new language just to write tests, especially when I thought I knew how to write tests. But seeing Ken talk about Groovy for Java programmers taught me a lot of what I needed to know without repeating things I already understood. It made me realise that with the right learning material I didn't need to wade through all the details of a language just to learn the bits I cared about. I bought his book immediately.

This new book on Modern Java Recipes follows a similar theme—as experienced developers, we don't need to learn everything about all the new features in Java 8 and 9 as if we're new to the language, nor do we have the time to do that. What we need is a guide that quickly makes the relevant features available to us, that gives us real examples that apply to our jobs. This book is that guide. By presenting recipes based on the sorts of problems we encounter daily, and showing how to solve those using new features in Java 8 and 9, we become familiar with the updates to the language in a way that's much more natural for us. We can evolve our skills.

Even those who've been using Java 8 and 9 can learn something. The section on Reduction Operators really helped me understand this functional-style programming without having to reprogram my brain. The Java 9 features that are covered are exactly the ones that are useful to us as developers, and they are not (yet) well known. This is an excellent way to get up to speed on the newest version of Java in a quick and effective fashion. There's something in this book for every Java developer who wants to level up their knowledge.

*—Trisha Gee*
*Java Champion &*
*Java Developer Advocate for JetBrains*
*July 2017*

# Preface

## Modern Java

Sometimes it's hard to believe that a language with literally 20 years of backward compatibility could change so drastically. Prior to the release of Java SE 8 in March of 2014,[1] for all of its success as the definitive server-side programming language, Java had acquired the reputation of being "the COBOL of the 21st century." It was stable, pervasive, and solidly focused on performance. Changes came slowly when they came at all, and companies felt little urgency to upgrade when new versions became available.

That all changed when Java SE 8 was released. Java SE 8 included "Project Lambda," the major innovation that introduced functional programming concepts into what was arguably the world's leading object-oriented language. Lambda expressions, method references, and streams fundamentally changed the idioms of the language, and developers have been trying to catch up ever since.

The attitude of this book is not to judge whether the changes are good or bad or could have been done differently. The goal here is to say, "this is what we have, and this is how you use it to get your job done." That's why this book is designed as a recipes book. It's all about what you need to do, and how the new features in Java help you do it.

That said, there are a lot of advantages to the new programming model, once you get used to them. Functional code tends to be simpler and easier to both write and understand. The functional approach favors immutability, which makes writing concurrent code cleaner and more likely to be successful. Back when Java was created, you could still rely on Moore's law to double your processor speed roughly every 18

1 Yes, it's actually been over three years since the first release of Java SE 8. I can't believe it either.

months. These days performance improvements come from the fact that even most phones have multiple processors.

Since Java has always been sensitive to backward compatibility, many companies and developers have moved to Java SE 8 without adopting the new idioms. The platform is more powerful even so, and is worth using, not to mention the fact that Oracle formally declared Java 7 end-of-life in April 2015.

It has taken a couple of years, but most Java developers are now working with the Java 8 JDK, and it's time to dig in and understand what that means and what consequences it has for your future development. This book is designed to make that process easier.

## Who Should Read This Book

The recipes in this book assume that the typical reader already is comfortable with Java versions prior to Java SE 8. You don't need to be an expert, and some older concepts are reviewed, but the book is not intended to be a beginner's guide to Java or object-oriented programming. If you have used Java on a project before and you are familiar with the standard library, you'll be fine.

This book covers almost all of Java SE 8, and includes one chapter focused on the new changes coming in Java 9. If you need to understand how the new functional idioms added to the language will change the way you write code, this book is a use-case-driven way of accomplishing that goal.

Java is pervasive on the server side, with a rich support system of open source libraries and tools. The Spring Framework and Hibernate are two of the most popular open source frameworks, and both either require Java 8 as a minimum or will very soon. If you plan to operate in this ecosystem, this book is for you.

## How This Book Is Organized

This book is organized into recipes, but it's difficult to discuss recipes containing lambda expressions, method references, and streams individually without referring to the others. In fact, the first six chapters discuss related concepts, though you don't have to read them in any particular order.

The chapters are organized as follows:

- Chapter 1, *The Basics*, covers the basics of *lambda expressions* and *method references*, and follows with the new features of interfaces: *default methods* and *static methods*. It also defines the term "functional interface" and explains how it is key to understanding lambda expressions.
- Chapter 2, *The java.util.function Package*, presents the new `java.util.function` package, which was added to the language in Java 8. The interfaces in that pack-

age fall into four special categories (consumers, suppliers, predicates, and functions) that are used throughout the rest of the standard library.

- Chapter 3, *Streams*, adds in the concept of *streams*, and how they represent an abstraction that allows you to transform and filter data rather than process it iteratively. The concepts of "map," "filter," and "reduce" relate to streams, as shown in the recipes in this chapter. They ultimately lead to the ideas of parallelism and concurrency covered in Chapter 9.
- Chapter 4, *Comparators and Collectors*, involves the sorting of streaming data, and converting it back into collections. Partitioning and grouping is also part of this chapter, which turns what are normally considered database operations into easy library calls.
- Chapter 5, *Issues with Streams, Lambdas, and Method References*, is a miscellaneous chapter; the idea being that now that you know how to use lambdas, method references, and streams, you can look at ways they can be combined to solve interesting problems. The concepts of laziness, deferred execution, and closure composition are also covered, as is the annoying topic of exception handling.
- Chapter 6, *The Optional Type*, discusses one of the more controversial additions to the language—the `Optional` type. Recipes in this chapter describe how the new type is intended to be used and how you can both create instances and extract values from them. This chapter also revisits the functional idea of map and flat-map operations on `Optional`s, and how they differ from the same operations on streams.
- Chapter 7, *File I/O*, switches to the practical topic of input/output streams (as opposed to functional streams), and the additions made to the standard library to incorporate the new functional concepts when dealing with files and directories.
- Chapter 8, *The java.time Package*, shows the basics of the new Date-Time API, and how (at long last) they replace the legacy `Date` and `Calendar` classes. The new API is based on the Joda-Time library, which is backed by many developer-years of experience and use and has been rewritten to form the `java.time` package. Frankly, if this had been the only addition to Java 8, it would have been worth the upgrade.
- Chapter 9, *Parallelism and Concurrency*, addresses one of the implicit promises of the stream model: that you can change a sequential stream to a parallel one with a single method call, and thereby take advantage of all the processors available on your machine. Concurrency is a big topic, but this chapter presents the additions to the Java library that make it easy to experiment with and assess when the costs and benefits are worth the effort.
- Chapter 10, *Java 9 Additions*, covers many of the changes coming in Java 9, which is currently scheduled to be released September 21, 2017. The details of Jigsaw

can fill an entire book by themselves, but the basics are clear and are described in this chapter. Other recipes cover private methods in interfaces, the new methods added to streams, collectors, and `Optional`, and how to create a stream of dates.[2]

- Appendix A, *Generics and Java 8*, is about the generics capabilities in Java. While generics as a technology was added back in 1.5, most developers only learned the minimum they needed to know to make them work. One glance at the Javadocs for Java 8 and 9 shows that those days are over. The goal of the appendix is to show you how to read and interpret the API so you understand the much more complex method signatures involved.

The chapters, and indeed the recipes themselves, do not have to be read in any particular order. They do complement each other and each recipe ends with references to others, but you can start reading anywhere. The chapter groupings are provided as a way to put similar recipes together, but it is expected that you will jump from one to another to solve whatever problem you may have at the moment.

## Conventions Used in This Book

The following typographical conventions are used in this book:

*Italic*
: Indicates new terms, URLs, email addresses, filenames, and file extensions.

`Constant width`
: Used for program listings, as well as within paragraphs to refer to program elements such as variable or function names, databases, data types, environment variables, statements, and keywords.

**`Constant width bold`**
: Shows commands or other text that should be typed literally by the user.

*`Constant width italic`*
: Shows text that should be replaced with user-supplied values or by values determined by context.

This element signifies a tip or suggestion.

2 Yes, I too wish that the Java 9 chapter had been Chapter 9, but it didn't seem right to reorder the chapters just for that accidental symmetry. This footnote will have to suffice.

This element signifies a general note.

This element indicates a warning or caution.

## Using Code Examples

The source code for the book is located in three GitHub repositories: one for the Java 8 recipes (everything but Chapter 10) at *https://github.com/kousen/java_8_recipes*, one for the Java 9 recipes at *https://github.com/kousen/java_9_recipes*, and a special one for the larger `CompletableFuture` example in Recipe 9.7 at *https://github.com/kousen/cfboxscores*. All are configured as Gradle projects with tests and a build file.

This book is here to help you get your job done. In general, if example code is offered with this book, you may use it in your programs and documentation. You do not need to contact us for permission unless you're reproducing a significant portion of the code. For example, writing a program that uses several chunks of code from this book does not require permission. Selling or distributing a CD-ROM of examples from O'Reilly books does require permission. Answering a question by citing this book and quoting example code does not require permission. Incorporating a significant amount of example code from this book into your product's documentation does require permission.

We appreciate, but do not require, attribution. An attribution usually includes the title, author, publisher, and ISBN. For example: "*Modern Java Recipes* by Ken Kousen (O'Reilly). Copyright 2017 Ken Kousen, 978-0-491-97317-2."

If you feel your use of code examples falls outside fair use or the permission given above, feel free to contact us at *permissions@oreilly.com*.

## O'Reilly Safari

*Safari* (formerly Safari Books Online) is a membership-based training and reference platform for enterprise, government, educators, and individuals.

Members have access to thousands of books, training videos, Learning Paths, interactive tutorials, and curated playlists from over 250 publishers, including O'Reilly

Media, Harvard Business Review, Prentice Hall Professional, Addison-Wesley Professional, Microsoft Press, Sams, Que, Peachpit Press, Adobe, Focal Press, Cisco Press, John Wiley & Sons, Syngress, Morgan Kaufmann, IBM Redbooks, Packt, Adobe Press, FT Press, Apress, Manning, New Riders, McGraw-Hill, Jones & Bartlett, and Course Technology, among others.

For more information, please visit *http://oreilly.com/safari*.

## How to Contact Us

Please address comments and questions concerning this book to the publisher:

O'Reilly Media, Inc.
1005 Gravenstein Highway North
Sebastopol, CA 95472
800-998-9938 (in the United States or Canada)
707-829-0515 (international or local)
707-829-0104 (fax)

To comment or ask technical questions about this book, send email to *bookquestions@oreilly.com*.

For more information about our books, courses, conferences, and news, see our website at *http://www.oreilly.com*.

Find us on Facebook: *http://facebook.com/oreilly*

Follow us on Twitter: *http://twitter.com/oreillymedia*

Watch us on YouTube: *http://www.youtube.com/oreillymedia*

## Acknowledgments

This book is the unexpected result of a conversation I had with Jay Zimmerman back in late July 2015. I was (and still am) a member of the No Fluff, Just Stuff (*http://nofluffjuststuff.com*) conference tour, and that year several Java 8 talks were being given by Venkat Subramaniam. Jay told me that Venkat had decided to scale back his activity in the coming year and Jay was wondering whether I would be willing to do similar talks in the new season starting in early 2016. I had been coding in Java since the mid-'90s (I started with Java 1.0.6) and had been planning to learn the new APIs anyway, so I agreed.

I have now been giving presentations on the new functional features of Java for a couple of years. By the Fall of 2016 I had completed my last book,[3] and since the idea was to write another recipes book for the same publisher I foolishly thought the project would be easy.

Noted science fiction author Neil Gaiman famously once said that after finishing *American Gods* he thought he knew how to write a novel. His friend corrected him, saying he now knew how to write *this* novel. I now understand what he meant. The original proposal for this book anticipated about 25 to 30 recipes spanning about 150 pages. The final result you hold in your hand has more than 70 recipes filling nearly 300 pages, but the larger scope and greater detail has produced a much more valuable book than I intended.

Of course, that's because I had lots of help. The aforementioned Venkat Subramaniam has been extremely helpful, both through his talks, his other books, and private discussions. He also was kind enough to be a technical reviewer on this book, so any remaining errors are all his fault. (No, they're mine, but please don't tell him I admitted that.)

I also am very grateful to have had the frequent assistance of Tim Yates, who is one of the best coders I've ever met. I knew him from his work in the Groovy community, but his versatility goes well beyond that, as his Stack Overflow rating will show. Rod Hilton, who I met while giving Java 8 presentations on the NFJS tour, was also kind enough to offer a review. Both of their recommendations have been invaluable.

I have been fortunate enough to work with the excellent editors and staff at O'Reilly Media over the course of two books, over a dozen video courses, and many online training classes delivered on their Safari online platform. Brian Foster has been a constant source of support, not to mention his almost magical ability to cut through bureaucracy. I met him while writing my previous book, and though he wasn't the editor of this one, his help and friendship have been very valuable to me throughout the process.

My editor, Jeff Bleiel, was very understanding as the book doubled in length, and provided the structure and organization needed to keep making progress. I'm very glad we got to work together and hope we will continue to do so in the future.

I need to acknowledge many of my fellow speakers on the NFJS tour, including Nate Schutta, Michael Carducci, Matt Stine, Brian Sletten, Mark Richards, Pratik Patel, Neal Ford, Craig Walls, Raju Gandhi, Kirk Knoernschild, Dan "the Man" Hinojosa, and Janelle Klein for their constant perspective and encouragement. Both writing books and teaching training classes (my actual day job) are solitary pursuits. It's great

[3] *Gradle Recipes for Android*, also from O'Reilly Media, all about the Gradle build tool as it is applied to Android projects.

having a community of friends and colleagues that I can rely on for perspective, advice, and various forms of entertainment.

Finally, I need to express all my love to my wife Ginger and my son Xander. Without the support and kindness of my family I would not be the person I am today, a fact that grows more obvious to me with each passing year. I can never express what you both mean to me.

# CHAPTER 1
# The Basics

The biggest change in Java 8 is the addition of concepts from functional programming to the language. Specifically, the language added lambda expressions, method references, and streams.

If you haven't used the new functional features yet, you'll probably be surprised by how different your code will look from previous Java versions. The changes in Java 8 represent the biggest changes to the language ever. In many ways, it feels like you're learning a completely new language.

The question then becomes: Why do this? Why make such drastic changes to a language that's already twenty years old and plans to maintain backward compatibility? Why make such dramatic revisions to a language that has been, by all accounts, extremely successful? Why switch to a functional paradigm after all these years of being one of the most successful object-oriented languages ever?

The answer is that the software development world has changed, so languages that want to be successful in the future need to adapt as well. Back in the mid-'90s, when Java was shiny and new, Moore's law[1] was still fully in force. All you had to do was wait a couple of years and your computer would double in speed.

Today's hardware no longer relies on increasing chip density for speed. Instead, even most phones have multiple cores, which means software needs to be written expecting to be run in a multiprocessor environment. Functional programming, with its emphasis on "pure" functions (that return the same result given the same inputs, with no side effects) and immutability simplifies programming in parallel environments. If

1 Coined by Gordon Moore, one of the co-founders of Fairchild Semiconductor and Intel, based on the observation that the number of transistors that could be packed into an integrated circuit doubled roughly every 18 months. See Wikipedia's Moore's law entry (*https://en.wikipedia.org/wiki/Moore%27s_law*) for details.

you don't have any shared, mutable state, and your program can be decomposed into collections of simple functions, it is easier to understand and predict its behavior.

This, however, is not a book about Haskell, or Erlang, or Frege, or any of the other functional programming languages. This book is about Java, and the changes made to the language to add functional concepts to what is still fundamentally an object-oriented language.

Java now supports lambda expressions, which are essentially methods treated as though they were first-class objects. The language also has method references, which allow you to use an existing method wherever a lambda expression is expected. In order to take advantage of lambda expressions and method references, the language also added a stream model, which produces elements and passes them through a pipeline of transformations and filters without modifying the original source.

The recipes in this chapter describe the basic syntax for lambda expressions, method references, and functional interfaces, as well the new support for static and default methods in interfaces. Streams are discussed in detail in Chapter 3.

# 1.1 Lambda Expressions

## Problem

You want to use lambda expressions in your code.

## Solution

Use one of the varieties of lambda expression syntax and assign the result to a reference of functional interface type.

## Discussion

A *functional interface* is an interface with a single abstract method (SAM). A class implements any interface by providing implementations for all the methods in it. This can be done with a top-level class, an inner class, or even an anonymous inner class.

For example, consider the `Runnable` interface, which has been in Java since version 1.0. It contains a single abstract method called `run`, which takes no arguments and returns `void`. The `Thread` class constructor takes a `Runnable` as an argument, so an anonymous inner class implementation is shown in Example 1-1.

*Example 1-1. Anonymous inner class implementation of Runnable*

```
public class RunnableDemo {
    public static void main(String[] args) {
```

```
        new Thread(new Runnable() { ❶
            @Override
            public void run() {
                System.out.println(
                    "inside runnable using an anonymous inner class");
            }
        }).start();
    }
}
```

❶ Anonymous inner class

The anonymous inner class syntax consists of the word `new` followed by the `Runnable` interface name and parentheses, implying that you're defining a class without an explicit name that implements that interface. The code in the braces (`{}`) then overrides the `run` method, which simply prints a string to the console.

The code in Example 1-2 shows the same example using a lambda expression.

*Example 1-2. Using a lambda expression in a Thread constructor*

```
new Thread(() -> System.out.println(
    "inside Thread constructor using lambda")).start();
```

The syntax uses an arrow to separate the arguments (since there are zero arguments here, only a pair of empty parentheses is used) from the body. In this case, the body consists of a single line, so no braces are required. This is known as an expression lambda. Whatever value the expression evaluates to is returned automatically. In this case, since `println` returns `void`, the return from the expression is also `void`, which matches the return type of the `run` method.

A lambda expression must match the argument types and return type in the signature of the single abstract method in the interface. This is called being *compatible* with the method signature. The lambda expression is thus the implementation of the interface method, and can also be assigned to a reference of that interface type.

As a demonstration, Example 1-3 shows the lambda assigned to a variable.

*Example 1-3. Assigning a lambda expression to a variable*

```
Runnable r = () -> System.out.println(
    "lambda expression implementing the run method");
new Thread(r).start();
```

There is no class in the Java library called `Lambda`. Lambda expressions can only be assigned to functional interface references.

Assigning a lambda to the functional interface is the same as saying the lambda is the implementation of the single abstract method inside it. You can think of the lambda as the body of an anonymous inner class that implements the interface. That is why the lambda must be compatible with the abstract method; its argument types and return type must match the signature of that method. Notably, however, the name of the method being implemented is not important. It does not appear anywhere as part of the lambda expression syntax.

This example was especially simple because the `run` method takes no arguments and returns `void`. Consider instead the functional interface `java.io.FilenameFilter`, which again has been part of the Java standard library since version 1.0. Instances of `FilenameFilter` are used as arguments to the `File.list` method to restrict the returned files to only those that satisfy the method.

From the Javadocs, the `FilenameFilter` class contains the single abstract method `accept`, with the following signature:

```
boolean accept(File dir, String name)
```

The `File` argument is the directory in which the file is found, and the `String` name is the name of the file.

The code in Example 1-4 implements `FilenameFilter` using an anonymous inner class to return only Java source files.

*Example 1-4. An anonymous inner class implementation of FilenameFilter*

```
File directory = new File("./src/main/java");

String[] names = directory.list(new FilenameFilter() {  ❶
    @Override
    public boolean accept(File dir, String name) {
        return name.endsWith(".java");
    }
});
System.out.println(Arrays.asList(names));
```

❶ Anonymous inner class

In this case, the `accept` method returns true if the filename ends with *.java* and false otherwise.

The lambda expression version is shown in Example 1-5.

*Example 1-5. Lambda expression implementing FilenameFilter*

```
File directory = new File("./src/main/java");

String[] names = directory.list((dir, name) -> name.endsWith(".java")); ❶
    System.out.println(Arrays.asList(names));
}
```

❶ Lambda expression

The resulting code is much simpler. This time the arguments are contained within parentheses, but do not have types declared. At compile time, the compiler knows that the `list` method takes an argument of type `FilenameFilter`, and therefore knows the signature of its single abstract method (`accept`). It therefore knows that the arguments to `accept` are a `File` and a `String`, so that the compatible lambda expression arguments must match those types. The return type on `accept` is a boolean, so the expression to the right of the arrow must also return a boolean.

If you wish to specify the data types in the code, you are free to do so, as in Example 1-6.

*Example 1-6. Lambda expression with explicit data types*

```
File directory = new File("./src/main/java");

String[] names = directory.list((File dir, String name) -> ❶
    name.endsWith(".java"));
```

❶ Explicit data types

Finally, if the implementation of the lambda requires more than one line, you need to use braces and an explicit return statement, as shown in Example 1-7.

*Example 1-7. A block lambda*

```
File directory = new File("./src/main/java");

String[] names = directory.list((File dir, String name) -> {  ❶
    return name.endsWith(".java");
});
System.out.println(Arrays.asList(names));
```

❶ Block syntax

This is known as a block lambda. In this case the body still consists of a single line, but the braces now allow for multiple statements. The `return` keyword is now required.

Lambda expressions never exist alone. There is always a *context* for the expression, which indicates the functional interface to which the expression is assigned. A lambda can be an argument to a method, a return type from a method, or assigned to a reference. In each case, the type of the assignment must be a functional interface.

# 1.2 Method References

## Problem

You want to use a method reference to access an existing method and treat it like a lambda expression.

## Solution

*Use the double-colon notation to separate an instance reference or class name from the method.(((”*
(double colon) notation in method references”)))

## Discussion

If a lambda expression is essentially treating a method as though it was a object, then a method reference treats an existing method as though it was a lambda.

For example, the `forEach` method in `Iterable` takes a `Consumer` as an argument. Example 1-8 shows that the `Consumer` can be implemented as either a lambda expression or as a method reference.

*Example 1-8. Using a method reference to access println*

```
Stream.of(3, 1, 4, 1, 5, 9)
        .forEach(x -> System.out.println(x));       ❶

Stream.of(3, 1, 4, 1, 5, 9)
        .forEach(System.out::println);              ❷

Consumer<Integer> printer = System.out::println;    ❸
Stream.of(3, 1, 4, 1, 5, 9)
        .forEach(printer);
```

❶ Using a lambda expression

❷ Using a method reference

❸ Assigning the method reference to a functional interface

The double-colon notation provides the reference to the `println` method on the `System.out` instance, which is a reference of type `PrintStream`. No parentheses are placed at the end of the method reference. In the example shown, each element of the stream is printed to standard output.[2]

If you write a lambda expression that consists of one line that invokes a method, consider using the equivalent method reference instead.

The method reference provides a couple of (minor) advantages over the lambda syntax. First, it tends to be shorter, and second, it often includes the name of the class containing the method. Both make the code easier to read.

Method references can be used with static methods as well, as shown in Example 1-9.

*Example 1-9. Using a method reference to a static method*

```
Stream.generate(Math::random)          ❶
        .limit(10)
        .forEach(System.out::println); ❷
```

❶ Static method

❷ Instance method

The `generate` method on `Stream` takes a `Supplier` as an argument, which is a functional interface whose single abstract method takes no arguments and produces a single result. The `random` method in the `Math` class is compatible with that signature, because it also takes no arguments and produces a single, uniformly distributed, pseudorandom double between 0 and 1. The method reference `Math::random` refers to that method as the implementation of the `Supplier` interface.

Since `Stream.generate` produces an infinite stream, the `limit` method is used to ensure only 10 values are produced, which are then printed to standard output using the `System.out::println` method reference as an implementation of `Consumer`.

2 It is difficult to discuss lambdas or method references without discussing streams, which have their own chapter later. Suffice it to say that a stream produces a series of elements sequentially, does not store them anywhere, and does not modify the original source.

## Syntax

There are three forms of the method reference syntax, and one is a bit misleading:

`object::instanceMethod`
: Refer to an instance method using a reference to the supplied object, as in `System.out::println`

`Class::staticMethod`
: Refer to static method, as in `Math::max`

`Class::instanceMethod`
: Invoke the instance method on a reference to an object supplied by the context, as in `String::length`

That last example is the confusing one, because as Java developers we're accustomed to seeing only static methods invoked via a class name. Remember that lambda expressions and method references never exist in a vacuum—there's always a context. In the case of an object reference, the context will supply the argument(s) to the method. In the printing case, the equivalent lambda expression is (as shown in context in Example 1-8):

```
// equivalent to System.out::println
x -> System.out.println(x)
```

The context provides the value of `x`, which is used as the method argument.

The situation is similar for the static `max` method:

```
// equivalent to Math::max
(x,y) -> Math.max(x,y)
```

Now the context needs to supply two arguments, and the lambda returns the greater one.

The "instance method through the class name" syntax is interpreted differently. The equivalent lambda is:

```
// equivalent to String::length
x -> x.length()
```

This time, when the context provides `x`, it is used as the target of the method, rather than as an argument.

If you refer to a method that takes multiple arguments via the class name, the first element supplied by the context becomes the target and the remaining elements are arguments to the method.

Example 1-10 shows the sample code.

*Example 1-10. Invoking a multiple-argument instance method from a class reference*

```
List<String> strings =
    Arrays.asList("this", "is", "a", "list", "of", "strings");
List<String> sorted = strings.stream()
        .sorted((s1, s2) -> s1.compareTo(s2))  ❶
        .collect(Collectors.toList());

List<String> sorted = strings.stream()
        .sorted(String::compareTo)             ❶
        .collect(Collectors.toList());
```

❶ Method reference and equivalent lambda

The `sorted` method on `Stream` takes a `Comparator<T>` as an argument, whose single abstract method is `int compare(String other)`. The `sorted` method supplies each pair of strings to the comparator and sorts them based on the sign of the returned integer. In this case, the context is a pair of strings. The method reference syntax, using the class name `String`, invokes the `compareTo` method on the first element (`s1` in the lambda expression) and uses the second element `s2` as the argument to the method.

In stream processing, you frequently access an instance method using the class name in a method reference if you are processing a series of inputs. The code in Example 1-11 shows the invocation of the `length` method on each individual `String` in the stream.

*Example 1-11. Invoking the length method on String using a method reference*

```
Stream.of("this", "is", "a", "stream", "of", "strings")
        .map(String::length)              ❶
        .forEach(System.out::println);    ❷
```

❶ Instance method via class name

❷ Instance method via object reference

This example transforms each string into an integer by invoking the `length` method, then prints each result.

A method reference is essentially an abbreviated syntax for a lambda. Lambda expressions are more general, in that each method reference has an equivalent lambda expression but not vice versa. The equivalent lambdas for the method references from Example 1-11 are shown in Example 1-12.

*Example 1-12. Lambda expression equivalents for method references*

```
Stream.of("this", "is", "a", "stream", "of", "strings")
        .map(s -> s.length())
        .forEach(x -> System.out.println(x));
```

As with any lambda expression, the context matters. You can also use `this` or `super` as the left side of a method reference if there is any ambiguity.

## See Also

You can also invoke constructors using the method reference syntax. Constructor references are shown in Recipe 1.3. The package of functional interfaces, including the `Supplier` interface discussed in this recipe, is covered in Chapter 2.

# 1.3 Constructor References

## Problem

You want to instantiate an object using a method reference as part of a stream pipeline.

## Solution

Use the `new` keyword as part of a method reference.

## Discussion

When people talk about the new syntax added to Java 8, they mention lambda expressions, method references, and streams. For example, say you had a list of people and you wanted to convert it to a list of names. One way to do so would be the snippet shown in Example 1-13.

*Example 1-13. Converting a list of people to a list of names*

```
List<String> names = people.stream()
    .map(person -> person.getName()) ❶
    .collect(Collectors.toList());

// or, alternatively,

List<String> names = people.stream()
    .map(Person::getName)            ❷
    .collect(Collectors.toList());
```

❶ Lambda expression

❷ Method reference

What if you want to go the other way? What if you have a list of strings and you want to create a list of `Person` references from it? In that case you can use a method reference, but this time using the keyword `new`. That syntax is called a *constructor reference*.

To show how it is used, start with a `Person` class, which is just about the simplest Plain Old Java Object (POJO) imaginable. All it does is wrap a simple string attribute called `name` in Example 1-14.

*Example 1-14. A Person class*

```
public class Person {
    private String name;

    public Person() {}

    public Person(String name) {
        this.name = name;
    }

    // getters and setters ...

    // equals, hashCode, and toString methods ...
}
```

Given a collection of strings, you can map each one into a `Person` using either a lambda expression or the constructor reference in Example 1-15.

*Example 1-15. Transforming strings into Person instances*

```
List<String> names =
    Arrays.asList("Grace Hopper", "Barbara Liskov", "Ada Lovelace",
        "Karen Spärck Jones");

List<Person> people = names.stream()
    .map(name -> new Person(name)) ❶
    .collect(Collectors.toList());

// or, alternatively,

List<Person> people = names.stream()
    .map(Person::new)              ❷
    .collect(Collectors.toList());
```

❶ Using a lambda expression to invoke the constructor

❷ Using a constructor reference instantiating `Person`

The syntax `Person::new` refers to the constructor in the `Person` class. As with all lambda expressions, the context determines which constructor is executed. Because the context supplies a string, the one-arg `String` constructor is used.

### Copy constructor

A copy constructor takes a `Person` argument and returns a new `Person` with the same attributes, as shown in Example 1-16.

*Example 1-16. A copy constructor for Person*

```
public Person(Person p) {
    this.name = p.name;
}
```

This is useful if you want to isolate streaming code from the original instances. For example, if you already have a list of people, convert the list into a stream, and then back into a list, the references are the same (see Example 1-17).

*Example 1-17. Converting a list to a stream and back*

```
Person before = new Person("Grace Hopper");

List<Person> people = Stream.of(before)
    .collect(Collectors.toList());
Person after = people.get(0);

assertTrue(before == after);                              ❶

before.setName("Grace Murray Hopper");                    ❷
assertEquals("Grace Murray Hopper", after.getName()); ❸
```

❶ Same object

❷ Change name using `before` reference

❸ Name has changed in the `after` reference

Using a copy constructor, you can break that connection, as in Example 1-18.

*Example 1-18. Using the copy constructor*

```
people = Stream.of(before)
      .map(Person::new)           ❶
      .collect(Collectors.toList());
```

```
after = people.get(0);
assertFalse(before == after);        ❷
assertEquals(before, after);         ❸

before.setName("Rear Admiral Dr. Grace Murray Hopper");
assertFalse(before.equals(after));
```

❶ Use copy constructor

❷ Different objects

❸ But equivalent

This time, when invoking the `map` method, the context is a stream of `Person` instances. Therefore the `Person::new` syntax invokes the constructor that takes a `Person` and returns a new, but equivalent, instance, and has broken the connection between the *before* reference and the *after* reference.[3]

### Varargs constructor

Consider now a varargs constructor added to the `Person` POJO, shown in Example 1-19.

*Example 1-19. A Person constructor that takes a variable argument list of String*

```
public Person(String... names) {
    this.name = Arrays.stream(names)
                      .collect(Collectors.joining(" "));
}
```

This constructor takes zero or more string arguments and concatenates them together with a single space as the delimiter.

How can that constructor get invoked? Any client that passes zero or more string arguments separated by commas will call it. One way to do that is to take advantage of the `split` method on `String` that takes a delimiter and returns a `String` array:

```
String[] split(String delimiter)
```

Therefore, the code in Example 1-20 splits each string in the list into individual words and invokes the varargs constructor.

3 I mean no disrespect by treating Admiral Hopper as an object. I have no doubt she could still kick my butt, and she passed away in 1992.

*Example 1-20. Using the varargs constructor*

```
names.stream()                          ❶
    .map(name -> name.split(" "))       ❷
    .map(Person::new)                   ❸
    .collect(Collectors.toList());      ❹
```

❶ Create a stream of strings

❷ Map to a stream of string arrays

❸ Map to a stream of `Person`

❹ Collect to a list of `Person`

This time, the context for the `map` method that contains the `Person::new` constructor reference is a stream of string arrays, so the varargs constructor is called. If you add a simple print statement to that constructor:

```
System.out.println("Varargs ctor, names=" + Arrays.toList(names));
```

then the result is:

```
Varargs ctor, names=[Grace, Hopper]
Varargs ctor, names=[Barbara, Liskov]
Varargs ctor, names=[Ada, Lovelace]
Varargs ctor, names=[Karen, Spärck, Jones]
```

### Arrays

Constructor references can also be used with arrays. If you want an array of `Person` instances, `Person[]`, instead of a list, you can use the `toArray` method on `Stream`, whose signature is:

```
<A> A[] toArray(IntFunction<A[]> generator)
```

This method uses `A` to represent the generic type of the array returned containing the elements of the stream, which is created using the provided generator function. The cool part is that a constructor reference can be used for that, too, as in Example 1-21.

*Example 1-21. Creating an array of Person references*

```
Person[] people = names.stream()
    .map(Person::new)           ❶
    .toArray(Person[]::new);    ❷
```

❶ Constructor reference for `Person`

❷ Constructor reference for an array of `Person`

The `toArray` method argument creates an array of `Person` references of the proper size and populates it with the instantiated `Person` instances.

Constructor references are just method references by another name, using the word `new` to invoke a constructor. Which constructor is determined by the context, as usual. This technique gives a lot of flexibility when processing streams.

### See Also

Method references are discussed in Recipe 1.2.

## 1.4 Functional Interfaces

### Problem

You want to use an existing functional interface, or write your own.

### Solution

Create an interface with a single, abstract method, and add the `@FunctionalInterface` annotation.

### Discussion

A functional interface in Java 8 is an interface with a single, abstract method. As such, it can be the target for a lambda expression or method reference.

The use of the term `abstract` here is significant. Prior to Java 8, all methods in interfaces were considered abstract by default—you didn't even need to add the keyword.

For example, here is the definition of an interface called `PalindromeChecker`, shown in Example 1-22.

*Example 1-22. A Palindrome Checker interface*

```
@FunctionalInterface
public interface PalindromeChecker {
    boolean isPalidrome(String s);
}
```

All methods in an interface are `public`,[4] so you can leave out the access modifier, just as you can leave out the `abstract` keyword.

---

4 At least until Java 9, when `private` methods are also allowed in interfaces. See Recipe 10.2 for details.

Since this interface has only a single, abstract method, it is a functional interface. Java 8 provides an annotation called `@FunctionalInterface` in the `java.lang` package that can be applied to the interface, as shown in the example.

This annotation is not required, but is a good idea, for two reasons. First, it triggers a compile-time check that the interface does, in fact, satisfy the requirement. If the interface has either zero abstract methods or more than one, you will get a compiler error.

The other benefit to adding the `@FunctionalInterface` annotation is that it generates a statement in the Javadocs as follows:

```
Functional Interface:
This is a functional interface and can therefore be used as the assignment
target for a lambda expression or method reference.
```

Functional interfaces can have `default` and `static` methods as well. Both default and static methods have implementations, so they don't count against the single abstract method requirement. Example 1-23 shows the sample code.

*Example 1-23. MyInterface is a functional interface with static and default methods*

```
@FunctionalInterface
public interface MyInterface {
    int myMethod();              ❶
    // int myOtherMethod();      ❷

    default String sayHello() {
        return "Hello, World!";
    }

    static void myStaticMethod() {
        System.out.println("I'm a static method in an interface");
    }
}
```

❶ Single abstract method

❷ If added, this would no longer be a functional interface

Note that if the commented method `myOtherMethod` was included, the interface would no longer satisfy the functional interface requirement. The annotation would generate an error of the form "multiple non-overriding abstract methods found."

Interfaces can extend other interfaces, even more than one. The annotation checks the current interface. So if one interface extends an existing functional interface and adds another abstract method, it is not itself a functional interface. See Example 1-24.

*Example 1-24. Extending a functional interface—no longer functional*

```
public interface MyChildInterface extends MyInterface {
    int anotherMethod(); ❶
}
```

❶ Additional abstract method

The `MyChildInterface` is not a functional interface, because it has two abstract methods: `myMethod`, which it inherits from `MyInterface`; and `anotherMethod`, which it declares. Without the `@FunctionalInterface` annotation, this compiles, because it's a standard interface. It cannot, however, be the target of a lambda expression.

One edge case should also be noted. The `Comparator` interface is used for sorting, which is discussed in other recipes. If you look at the Javadocs for that interface and select the Abstract Methods tab, you see the methods shown in Figure 1-1.

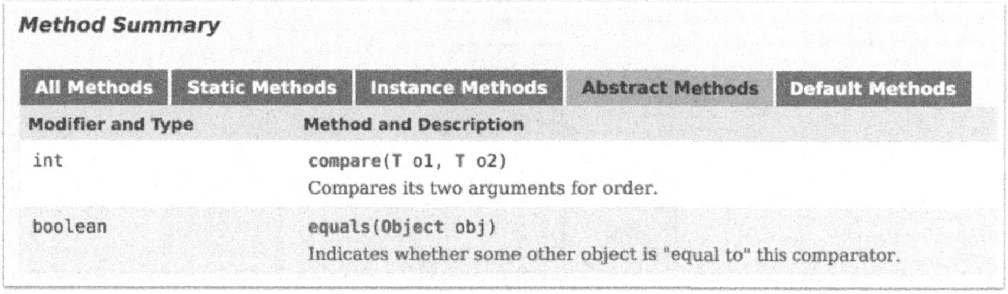

**Method Summary**

All Methods | Static Methods | Instance Methods | Abstract Methods | Default Methods

| Modifier and Type | Method and Description |
|---|---|
| int | compare(T o1, T o2)<br>Compares its two arguments for order. |
| boolean | equals(Object obj)<br>Indicates whether some other object is "equal to" this comparator. |

*Figure 1-1. Abstract methods in the Comparator class*

Wait, what? How can this be a functional interface if there are two abstract methods, especially if one of them is actually implemented in `java.lang.Object`?

As it turns out, this has always been legal. You can declare methods in `Object` as abstract in an interface, but that doesn't make them abstract. Usually the reason for doing so is to add documentation that explains the contract of the interface. In the case of `Comparator`, the contract is that if two elements return `true` from the `equals` method, the `compare` method should return zero. Adding the `equals` method to `Comparator` allows the associated Javadocs to explain that.

The rules for functional interfaces say that methods from `Object` don't count against the single abstract method limit, so `Comparator` is still a functional interface.

## See Also

Default methods in interfaces are discussed in Recipe 1.5, and static methods in interfaces are discussed in Recipe 1.6.

## 1.5 Default Methods in Interfaces

### Problem

You want to provide an implementation of a method inside an interface.

### Solution

Use the keyword `default` on the interface method, and add the implementation in the normal way.

### Discussion

The traditional reason Java never supported multiple inheritance is the so-called *diamond problem*. Say you have an inheritance hierarchy as shown in the (vaguely UML-like) Figure 1-2.

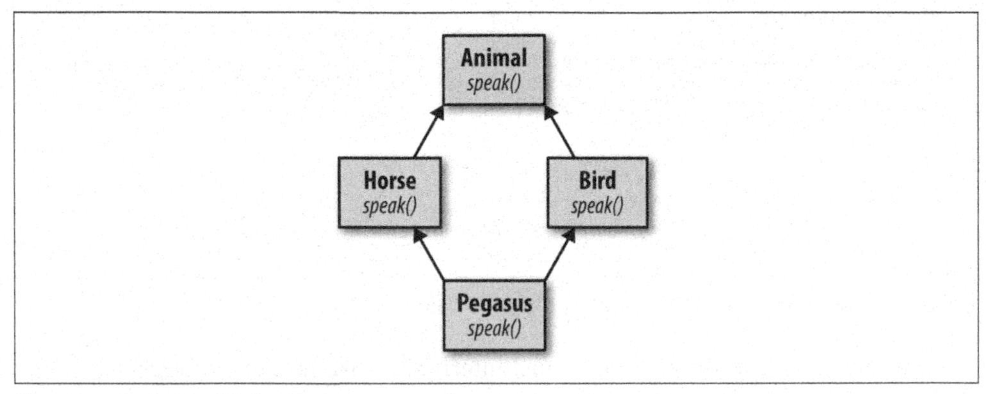


*Figure 1-2. Animal inheritance*

Class `Animal` has two child classes, `Bird` and `Horse`, each of which overrides the `speak` method from `Animal`, in `Horse` to say "whinny" and in `Bird` to say "chirp." What, then, does `Pegasus` (which multiply inherits from both `Horse` and `Bird`)[5] say? What if you have a reference of type `Animal` assigned to an instance of `Pegasus`? What then should the `speak` method return?

```
Animal animal = new Pegaus();
animal.speak(); // whinny, chirp, or other?
```

Different languages take different approaches to this problem. In C++, for example, multiple inheritance is allowed, but if a class inherits conflicting implementations, it

5 "A magnificent horse, with the brain of a bird." (Disney's *Hercules* movie, which is fun if you pretend you know nothing about Greek mythology and never heard of Hercules.)

won't compile.[6] In Eiffel,[7] the compiler allows you to choose which implementation you want.

Java's approach was to prohibit multiple inheritance, and interfaces were introduced as a workaround for when a class has an "is a kind of" relationship with more than one type. Since interfaces had only abstract methods, there were no implementations to conflict. Multiple inheritance is allowed with interfaces, but again that works because only the method signatures are inherited.

The problem is, if you can never implement a method in an interface, you wind up with some awkward designs. Among the methods in the `java.util.Collection` interface, for example, are:

```
boolean isEmpty()
int     size()
```

The `isEmpty` method returns true if there are no elements in the collection, and false otherwise. The `size` method returns the number of elements in the collections. Regardless of the underlying implementation, you can immediately implement the `isEmpty` method in terms of `size`, as in Example 1-25.

*Example 1-25. Implementation of isEmpty in terms of size*

```
public boolean isEmpty() {
    return size() == 0;
}
```

Since `Collection` is an interface, you can't do this in the interface itself. Instead, the standard library includes an abstract class called `java.util.AbstractCollection`, which includes, among other code, exactly the implementation of `isEmpty` shown here. If you are creating your own collection implementation and you don't already have a superclass, you can extend `AbstractCollection` and you get the `isEmpty` method for free. If you already have a superclass, you have to implement the `Collection` interface instead and remember to provide your own implementation of `isEmpty` as well as `size`.

All of this is quite familiar to experienced Java developers, but as of Java 8 the situation changes. Now you can add implementations to interface methods. All you have to do is add the keyword `default` to a method and provide an implementation. The code in Example 1-26 shows an interface with both abstract and default methods.

6 This can be solved by using virtual inheritance, but still.

7 There's an obscure reference for you, but Eiffel was one of the foundational languages of object-oriented programming. See Bertrand Meyer's *Object-Oriented Software Construction*, Second Edition (Prentice Hall, 1997).

*Example 1-26. An Employee interface with a default method*

```
public interface Employee {
    String getFirst();

    String getLast();

    void convertCaffeineToCodeForMoney();

    default String getName() {  ❶
        return String.format("%s %s", getFirst(), getLast());
    }
}
```

❶ Default method with an implementation

The `getName` method has the keyword `default`, and its implementation is in terms of the other, abstract, methods in the interface, `getFirst` and `getLast`.

Many of the existing interfaces in Java have been enhanced with default methods in order to maintain backward compatibility. Normally when you add a new method to an interface, you break all the existing implementations. By adding a new method as a default, all the existing implementations inherit the new method and still work. This allowed the library maintainers to add new default methods throughout the JDK without breaking existing implementations.

For example, `java.util.Collection` now contains the following default methods:

```
default boolean        removeIf(Predicate<? super E> filter)
default Stream<E>      stream()
default Stream<E>      parallelStream()
default Spliterator<E> spliterator()
```

The `removeIf` method removes all of the elements from the collection that satisfy the `Predicate`[8] argument, returning `true` if any elements were removed. The `stream` and `parallelStream` methods are factory methods for creating streams. The `spliterator` method returns an object from a class that implements the `Spliterator` interface, which is an object for traversing and partitioning elements from a source.

Default methods are used the same way any other methods are used, as Example 1-27 shows.

---

8 `Predicate` is one of the new functional interfaces in the `java.util.function` package, described in detail in Recipe 2.3.

*Example 1-27. Using default methods*

```
List<Integer> nums = Arrays.asList(3, 1, 4, 1, 5, 9);
boolean removed = nums.removeIf(n -> n <= 0);  ❶
System.out.println("Elements were " + (removed ? "" : "NOT") + " removed");
nums.forEach(System.out::println);             ❷
```

❶ Use the `default` method `removeIf` from `Collection`

❷ Use the `default` method `forEach` from `Iterator`

What happens when a class implements two interfaces with the same default method? That is the subject of Recipe 5.5, but the short answer is that if the class implements the method itself everything is fine. See Recipe 5.5 for details.

## See Also

Recipe 5.5 shows the rules that apply when a class implements multiple interfaces with default methods.

# 1.6 Static Methods in Interfaces

## Problem

You want to add a class-level utility method to an interface, along with an implementation.

## Solution

Make the method `static` and provide the implementation in the usual way.

## Discussion

Static members of Java classes are class-level, meaning they are associated with the class as a whole rather than with a particular instance. That makes their use in interfaces problematic from a design point of view. Some questions include:

- What does a class-level member mean when the interface is implemented by many different classes?
- Does a class need to implement an interface in order to use a static method?
- Static methods in classes are accessed by the class name. If a class implements an interface, does a static method get called from the class name or the interface name?

The designers of Java could have decided these questions in several different ways. Prior to Java 8, the decision was not to allow static members in interfaces at all.

Unfortunately, however, that led to the creation of *utility* classes: classes that contain only static methods. A typical example is `java.util.Collections`, which contains methods for sorting and searching, wrapping collections in synchronized or unmodifiable types, and more. In the NIO package, `java.nio.file.Paths` is another example. It contains only static methods that parse `Path` instances from strings or URIs.

Now, in Java 8, you can add static methods to interfaces whenever you like. The requirements are:

- Add the `static` keyword to the method.
- Provide an implementation (which cannot be overridden). In this way they are like `default` methods, and are included in the default tab in the Javadocs.
- Access the method using the interface name. Classes do *not* need to implement an interface to use its static methods.

One example of a convenient static method in an interface is the `comparing` method in `java.util.Comparator`, along with its primitive variants, `comparingInt`, `comparingLong`, and `comparingDouble`. The `Comparator` interface also has static methods `naturalOrder` and `reverseOrder`. Example 1-28 shows how they are used.

*Example 1-28. Sorting strings*

```
List<String> bonds = Arrays.asList("Connery", "Lazenby", "Moore",
    "Dalton", "Brosnan", "Craig");

List<String> sorted = bonds.stream()
    .sorted(Comparator.naturalOrder())                    ❶
    .collect(Collectors.toList());
// [Brosnan, Connery, Craig, Dalton, Lazenby, Moore]

sorted = bonds.stream()
    .sorted(Comparator.reverseOrder())                    ❷
    .collect(Collectors.toList());
// [Moore, Lazenby, Dalton, Craig, Connery, Brosnan]

sorted = bonds.stream()
    .sorted(Comparator.comparing(String::toLowerCase)) ❸
    .collect(Collectors.toList());
// [Brosnan, Connery, Craig, Dalton, Lazenby, Moore]

sorted = bonds.stream()
    .sorted(Comparator.comparingInt(String::length))   ❹
    .collect(Collectors.toList());
// [Moore, Craig, Dalton, Connery, Lazenby, Brosnan]
```

```
sorted = bonds.stream()
    .sorted(Comparator.comparingInt(String::length)     ❺
        .thenComparing(Comparator.naturalOrder()))
    .collect(Collectors.toList());
// [Craig, Moore, Dalton, Brosnan, Connery, Lazenby]
```

❶ Natural order (lexicographical)

❷ Reverse lexicographical

❸ Sort by lowercase name

❹ Sort by name length

❺ Sort by length, then equal lengths lexicographically

The example shows how to use several static methods in `Comparator` to sort the list of actors who have played James Bond over the years.[9] Comparators are discussed further in Recipe 4.1.

Static methods in interfaces remove the need to create separate utility classes, though that option is still available if a design calls for it.

The key points to remember are:

- Static methods must have an implementation
- You cannot override a static method
- Call static methods from the interface name
- You do not need to implement an interface to use its static methods

## See Also

Static methods from interfaces are used throughout this book, but Recipe 4.1 covers the static methods from `Comparator` used here.

9 The temptation to add Idris Elba to the list is almost overwhelming, but no such luck as yet.

CHAPTER 2

# The java.util.function Package

The previous chapter discussed the basic syntax of lambda expressions and method references. One basic principle is that for either, there is always a context. Lambda expressions and method references are always assigned to functional interfaces, which provide information about the single abstract method being implemented.

While many interfaces in the Java standard library contain only a single, abstract method and are thus functional interfaces, there is a new package that is specifically designed to contain only functional interfaces that are reused in the rest of the library. That package is called `java.util.function`.

The interfaces in `java.util.function` fall into four categories: (1) consumers, (2) suppliers, (3) predicates, and (4) functions. Consumers take a generic argument and return nothing. `Suppliers` take no arguments and return a value. Predicates take an argument and return a boolean. Functions take a single argument and return a value.

For each of the basic interfaces, there are several related ones. For example, `Consumer` has variations customized for primitive types (`IntConsumer`, `LongConsumer`, and `DoubleConsumer`) and a variation (`BiConsumer`) that takes two arguments and returns `void`.

Although by definition the interfaces in this chapter only contain a single abstract method, most also include additional methods that are either `static` or `default`. Becoming familiar with these methods will make your job as a developer easier.

## 2.1 Consumers

### Problem

You want to write lambda expressions that implement the `java.util.function.Consumer` package.

### Solution

Implement the `void accept(T t)` method using a lambda expression or a method reference.

### Discussion

The `java.util.function.Consumer` interface has as its single, abstract method, `void accept(T t)`. See Example 2-1.

*Example 2-1. Methods in java.util.function.Consumer*

```
        void        accept(T t)                          ❶
default Consumer<T> andThen(Consumer<? super T> after)   ❷
```

❶ Single abstract method

❷ Default method for composition

The `accept` method takes a generic argument and returns `void`. One of the most frequently used examples of a method that takes a `Consumer` as an argument is the default `forEach` method in `java.util.Iterable`, shown in Example 2-2.

*Example 2-2. The forEach method in Iterable*

```
default void forEach(Consumer<? super T> action)  ❶
```

❶ Passes each element of an iterable collection to the consumer argument

All linear collections implement this interface by performing the given action for each element of the collection, as in Example 2-3.

*Example 2-3. Printing the elements of a collection*

```
List<String> strings = Arrays.asList("this", "is", "a", "list", "of", "strings");

strings.forEach(new Consumer<String>() {         ❶
    @Override
```

```
    public void accept(String s) {
        System.out.println(s);
    }
});

strings.forEach(s -> System.out.println(s));  ❷
strings.forEach(System.out::println);          ❸
```

❶ Anonymous inner class implementation

❷ Expression lambda

❸ Method reference

The lambda expression conforms to the signature of the `accept` method, because it takes a single argument and returns nothing. The `println` method in `PrintStream`, accessed here via `System.out`, is compatible with `Consumer`. Therefore, either can be used as the target for an argument of type `Consumer`.

The `java.util.function` package also contains primitive variations of `Consumer<T>`, as well as a two-argument version. See Table 2-1 for details.

*Table 2-1. Additional Consumer interfaces*

| Interface | Single abstract method |
|---|---|
| `IntConsumer` | `void accept(int x)` |
| `DoubleConsumer` | `void accept(double x)` |
| `LongConsumer` | `void accept(long x)` |
| `BiConsumer` | `void accept(T t, U u)` |

Consumers are expected to operate via side effects, as shown in Recipe 2.3.

The `BiConsumer` interface has an `accept` method that takes two generic arguments, which are assumed to be of different types. The package contains three variations on `BiConsumer` where the second argument is a primitive. One is `ObjIntConsumer`, whose `accept` method takes two arguments, a generic and and an `int`. `ObjLong Consumer` and `ObjDoubleConsumer` are defined similarly.

Other uses of the `Consumer` interface in the standard library include:

`Optional.ifPresent(Consumer<? super T> consumer)`
: If a value is present, invoke the specified consumer. Otherwise do nothing.

`Stream.forEach(Consumer<? super T> action)`
: Performs an action for each element of the stream.[1] The `Stream.forEachOrdered` method is similar, accessing elements in encounter order.

`Stream.peek(Consumer<? super T> action)`
: Returns a stream with the same elements as the existing stream, first performing the given action. This is a very useful technique for debugging (see Recipe 3.5 for an example).

### See Also

The `andThen` method in `Consumer` is used for composition. Function composition is discussed further in Recipe 5.8. The `peek` method in `Stream` is examined in Recipe 3.5.

## 2.2 Suppliers

### Problem

You want to implement the `java.util.function.Supplier` interface.

### Solution

Implement the `T get()` method in `java.util.function.Supplier` using a lambda expression or a method reference.

### Discussion

The `java.util.function.Supplier` interface is particularly simple. It does not have any static or default methods. It contains only a single, abstract method, `T get()`.

Implementing `Supplier` means providing a method that takes no arguments and returns the generic type. As stated in the Javadocs, there is no requirement that a new or distinct result be returned each time the `Supplier` is invoked.

One simple example of a `Supplier` is the `Math.random` method, which takes no arguments and returns a `double`. That can be assigned to a `Supplier` reference and invoked at any time, as in Example 2-4.

1 This is such a common operation that `forEach` was also added directly to `Iterable`. The `Stream` variation is useful when the source elements do not come from a collection, or if you want to make the stream parallel.

*Example 2-4. Using Math.random() as a Supplier*

```
Logger logger = Logger.getLogger("...");

DoubleSupplier randomSupplier = new DoubleSupplier() { ❶
    @Override
    public double getAsDouble() {
        return Math.random();
    }
};

randomSupplier = () -> Math.random();                   ❷
randomSupplier = Math::random;                          ❸

logger.info(randomSupplier);
```

❶ Anonymous inner class implementation

❷ Expression lambda

❸ Method reference

The single abstract method in `DoubleSupplier` is `getAsDouble`, which returns a `double`. The other associated `Supplier` interfaces in the `java.util.function` package are shown in Table 2-2.

*Table 2-2. Additional Supplier interfaces*

| Interface | Single abstract method |
|---|---|
| `IntSupplier` | `int getAsInt()` |
| `DoubleSupplier` | `double getAsDouble()` |
| `LongSupplier` | `long getAsLong()` |
| `BooleanSupplier` | `boolean getAsBoolean()` |

One of the primary use cases for `Suppliers` is to support the concept of *deferred execution*. The `info` method in `java.util.logging.Logger` takes a `Supplier`, whose `get` method is only called if the log level means the message will be seen (shown in detail in Recipe 5.7). This process of deferred execution can be used in your own code, to ensure that a value is retrieved from a `Supplier` only when appropriate.

Another example from the standard library is the `orElseGet` method in `Optional`, which also takes a `Supplier`. The `Optional` class is discussed in Chapter 6, but the short explanation is that an `Optional` is a nonnull object that either wraps a value or is empty. It is typically returned by methods that may reasonably expect to have no result, like finding a value in an empty collection.

To see how that might work, consider searching for a name in a collection, as shown in Example 2-5.

*Example 2-5. Finding a name from a collection*

```
List<String> names = Arrays.asList("Mal", "Wash", "Kaylee", "Inara",
    "Zoë", "Jayne", "Simon", "River", "Shepherd Book");

Optional<String> first = names.stream()
    .filter(name -> name.startsWith("C"))
    .findFirst();

System.out.println(first);                   ❶
System.out.println(first.orElse("None")); ❷

System.out.println(first.orElse(String.format("No result found in %s",
    names.stream().collect(Collectors.joining(", "))))); ❸

System.out.println(first.orElseGet(() ->
    String.format("No result found in %s",
    names.stream().collect(Collectors.joining(", "))))); ❹
```

❶ Prints `Optional.empty`

❷ Prints the string `"None"`

❸ Forms the comma-separated collection, even when name is found

❹ Forms the comma-separated collection only if the `Optional` is empty

The `findFirst` method on `Stream` returns the first encountered element in an ordered stream.[2] Since it's possible to apply a filter so there are no elements remaining in the stream, the method returns an `Optional`. That `Optional` either contains the desired element, or is empty. In this case, none of the names in the list pass the filter, so the result is an empty `Optional`.

The `orElse` method on `Optional` returns either the contained element, or a specified default. That's fine if the default is a simple string, but can be wasteful if processing is necessary to return a value.

2 Streams may have an encounter order or they may not, just as lists are assumed to be ordered by index and sets are not. This can be different from the order in which elements are processed. See Recipe 3.9 for more information.

In this case, the returned value shows the complete list of names in comma-separated form. The `orElse` method creates the complete string, whether the `Optional` contains a value or not.

The `orElseGet` method, however, takes a `Supplier` as an argument. The advantage is that the `get` method on the `Supplier` will only be invoked when the `Optional` is empty, so the complete name string is not formed unless it is necessary.

Other examples from the standard library that use `Suppliers` include:

- The `orElseThrow` method in `Optional`, which takes a `Supplier<X extends Exception>`. The `Supplier` is only executed if an exception occurs.
- `Objects.requireNonNull(T obj, Supplier<String> messageSupplier)` only customizes its response if the first argument is null.
- `CompletableFuture.supplyAsync(Supplier<U> supplier)` returns a `CompletableFuture` that is asynchronously completed by a task running with the value obtained by calling the given `Supplier`.
- The `Logger` class has overloads for all its logging methods that takes a `Supplier<String>` rather than just a string (used as an example in Recipe 5.7).

## See Also

Using the overloaded logging methods that take a `Supplier` is discussed in Recipe 5.7. Finding the first element in a collection is discussed in Recipe 3.9. Completable futures are part of several recipes in Chapter 9, and `Optional` is the topic of recipes in Chapter 6.

# 2.3 Predicates

## Problem

You want to filter data using the `java.util.function.Predicate` interface.

## Solution

Implement the `boolean test(T t)` method in the `Predicate` interface using a lambda expression or a method reference.

## Discussion

Predicates are used primarily to filter streams. Given a stream of items, the `filter` method in `java.util.stream.Stream` takes a `Predicate` and returns a new stream that includes only the items that satisfy the given predicate.

The single abstract method in `Predicate` is `boolean test(T t)`, which takes a single generic argument and returns true or false. The complete set of methods in `Predicate`, including state and defaults, is given in Example 2-6.

*Example 2-6. Methods in java.util.function.Predicate*

```
default     Predicate<T> and(Predicate<? super T> other)
static <T> Predicate<T> isEquals(Object targetRef)
default     Predicate<T> negate()
default     Predicate<T> or(Predicate<? super T> other)
boolean     test(T t)  ❶
```

❶ Single abstract method

Say you have a collection of names and you want to find all the instances that have a particular length. Example 2-7 shows an example of how to use stream processing to do so.

*Example 2-7. Finding strings of a given length*

```
public String getNamesOfLength(int length, String... names) {
    return Arrays.stream(names)
        .filter(s -> s.length() == length)   ❶
        .collect(Collectors.joining(", "));
}
```

❶ Predicate for strings of given length only

Alternatively, perhaps you want only the names that start with a particular string, as in Example 2-8.

*Example 2-8. Finding strings that start with a given string*

```
public String getNamesStartingWith(String s, String... names) {
    return Arrays.stream(names)
        .filter(s -> s.startsWith(s)) ❶
        .collect(Collectors.joining(", "));
}
```

❶ Predicate to return strings starting with a given string

These can be made more general by allowing the condition to be specified by the client. Example 2-9 shows a method to do that.

*Example 2-9. Finding strings that satisfy an arbitrary predicate*

```
public class ImplementPredicate {
    public String getNamesSatisfyingCondition(
        Predicate<String> condition, String... names) {
            return Arrays.stream(names)
                .filter(condition) ❶
                .collect(Collectors.joining(", "));
        }
    }

    // ... other methods ...
}
```

❶ Filter by supplied predicate

This is quite flexible, but it may be a bit much to expect the clients to write every predicate themselves. One option is to add constants to the class representing the most common cases, as in Example 2-10.

*Example 2-10. Adding constants for common cases*

```
public class ImplementPredicate {
    public static final Predicate<String> LENGTH_FIVE = s -> s.length() == 5;
    public static final Predicate<String> STARTS_WITH_S =
        s -> s.startsWith("S");

    // ... rest as before ...
}
```

The other advantage to supplying a predicate as an argument is that you can also use the default methods `and`, `or`, and `negate` to create a composite predicate from a series of individual elements.

The test case in Example 2-11 demonstrates all of these techniques.

*Example 2-11. JUnit test for predicate methods*

```
import static functionpackage.ImplementPredicate.*; ❶
import static org.junit.Assert.assertEquals;

// ... other imports ...

public class ImplementPredicateTest {
    private ImplementPredicate demo = new ImplementPredicate();
    private String[] names;
```

```
    @Before
    public void setUp() {
        names = Stream.of("Mal", "Wash", "Kaylee", "Inara", "Zoë",
            "Jayne", "Simon", "River", "Shepherd Book")
            .sorted()
            .toArray(String[]::new);
    }

    @Test
    public void getNamesOfLength5() throws Exception {
        assertEquals("Inara, Jayne, River, Simon",
            demo.getNamesOfLength(5, names));
    }

    @Test
    public void getNamesStartingWithS() throws Exception {
        assertEquals("Shepherd Book, Simon",
            demo.getNamesStartingWith("S", names));
    }

    @Test
    public void getNamesSatisfyingCondition() throws Exception {
        assertEquals("Inara, Jayne, River, Simon",
            demo.getNamesSatisfyingCondition(s -> s.length() == 5, names));
        assertEquals("Shepherd Book, Simon",
            demo.getNamesSatisfyingCondition(s -> s.startsWith("S"),
            names));
        assertEquals("Inara, Jayne, River, Simon",
            demo.getNamesSatisfyingCondition(LENGTH_FIVE, names));
        assertEquals("Shepherd Book, Simon",
            demo.getNamesSatisfyingCondition(STARTS_WITH_S, names));
    }

    @Test
    public void composedPredicate() throws Exception {
        assertEquals("Simon",
            demo.getNamesSatisfyingCondition(
                LENGTH_FIVE.and(STARTS_WITH_S), names));  ❷
        assertEquals("Inara, Jayne, River, Shepherd Book, Simon",
            demo.getNamesSatisfyingCondition(
                LENGTH_FIVE.or(STARTS_WITH_S), names));  ❷
        assertEquals("Kaylee, Mal, Shepherd Book, Wash, Zoë",
            demo.getNamesSatisfyingCondition(LENGTH_FIVE.negate(), names)); ❸
    }
}
```

❶ Static import to make using constants simpler

❷ Composition

❸ Negation

Other methods in the standard library that use predicates include:

`Optional.filter(Predicate<? super T> predicate)`
: If a value is present, and the value matches the given predicate, returns an `Optional` describing the value, otherwise returns an empty `Optional`.

`Collection.removeIf(Predicate<? super E> filter)`
: Removes all elements of this collection that satisfy the predicate.

`Stream.allMatch(Predicate<? super T> predicate)`
: Returns true if all elements of the stream satisfy the given predicate. The methods `anyMatch` and `noneMatch` work similarly.

`Collectors.partitioningBy(Predicate<? super T> predicate)`
: Returns a `Collector` that splits a stream into two categories: those that satisfy the predicate and those that do not.

Predicates are useful whenever a stream should only return certain elements. This recipe hopefully gives you an idea where and when that might be useful.

### See Also

Closure composition is also discussed in Recipe 5.8. The `allMatch`, `anyMatch`, and `noneMatch` methods are discussed in Recipe 3.10. Partitioning and group by operations are discussed in Recipe 4.5.

## 2.4 Functions

### Problem

You need to implement the `java.util.function.Function` interface to transform an input parameter into an output value.

### Solution

Provide a lambda expression that implements the `R apply(T t)` method.

### Discussion

The functional interface `java.util.function.Function` contains the single abstract method `apply`, which is invoked to transform a generic input parameter of type `T` into a generic output value of type `R`. The methods in `Function` are shown in Example 2-12.

*Example 2-12. Methods in the java.util.function.Function interface*

```
default <V> Function<T,V> andThen(Function<? super R,? extends V> after)
            R             apply(T t)
default <V> Function<V,R> compose(Function<? super V,? extends T> before)
static  <T> Function<T,T> identity()
```

The most common usage of `Function` is as an argument to the `Stream.map` method. For example, one way to transform a `String` into an integer would be to invoke the length method on each instance, as in Example 2-13.

*Example 2-13. Mapping strings to their lengths*

```
List<String> names = Arrays.asList("Mal", "Wash", "Kaylee", "Inara",
        "Zoë", "Jayne", "Simon", "River", "Shepherd Book");

List<Integer> nameLengths = names.stream()
        .map(new Function<String, Integer>() { ❶
            @Override
            public Integer apply(String s) {
                return s.length();
            }
        })
        .collect(Collectors.toList());

nameLengths = names.stream()
        .map(s -> s.length())                ❷
        .collect(Collectors.toList());

nameLengths = names.stream()
        .map(String::length)                 ❸
        .collect(Collectors.toList());

System.out.printf("nameLengths = %s%n", nameLengths);
// nameLengths == [3, 4, 6, 5, 3, 5, 5, 5, 13]
```

❶ Anonymous inner class

❷ Lambda expression

❸ Method reference

The complete list of primitive variations for both the input and the output generic types are shown in Table 2-3.

*Table 2-3. Additional Function interfaces*

| Interface | Single abstract method |
|---|---|
| `IntFunction` | `R apply(int value)` |
| `DoubleFunction` | `R apply(double value)` |
| `LongFunction` | `R apply(long value)` |
| `ToIntFunction` | `int applyAsInt(T value)` |
| `ToDoubleFunction` | `double applyAsDouble(T value)` |
| `ToLongFunction` | `long applyAsLong(T value)` |
| `DoubleToIntFunction` | `int applyAsInt(double value)` |
| `DoubleToLongFunction` | `long applyAsLong(double value)` |
| `IntToDoubleFunction` | `double applyAsDouble(int value)` |
| `IntToLongFunction` | `long applyAsLong(int value)` |
| `LongToDoubleFunction` | `double applyAsDouble(long value)` |
| `LongToIntFunction` | `int applyAsInt(long value)` |
| `BiFunction` | `void accept(T t, U u)` |

The argument to the `map` method in Example 2-13 could have been a `ToIntFunction`, because the return type on the method is an `int` primitive. The `Stream.mapToInt` method takes a `ToIntFunction` as an argument, and `mapToDouble` and `mapToLong` are analogous. The return types on `mapToInt`, `mapToDouble`, and `mapToLong` are `IntStream`, `DoubleStream`, and `LongStream`, respectively.

What if the argument and return type are the same? The `java.util.function` package defines `UnaryOperator` for that. As you might expect, there are also interfaces called `IntUnaryOperator`, `DoubleUnaryOperator`, and `LongUnaryOperator`, where the input and output arguments are `int`, `double`, and `long`, respectively. An example of a `UnaryOperator` would be the `reverse` method in `StringBuilder`, because both the input type and the output type are strings.

The `BiFunction` interface is defined for two generic input types and one generic output type, all of which are assumed to be different. If all three are the same, the package includes the `BinaryOperator` interface. An example of a binary operator would be `Math.max`, because both inputs and the output are either `int`, `double`, `float`, or `long`. Of course, the interface also defines interfaces called `IntBinaryOperator`, `DoubleBinaryOperator`, and `LongBinaryOperator` for those situations.[3]

3 See Recipe 3.3 for more on `BinaryOperator` uses in the standard library.

To complete the set, the package also has primitive variations of `BiFunction`, which are summarized in Table 2-4.

*Table 2-4. Additional BiFunction interfaces*

| Interface | Single abstract method |
| --- | --- |
| `ToIntBiFunction` | `int applyAsInt(T t, U u)` |
| `ToDoubleBiFunction` | `double applyAsDouble(T t, U u)` |
| `ToLongBiFunction` | `long applyAsLong(T t, U u)` |

While the various `Stream.map` methods are the primary usages of `Function`, they do appear in other contexts. Among them are:

`Map.computeIfAbsent(K key, Function<? super K,? extends V> mappingFunction)`
: If the specified key does not have a value, use the provided `Function` to compute one and add it to a `Map`.

`Comparator.comparing(Function<? super T,? extends U> keyExtractor)`
: Discussed in Recipe 4.1, this method generates a `Comparator` that sorts a collection by the key generated from the given `Function`.

`Comparator.thenComparing(Function<? super T,? extends U> keyExtractor)`
: An instance method, also used in sorting, that adds an additional sorting mechanism if the collection has equal values by the first sort.

Functions are also used extensively in the `Collectors` utility class for grouping and downstream collectors.

The `andThen` and `compose` methods are discussed in Recipe 5.8. The `identity` method is simply the lambda expression `e -> e`. One usage is shown in Recipe 4.3.

## See Also

See Recipe 5.8 for examples of the `andThen` and `compose` methods in the `Function` interface. See Recipe 4.3 for an example of `Function.identity`. See Recipe 4.6 for examples of using functions as downstream collectors. The `computeIfAbsent` method is discussed in Recipe 5.4. Binary operators are also covered in Recipe 3.3.

CHAPTER 3

# Streams

Java 8 introduces a new streaming metaphor to support functional programming. A stream is a sequence of elements that does not save the elements or modify the original source. Functional programming in Java often involves generating a stream from some source of data, passing the elements through a series of intermediate operations (called a *pipeline*), and completing the process with a *terminal expression*.

Streams can only be used once. After a stream has passed through zero or more intermediate operations and reached a terminal operation, it is finished. To process the values again, you need to make a new stream.

Streams are also lazy. A stream will only process as much data as is necessary to reach the terminal condition. Recipe 3.13 shows this in action.

The recipes in this chapter demonstrate various typical stream operations.

## 3.1 Creating Streams

### Problem

You want to create a stream from a source of data.

### Solution

Use the static factory methods in the `Stream` interface, or the `stream` methods on `Iterable` or `Arrays`.

## Discussion

The new `java.util.stream.Stream` interface in Java 8 provides several static methods for creating streams. Specifically, you can use the static methods `Stream.of`, `Stream.iterate`, and `Stream.generate`.

The `Stream.of` method takes a variable argument list of elements:

```
static <T> Stream<T> of(T... values)
```

The implementation of the `of` method in the standard library actually delegates to the `stream` method in the `Arrays` class, shown in Example 3-1.

*Example 3-1. Reference implementation of Stream.of*

```
@SafeVarargs
public static<T> Stream<T> of(T... values) {
    return Arrays.stream(values);
}
```

The `@SafeVarargs` annotation is part of Java generics. It comes up when you have an array as an argument, because it is possible to assign a typed array to an `Object` array and then violate type safety with an added element. The `@SafeVarargs` annotation tells the compiler that the developer promises not to do that. See Appendix A for additional details.

As a trivial example, see Example 3-2.

Since streams do not process any data until a terminal expression is reached, each of the examples in this recipe will add a terminal method like `collect` or `forEach` at the end.

*Example 3-2. Creating a stream using Stream.of*

```
String names = Stream.of("Gomez", "Morticia", "Wednesday", "Pugsley")
    .collect(Collectors.joining(","));
System.out.println(names);
// prints Gomez,Morticia,Wednesday,Pugsley
```

The API also includes an overloaded `of` method that takes a single element `T t`. This method returns a singleton sequential stream containing a single element.

Speaking of the `Arrays.stream` method, Example 3-3 shows an example.

*Example 3-3. Creating a stream using Arrays.stream*

```
String[] munsters = { "Herman", "Lily", "Eddie", "Marilyn", "Grandpa" };
names = Arrays.stream(munsters)
    .collect(Collectors.joining(","));
System.out.println(names);
// prints Herman,Lily,Eddie,Marilyn,Grandpa
```

Since you have to create an array ahead of time, this approach is less convenient, but works well for variable argument lists. The API includes overloads of `Arrays.stream` for arrays of `int`, `long`, and `double`, as well as the generic type used here.

Another static factory method in the `Stream` interface is `iterate`. The signature of the `iterate` method is:

```
static <T> Stream<T> iterate(T seed, UnaryOperator<T> f)
```

According to the Javadocs, this method "returns an *infinite* (emphasis added) sequential ordered `Stream` produced by iterative application of a function `f` to an initial element seed." Recall that a `UnaryOperator` is a function whose single input and output types are the same (discussed in Recipe 2.4). This is useful when you have a way to produce the next value of the stream from the current value, as in Example 3-4.

*Example 3-4. Creating a stream using Stream.iterate*

```
List<BigDecimal> nums =
    Stream.iterate(BigDecimal.ONE, n -> n.add(BigDecimal.ONE) )
        .limit(10)
        .collect(Collectors.toList());
System.out.println(nums);
// prints [1, 2, 3, 4, 5, 6, 7, 8, 9, 10]

Stream.iterate(LocalDate.now(), ld -> ld.plusDays(1L))
    .limit(10)
    .forEach(System.out::println)
// prints 10 days starting from today
```

The first example counts from one using `BigDecimal` instances. The second uses the new `LocalDate` class in `java.time` and adds one day to it repeatedly. Since the resulting streams are both unbounded, the intermediate operation `limit` is needed.

The other factory method in the `Stream` class is `generate`, whose signature is:

```
static <T> Stream<T> generate(Supplier<T> s)
```

This method produces a sequential, unordered stream by repeatedly invoking the `Supplier`. A simple example of a `Supplier` in the standard library (a method that takes no arguments but produces a return value) is the `Math.random` method, which is used in Example 3-5.

*Example 3-5. Creating a stream of random doubles*

```
long count = Stream.generate(Math::random)
    .limit(10)
    .forEach(System.out::println)
```

If you already have a collection, you can take advantage of the `default` method `stream` that has been added to the `Collection` interface, as in Example 3-6.[1]

*Example 3-6. Creating a stream from a collection*

```
List<String> bradyBunch = Arrays.asList("Greg", "Marcia", "Peter", "Jan",
    "Bobby", "Cindy");
names = bradyBunch.stream()
    .collect(Collectors.joining(","));
System.out.println(names);
// prints Greg,Marcia,Peter,Jan,Bobby,Cindy
```

There are three child interfaces of `Stream` specifically for working with primitives: `IntStream`, `LongStream`, and `DoubleStream`. `IntStream` and `LongStream` each have two additional factory methods for creating streams, `range` and `rangeClosed`. Their method signatures from `IntStream` are (`LongStream` is similar):

```
static IntStream  range(int startInclusive, int endExclusive)
static IntStream  rangeClosed(int startInclusive, int endInclusive)
static LongStream range(long startInclusive, long endExclusive)
static LongStream rangeClosed(long startInclusive, long endInclusive)
```

The arguments show the difference between the two: `rangeClosed` includes the end value, and `range` doesn't. Each returns a sequential, ordered stream that starts at the first argument and increments by one after that. An example of each is shown in Example 3-7.

*Example 3-7. The range and rangeClosed methods*

```
List<Integer> ints = IntStream.range(10, 15)
    .boxed()  ❶
    .collect(Collectors.toList());
System.out.println(ints);
// prints [10, 11, 12, 13, 14]

List<Long> longs = LongStream.rangeClosed(10, 15)
    .boxed()  ❶
    .collect(Collectors.toList());
```

1 Hopefully it doesn't destroy my credibility entirely to admit that I was able to recall the names of all six Brady Bunch kids without looking them up. Believe me, I'm as horrified as you are.

```
System.out.println(longs);
// prints [10, 11, 12, 13, 14, 15]
```

❶ Necessary for `Collectors` to convert primitives to `List<T>`

The only quirk in that example is the use of the `boxed` method to convert the `int` values to `Integer` instances, which is discussed further in Recipe 3.2.

To summarize, here are the methods to create streams:

- `Stream.of(T... values)` and `Stream.of(T t)`
- `Arrays.stream(T[] array)`, with overloads for `int[]`, `double[]`, and `long[]`
- `Stream.iterate(T seed, UnaryOperator<T> f)`
- `Stream.generate(Supplier<T> s)`
- `Collection.stream()`
- Using `range` and `rangeClosed`:
  - `IntStream.range(int startInclusive, int endExclusive)`
  - `IntStream.rangeClosed(int startInclusive, int endInclusive)`
  - `LongStream.range(long startInclusive, long endExclusive)`
  - `LongStream.rangeClosed(long startInclusive, long endInclusive)`

## See Also

Streams are used throughout this book. The process of converting streams of primitives to wrapper instances is discussed in Recipe 3.2.

# 3.2 Boxed Streams

## Problem

You want to create a collection from a primitive stream.

## Solution

Use the `boxed` method on `Stream` to wrap the elements. Alternatively, map the values using the appropriate wrapper class, or use the three-argument form of the `collect` method.

## Discussion

When dealing with streams of objects, you can convert from a stream to a collection using one of the static methods in the `Collectors` class. For example, given a stream of strings, you can create a `List<String>` using the code in Example 3-8.

*Example 3-8. Converting a stream of strings to a list*

```
List<String> strings = Stream.of("this", "is", "a", "list", "of", "strings")
    .collect(Collectors.toList());
```

The same process doesn't work on streams of primitives, however. The code in Example 3-9 does not compile.

*Example 3-9. Converting a stream of int to a list of Integer (DOES NOT COMPILE)*

```
IntStream.of(3, 1, 4, 1, 5, 9)
    .collect(Collectors.toList());  // does not compile
```

You have three alternatives available as workarounds. First, use the `boxed` method on `Stream` to convert the `IntStream` to a `Stream<Integer>`, as shown in Example 3-10.

*Example 3-10. Using the boxed method*

```
List<Integer> ints = IntStream.of(3, 1, 4, 1, 5, 9)
    .boxed() ❶
    .collect(Collectors.toList());
```

❶ Converts `int` to `Integer`

One alternative is to use the `mapToObj` method to convert each element from a primitive to an instance of the wrapper class, as in Example 3-11.

*Example 3-11. Using the mapToObj method*

```
List<Integer> ints = IntStream.of(3, 1, 4, 1, 5, 9)
    .mapToObj(Integer::valueOf)
    .collect(Collectors.toList())
```

Just as `mapToInt`, `mapToLong`, and `mapToDouble` parse streams of objects into the associated primitives, the `mapToObj` method from `IntStream`, `LongStream`, and `DoubleStream` converts primitives to instances of the associated wrapper classes. The argument to `mapToObj` in this example uses the `Integer` constructor.

In JDK 9, the `Integer(int val)` constructor is deprecated for performance reasons. The recommendation is to use `Integer.valueOf(int)` instead.

Another alternative is to use the three-argument version of `collect`, whose signature is:

```
<R> R collect(Supplier<R> supplier,
              ObjIntConsumer<R> accumulator,
              BiConsumer<R,R> combiner)
```

Example 3-12 shows how to use this method.

*Example 3-12. Using the three-argument version of collect*

```
List<Integer> ints = IntStream.of(3, 1, 4, 1, 5, 9)
    .collect(ArrayList<Integer>::new, ArrayList::add, ArrayList::addAll);
```

In this version of `collect`, the `Supplier` is the constructor for `ArrayList<Integer>`, the accumulator is the `add` method, which represents how to add a single element to a list, and the combiner (which is only used during parallel operations) is `addAll`, which combines two lists into one. Using the three-argument version of `collect` is not very common, but understanding how it works is a useful skill.

Any of these approaches work, so the choice is just a matter of style.

Incidentally, if you want to convert to an array rather than a list, then the `toArray` method works just as well if not better. See Example 3-13.

*Example 3-13. Convert an IntStream to an int array*

```
int[] intArray = IntStream.of(3, 1, 4, 1, 5, 9).toArray();

// or

int[] intArray = IntStream.of(3, 1, 4, 1, 5, 9).toArray(int[]::new);
```

The first demo uses the default form of `toArray`, which returns `Object[]`. The second uses an `IntFunction<int[]>` as a generator, which creates an `int[]` of the proper size and populates it.

The fact that any of these approaches is necessary is yet another consequence of the original decision in Java to treat primitives differently from objects, complicated by the introduction of generics. Still, using `boxed` or `mapToObj` is easy enough once you know to look for them.

## See Also

Collectors are discussed in Chapter 4. Constructor references are covered in Recipe 1.3.

# 3.3 Reduction Operations Using Reduce

## Problem

You want to produce a single value from stream operations.

## Solution

Use the `reduce` method to accumulate calculations on each element.

## Discussion

The functional paradigm in Java often uses a process known as map-filter-reduce. The `map` operation transforms a stream of one type (like a `String`) into another (like an `int`, by invoking the `length` method). Then a `filter` is applied to produce a new stream with only the desired elements in it (e.g., strings with length below a certain threshold). Finally, you may wish to provide a terminal operation that generates a single value from the stream (like a sum or average of the lengths).

### Built-in reduction operations

The primitive streams `IntStream`, `LongStream`, and `DoubleStream` have several reduction operations built into the API.

For example, Table 3-1 shows the reduction operations from the `IntStream` class.

*Table 3-1. Reduction operations in the IntStream class*

| Method | Return type |
| --- | --- |
| `average` | `OptionalDouble` |
| `count` | `long` |
| `max` | `OptionalInt` |
| `min` | `OptionalInt` |
| `sum` | `int` |
| `summaryStatistics` | `IntSummaryStatistics` |
| `collect(Supplier<R> supplier, ObjIntConsumer<R> accumulator, BiConsumer<R,R> combiner)` | `R` |
| `reduce` | `int, OptionalInt` |

Reduction operations like `sum`, `count`, `max`, `min`, and `average` do what you would expect. The only interesting part is that some of them return `Optionals`, because if there are no elements in the stream (perhaps after a filtering operation) the result is undefined or null.

For example, consider reduction operations involving the lengths of a collection of strings, as in Example 3-14.

*Example 3-14. Reduction operations on IntStream*

```
String[] strings = "this is an array of strings".split(" ");
long count = Arrays.stream(strings)
        .map(String::length)          ❶
        .count();
System.out.println("There are " + count + " strings");

int totalLength = Arrays.stream(strings)
        .mapToInt(String::length)     ❷
        .sum();
System.out.println("The total length is " + totalLength);

OptionalDouble ave = Arrays.stream(strings)
        .mapToInt(String::length)     ❷
        .average();
System.out.println("The average length is " + ave);

OptionalInt max = Arrays.stream(strings)
        .mapToInt(String::length)     ❷
        .max();                       ❸

OptionalInt min = Arrays.stream(strings)
        .mapToInt(String::length)     ❷
        .min();                       ❸

System.out.println("The max and min lengths are " + max + " and " + min);
```

❶ `count` is a `Stream` method, so no need to map to `IntStream`

❷ `sum` and `average` are on the primitive streams only

❸ `max` and `min` without `Comparator` only on primitive streams

The program prints:

```
There are 6 strings
The total length is 22
The average length is OptionalDouble[3.6666666666666665]
The max and min lengths are OptionalInt[7] and OptionalInt[2]
```

Note how the average, max, and min methods return Optionals, because in principle you could have applied a filter that removed all the elements from the stream.

The count method is actually quite interesting, and is discussed in Recipe 3.7.

The Stream interface has max(Comparator) and min(Comparator), where the comparators are used to determine the max or min element. In IntStream, there are overloaded versions of both methods that do not need an argument, because the comparison is done using the natural order of integers.

The summaryStatistics method is discussed in Recipe 3.8.

The last two operations in the table, collect and reduce, bear further discussion. The collect method is used throughout this book to convert a stream into a collection, usually in combination with one of the static helper methods in the Collectors class, like toList or toSet. That version of collect does not exist on the primitive streams. The three-argument version shown here takes a collection to populate, a way to add a single element to that collection, and a way to add multiple elements to the collection. An example is shown in Recipe 3.2.

#### Basic reduce implementations

The behavior of the reduce method, however, is not necessarily intuitive until you've seen it in action.

There are two overloaded versions of the reduce method in IntStream:

```
OptionalInt reduce(IntBinaryOperator op)
int         reduce(int identity, IntBinaryOperator op)
```

The first takes an IntBinaryOperator and returns an OptionalInt. The second asks you to supply an int called identity along with an IntBinaryOperator.

Recall that a java.util.function.BiFunction takes two arguments and returns a single value, all three of which can be of different types. If both input types and the return type are all the same, the function is a BinaryOperator (think, for example, Math.max). An IntBinaryOperator is a BinaryOperator where the both inputs and the output type are all ints.

Pretend, for the moment, that you didn't think to use sum. One way to sum a series of integers would be to use the reduce method shown in Example 3-15.

*Example 3-15. Summing numbers using reduce*

```
int sum = IntStream.rangeClosed(1, 10)
    .reduce((x, y) -> x + y).orElse(0); ❶
```

❶ The value of sum is 55

Normally stream pipelines are written vertically, an approach based on a *fluent* API where the result of one method becomes the target of the next. In this case, the `reduce` method returns something other than a stream, so `orElse` is written on the same line rather than below because it's not part of the pipeline. That's just a convenience—use any formatting approach that works for you.

The `IntBinaryOperator` here is supplied by a lambda expression that takes two ints and returns their sum. Since it is conceivable that the stream could be empty if we had added a filter, the result is an `OptionalInt`. Chaining the `orElse` method to it indicates that if there are no elements in the stream, the return value should be zero.

In the lambda expression, you can think of the first argument of the binary operator as an accumulator, and the second argument as the value of each element in the stream. This is made clear if you print each one as it goes by, as shown in Example 3-16.

*Example 3-16. Printing the values of x and y*

```
int sum = IntStream.rangeClosed(1, 10)
    .reduce((x, y) -> {
        System.out.printf("x=%d, y=%d%n", x, y);
        return x + y;
    }).orElse(0);
```

The output is shown in Example 3-17.

*Example 3-17. The output of printing each value as it passes*

```
x=1, y=2
x=3, y=3
x=6, y=4
x=10, y=5
x=15, y=6
x=21, y=7
x=28, y=8
x=36, y=9
x=45, y=10

sum=55
```

As the output shows, the initial values of `x` and `y` are the first two values of the range. The value returned by the binary operator becomes the value of `x` (i.e., the accumulator) on the next iteration, while `y` takes on each value in the stream.

This is fine, but what if you wanted to process each number before summing them? Say, for example, you wanted to double all the numbers before summing them.[2] A naïve approach would be simply to try the code shown in Example 3-18.

*Example 3-18. Doubling the values during the sum (NOTE: NOT CORRECT)*

```
int doubleSum = IntStream.rangeClosed(1, 10)
    .reduce((x, y) -> x + 2 * y).orElse(0);  ❶
```

❶ The value of `doubleSum` is 109 (oops! off by one!)

Since the sum of the integers from 1 to 10 is 55, the resulting sum should be 110, but this calculation produces 109. The reason is that in the lambda expression in the `reduce` method, the initial values of `x` and `y` are 1 and 2 (the first two values of the stream), so that first value of the stream doesn't get doubled.

That's why there's an overloaded version of `reduce` that takes an initial value for the accumulator. The resulting code is shown in Example 3-19.

*Example 3-19. Doubling the values during the sum (WORKS)*

```
int doubleSum = IntStream.rangeClosed(1, 10)
    .reduce(0, (x, y) -> x + 2 * y);  ❶
```

❶ The value of `doubleSum` is 110, as it should be

By providing the initial value of zero for the accumulator `x`, the value of `y` is assigned to each of the elements in the stream, doubling them all. The values of `x` and `y` during each iteration are shown in Example 3-20.

*Example 3-20. The values of the lambda parameters during each iteration*

```
Acc=0, n=1
Acc=2, n=2
Acc=6, n=3
Acc=12, n=4
Acc=20, n=5
Acc=30, n=6
Acc=42, n=7
Acc=56, n=8
Acc=72, n=9
Acc=90, n=10
```

---

2 There are many ways to solve this problem, including just doubling the value returned by the `sum` method. The approach taken here illustrates how to use the two-argument form of `reduce`.

```
sum=110
```

Note also that when you use the version of reduce with an initial value for the accumulator, the return type is `int` rather than `OptionalInt`.

> **Identity Values of Binary Operators**
>
> The demonstrations used in this recipe referred to the first argument as an initial value for the accumulator, even though the method signature called it `identity`. The word `identity` means that you should supply a value to the binary operator that, when combined with any other value, returns the other value. For addition, the identity is zero. For multiplication, the identity is 1. For string concatenation, the identity is the empty string.
>
> For the summing operation demonstrated here, the result is the same, but it's worth keeping in mind that the actual requirement for the first argument of `reduce` is the identity value for whatever operation you are planning to use as the binary operator. Internally this becomes the initial value of the accumulator.

The standard library provides many reduction methods, but if none of them directly apply to your problem, the two forms of the `reduce` method shown here can be very helpful.

#### Binary operators in the library

A few methods have been added to the standard library that make reduction operations particularly simple. For example, `Integer`, `Long`, and `Double` all have a `sum` method that does exactly what you would expect. The implementation of the `sum` method in `Integer` is:

```
public static int sum(int a, int b) {
    return a + b;
}
```

Why bother creating a method just to add two integers, as done here? The `sum` method is a `BinaryOperator` (more specifically, an `IntBinaryOperator`) and can therefore be used easily in a `reduce` operation, as in Example 3-21.

*Example 3-21. Performing a reduce with a binary operator*

```
int sum = Stream.of(1, 2, 3, 4, 5, 6, 7, 8, 9, 10)
                .reduce(0, Integer::sum);
System.out.println(sum);
```

This time you don't even need an `IntStream`, but the result is the same. Likewise the `Integer` class now has a `max` and a `min` method, both of which are also binary operators and can be used the same way, as in Example 3-22.

*Example 3-22. Finding the max using reduce*

```
Integer max = Stream.of(3, 1, 4, 1, 5, 9)
        .reduce(Integer.MIN_VALUE, Integer::max); ❶
System.out.println("The max value is " + max);
```

❶ The identity for `max` is the minimum integer

Another interesting example is the `concat` method in `String`, which doesn't actually look like a `BinaryOperator` because the method only takes a single argument:

```
String concat(String str)
```

You can use this in a `reduce` operation anyway, as shown in Example 3-23.

*Example 3-23. Concatenating strings from a stream using reduce*

```
String s = Stream.of("this", "is", "a", "list")
        .reduce("", String::concat);
System.out.println(s);      ❶
```

❶ Prints `thisisalist`

The reason this works is that when you use a method reference via the class name (as in `String::concat`), the first parameter becomes the target of the `concat` method and the second parameter is the argument to `concat`. Since the result returns a `String`, the target, parameter, and return type are all of the same type and once again you can treat this as a binary operator for the `reduce` method.

This technique can greatly reduce[3] the size of your code, so keep that in mind when you're browsing the API.

3 Sorry about the pun.

### Using a Collector

While using concat this way works, it is inefficient because String concatenation creates and destroys objects. A better approach would be to use the collect method with a Collector.

One overload of the collect method on Stream takes a Supplier for the collection, a BiConsumer that adds a single element to the collection, and a BiConsumer that combines two collections. With strings, the natural accumulator would be a StringBuilder. The corresponding collect implementation would look like Example 3-24.

*Example 3-24. Collecting strings using a StringBuilder*

```
String s = Stream.of("this", "is", "a", "list")
        .collect(() -> new StringBuilder(),        ❶
                (sb, str) -> sb.append(str),       ❷
                (sb1, sb2) -> sb1.append(sb2))     ❸
        .toString();
```

❶ Result Supplier

❷ Add a single value to the result

❸ Combine two results

This approach can be more simply expressed using method references, as in Example 3-25.

*Example 3-25. Collecting strings, with method references*

```
String s = Stream.of("this", "is", "a", "list")
        .collect(StringBuilder::new,
                StringBuilder::append,
                StringBuilder::append)
        .toString();
```

Simplest of all, however, would be to use the joining method in the Collectors utility class, as in Example 3-26.

*Example 3-26. Joining strings using Collectors*

```
String s = Stream.of("this", "is", "a", "list")
        .collect(Collectors.joining());
```

The joining method is overloaded to also take a string delimiter. It's hard to beat that for simplicity. For more details and examples, see Recipe 4.2.

### The most general form of reduce

The third form of the `reduce` method is:

```
<U> U reduce(U identity,
             BiFunction<U,? super T,U> accumulator,
             BinaryOperator<U> combiner)
```

This is a bit more complicated, and there are normally easier ways to accomplish the same goal, but an example of how to use it might be useful.

Consider a `Book` class with simply an integer ID and a string title, as in Example 3-27.

*Example 3-27. A simple Book class*

```
public class Book {
    private Integer id;
    private String title;

    // ... constructors, getters and setters, toString, equals, hashCode ...
}
```

Say you have a list of books and you want to add them to a `Map`, where the keys are the IDs and the values are the books themselves.

The example shown here can be solved much more easily using the `Collectors.toMap` method, which is demonstrated in Recipe 4.3. It is used here because its simplicity will hopefully make it easier to focus on the more complex version of `reduce`.

One way to accomplish that is shown in Example 3-28.

*Example 3-28. Accumulating Books into a Map*

```
HashMap<Integer, Book> bookMap = books.stream()
    .reduce(new HashMap<Integer, Book>(),  ❶
            (map, book) -> {               ❷
                map.put(book.getId(), book);
                return map;
            },
            (map1, map2) -> {              ❸
                map1.putAll(map2);
                return map1;
            });

bookMap.forEach((k,v) -> System.out.println(k + ": " + v));
```

❶ Identity value for `putAll`

❷ Accumulate a single book into `Map` using `put`

❸ Combine multiple `Maps` using `putAll`

It's easiest to examine the arguments to the `reduce` method in reverse order.

The last argument is a `combiner`, which is required to be a `BinaryOperator`. In this case, the provided lambda expression takes two maps and copies all the keys from the second map into the first one and returns it. The lambda expression would be simpler if the `putAll` method returned the map, but no such luck. The combiner is only relevant if the `reduce` operation is done in parallel, because then you need to combine maps produced from each portion of the range.

The second argument is a function that adds a single book to a `Map`. This too would be simpler if the `put` method on `Map` returned the `Map` after the new entry was added.

The first argument to the `reduce` method is the identity value for the `combiner` function. In this case, the identity value is an empty `Map`, because that combined with any other `Map` returns the other `Map`.

The output from this program is:

```
1: Book{id=1, title='Modern Java Recipes'}
2: Book{id=2, title='Making Java Groovy'}
3: Book{id=3, title='Gradle Recipes for Android'}
```

Reduction operations are fundamental to the functional programming idiom. In many common cases, the `Stream` interfaces provide a built-in method for you, like `sum` or `collect(Collectors.joining(',')`. If you need to write your own, however, this recipe shows how to use the `reduce` operation directly.

The best news is that once you understand how to use `reduce` in Java 8, you know how to use the same operation in other languages, even if it goes by different names (like `inject` in Groovy or `fold` in Scala). They all work the same way.

## See Also

A much simpler way to turn a list of POJOs into a `Map` is shown in Recipe 4.3. Summary statistics are discussed in Recipe 3.8. Collectors are discussed in Chapter 4.

# 3.4 Check Sorting Using Reduce

## Problem

You want to check that a sort is correct.

## Solution

Use the `reduce` method to check each pair of elements.

## Discussion

The `reduce` method on `Stream` takes a `BinaryOperator` as an argument:

```
Optional<T> reduce(BinaryOperator<T> accumulator)
```

A `BinaryOperator` is a `Function` where both input types and the output type are all the same. As shown in Recipe 3.3, the first element in the `BinaryOperator` is normally an accumulator, while the second element takes each value of the stream, as in Example 3-29.

*Example 3-29. Summing BigDecimals with reduce*

```
BigDecimal total = Stream.iterate(BigDecimal.ONE, n -> n.add(BigDecimal.ONE))
        .limit(10)
        .reduce(BigDecimal.ZERO, (acc, val) -> acc.add(val)); ❶
System.out.println("The total is " + total);
```

❶ Using the `add` method in `BigDecimal` as a `BinaryOperator`

As usual, whatever is returned by the lambda expression becomes the value of the `acc` variable on the next iteration. In this way, the calculation accumulates the values of the first 10 `BigDecimal` instances.

This is the most typical way of using the `reduce` method, but just because `acc` here is used as an accumulator doesn't mean it has to be thought of as such. Consider sorting strings instead, using the approach discussed in Recipe 4.1. The code snippet shown in Example 3-30 sorts strings by length.

*Example 3-30. Sorting strings by length*

```
List<String> strings = Arrays.asList(
    "this", "is", "a", "list", "of", "strings");

List<String> sorted = strings.stream()
    .sorted(Comparator.comparingInt(String::length))
    .collect(toList());    ❶
```

❶ Result is `["a", "is", "of", "this", "list", "strings"]`

The question is, how do you test this? Each adjacent pair of strings has to be compared by length to make sure the first is equal to or shorter than the second. The reduce method here works well, however, as Example 3-31 shows (part of a JUnit test case).

*Example 3-31. Testing that strings are sorted properly*

```
strings.stream()
    .reduce((prev, curr) -> {
        assertTrue(prev.length() <= curr.length());  ❶
        return curr;                                  ❷
    });
```

❶ Check each pair is sorted properly

❷ curr becomes the next value of prev

For each consecutive pair, the previous and current parameters are assigned to variables prev and curr. The assertion tests that the previous length is less than or equal to the current length. The important part is that the argument to reduce returns the value of the current string, curr, which becomes the value of prev on the next iteration.

The only thing required to make this work is for the stream to be sequential and ordered, as here.

## See Also

The reduce method is discussed in Recipe 3.3. Sorting is discussed in Recipe 4.1.

# 3.5 Debugging Streams with peek

## Problem

You want to see the individual elements of a stream as they are processed.

## Solution

Invoke the peek intermediate operation wherever you need it in a stream pipeline.

## Discussion

Stream processing consists of a series of zero or more intermediate operations followed by a terminal operation. Each intermediate operation returns a new stream. The terminal operation returns something other than a stream.

Newcomers to Java 8 sometimes find the sequence of intermediate operations on a stream pipeline confusing, because they have trouble visualizing the stream values as they are processed.

Consider a simple method that accepts a start and end range for a stream of integers, doubles each number, and then sums up only the resulting values divisible by 3, as shown in Example 3-32.

*Example 3-32. Doubling integers, filtering, and summing*

```
public int sumDoublesDivisibleBy3(int start, int end) {
    return IntStream.rangeClosed(start, end)
        .map(n -> n * 2)
        .filter(n -> n % 3 == 0)
        .sum();
}
```

A simple test could prove that this is working properly:

```
@Test
public void sumDoublesDivisibleBy3() throws Exception {
    assertEquals(1554, demo.sumDoublesDivisibleBy3(100, 120));
}
```

That's helpful, but doesn't deliver a lot of insight. If the code wasn't working, it would be very difficult to figure out where the problem lay.

Imagine that you added a `map` operation to the pipeline that took each value, printed it, and then returned the value again, as in Example 3-33.

*Example 3-33. Adding an identity map for printing*

```
public int sumDoublesDivisibleBy3(int start, int end) {
    return IntStream.rangeClosed(start, end)
        .map(n -> { ❶
            System.out.println(n);
            return n;
        })
        .map(n -> n * 2)
        .filter(n -> n % 3 == 0)
        .sum();
}
```

❶ Identity map that prints each element before returning it

The result prints the numbers from `start` to `end`, inclusive, with one number per line. While you might not want this in production code, it gives you a look inside the stream processing without interfering with it.

This behavior is exactly how the `peek` method in `Stream` works. The declaration of the `peek` method is:

```
Stream<T> peek(Consumer<? super T> action)
```

According to the Javadocs, the `peek` method "returns a stream consisting of the elements of this stream, additionally performing the provided action on each element as they are consumed from the resulting stream." Recall that a `Consumer` takes a single input but returns nothing, so any provided `Consumer` will not corrupt each value as it streams by.

Since `peek` is an intermediate operation, the `peek` method can be added multiple times if you wish, as in Example 3-34.

*Example 3-34. Using multiple peek methods*

```
public int sumDoublesDivisibleBy3(int start, int end) {
    return IntStream.rangeClosed(start, end)
        .peek(n -> System.out.printf("original: %d%n", n)) ❶
        .map(n -> n * 2)
        .peek(n -> System.out.printf("doubled : %d%n", n)) ❷
        .filter(n -> n % 3 == 0)
        .peek(n -> System.out.printf("filtered: %d%n", n)) ❸
        .sum();
}
```

❶ Print value before doubling

❷ Print value after doubling but before filtering

❸ Print value after filtering but before summing

The result will show each element in its original form, then after it has been doubled, and finally only if it passes the filter. The output is:

```
original: 100
doubled : 200
original: 101
doubled : 202
original: 102
doubled : 204
filtered: 204
...
original: 119
doubled : 238
original: 120
doubled : 240
filtered: 240
```

Unfortunately, there's no easy way to make the peek code optional, so this is a convenient step to use for debugging but should be removed in production code.

## 3.6 Converting Strings to Streams and Back

### Problem

Rather than loop over individual characters of a `String`, you would like to use the idiomatic `Stream` processing techniques.

### Solution

Use the default methods `chars` and `codePoints` from the `java.lang.CharSequence` interface to convert a `String` into an `IntStream`. To convert back to a `String`, use the overload of the `collect` method on `IntStream` that takes a `Supplier`, a `BiConsumer` representing an accumulator, and a `BiConsumer` representing a combiner.

### Discussion

Strings are collections of characters, so in principle it should be as easy to convert a string into a stream as it is any other collection or array. Unfortunately, `String` is not part of the Collections framework, and therefore does not implement `Iterable`, so there is no `stream` factory method to convert one into a `Stream`. The other option would be the static `stream` methods in the `java.util.Arrays` class, but while there are versions of `Arrays.stream` for `int[]`, `long[]`, `double[]`, and even `T[]`, there isn't one for `char[]`. It's almost as if the designers of the API didn't want you to process a `String` using stream techniques.

Still, there is an approach that works. The `String` class implements the `CharSequence` interface, and that interface contains two new methods that produce an `IntStream`. Both methods are default methods in the interface, so they have an implementation available. The signatures are in Example 3-35.

*Example 3-35. Stream methods in java.lang.CharSequence*

```
default IntStream chars()
default IntStream codePoints()
```

The difference between the two methods has to do with how Java handles UTF-16-encoded characters as opposed to the full Unicode set of code points. If you're interested, the differences are explained in the Javadocs for `java.lang.Character`. For the methods shown here, the difference is only in the type of integers returned. The former returns a `IntStream` consisting of `char` values from this sequence, while the latter returns an `IntStream` of Unicode code points.

The opposite question is how to convert a stream of characters back into a `String`. The `Stream.collect` method is used to perform a mutable reduction on the elements of a stream to produce a collection. The version of `collect` that takes a `Collector` is most commonly used, because the `Collectors` utility class provides many static methods (like `toList`, `toSet`, `toMap`, `joining`, and many others discussed in this book) that produce the desired `Collector`.

Conspicuous by its absence, however, is a `Collector` that will take a stream of characters and assemble it into a `String`. Fortunately, that code isn't difficult to write, using the other overload of `collect`, which takes a `Supplier` and two `BiConsumer` arguments, one as an accumulator and one as a combiner.

This all sounds a lot more complicated than it is in practice. Consider writing a method to check if a string is a palindrome. Palindromes are not case sensitive, and they remove all punctuation before checking whether the resulting string is the same forward as backward. In Java 7 or earlier, Example 3-36 shows one way to write a method that tests strings.

*Example 3-36. Checking for palindromes in Java 7 or earlier*

```
public boolean isPalindrome(String s) {
    StringBuilder sb = new StringBuilder();
    for (char c : s.toCharArray()) {
        if (Character.isLetterOrDigit(c)) {
            sb.append(c);
        }
    }
    String forward = sb.toString().toLowerCase();
    String backward = sb.reverse().toString().toLowerCase();
    return forward.equals(backward);
}
```

As is typical in code written in a nonfunctional style, the method declares a separate object with mutable state (the `StringBuilder` instance), then iterates over a collection (the `char[]` returned by the `toCharArray` method in `String`), using an `if` condition to decide whether to append a value to the buffer. The `StringBuilder` class also has a `reverse` method to make checking for palindromes easier, while the `String` class does not. This combination of mutable state, iteration, and decision statements cries out for an alternative stream-based approach.

That stream-based alternative is shown in Example 3-37.

*Example 3-37. Checking for palindromes using Java 8 streams*

```
public boolean isPalindrome(String s) {
    String forward = s.toLowerCase().codePoints()  ❶
        .filter(Character::isLetterOrDigit)
        .collect(StringBuilder::new,
                 StringBuilder::appendCodePoint,
                 StringBuilder::append)
        .toString();

  String backward = new StringBuilder(forward).reverse().toString();
  return forward.equals(backward);
}
```

❶ Returns an `IntStream`

The `codePoints` method returns an `IntStream`, which can then be filtered using the same condition as in Example 3-37. The interesting part is in the `collect` method, whose signature is:

```
<R> R collect(Supplier<R> supplier,
              BiConsumer<R,? super T> accumulator,
              BiConsumer<R,R> combiner)
```

The arguments are:

- A `Supplier`, which produces the resulting reduced object, in this case a `StringBuilder`.
- A `BiConsumer` used to accumulate each element of the stream into the resulting data structure; this example uses the `appendCodePoint` method.
- A `BiConsumer` representing a combiner, which is a "non-interfering, stateless function" for combining two values that must be compatible with the accumulator; in this case, the `append` method. Note that the combiner is only used if the operation is done in parallel.

That sounds like a lot, but the advantage in this case is that the code doesn't have to make a distinction between characters and integers, which is often an issue when working with elements of strings.

Example 3-38 shows a simple test of the method.

*Example 3-38. Testing the palindrome checker*

```
private PalindromeEvaluator demo = new PalindromeEvaluator();

@Test
public void isPalindrome() throws Exception {
    assertTrue(
```

```
        Stream.of("Madam, in Eden, I'm Adam",
                  "Go hang a salami; I'm a lasagna hog",
                  "Flee to me, remote elf!",
                  "A Santa pets rats as Pat taps a star step at NASA")
              .allMatch(demo::isPalindrome));

    assertFalse(demo.isPalindrome("This is NOT a palindrome"));
}
```

Viewing strings as arrays of characters doesn't quite fit the functional idioms in Java 8, but the mechanisms in this recipe hopefully show how they can be made to work.

## See Also

Collectors are discussed further in Chapter 4, with the case of implementing your own collector the subject of Recipe 4.9. The `allMatch` method is discussed in Recipe 3.10.

# 3.7 Counting Elements

## Problem

You want to know how many elements are in a stream.

## Solution

Use either the `Stream.count` or `Collectors.counting` methods.

## Discussion

This recipe is almost too easy, but does serve to demonstrate a technique that will be revisited later in Recipe 4.6.

The `Stream` interface has a default method called `count` that returns a `long`, which is demonstrated in Example 3-39.

*Example 3-39. Counting elements in a stream*

```
long count = Stream.of(3, 1, 4, 1, 5, 9, 2, 6, 5).count();
System.out.printf("There are %d elements in the stream%n", count); ❶
```

❶ Prints `There are 9 elements in the stream`

One interesting feature of the `count` method is that the Javadocs show how it is implemented. The docs say, "this is a special case of a reduction and is equivalent to":

```
return mapToLong(e -> 1L).sum();
```

First every element in the stream is mapped to `1` as a `long`. Then the `mapToLong` method produces a `LongStream`, which has a `sum` method. In other words, map all the elements to ones and add them up. Nice and simple.

An alternative is to notice that the `Collectors` class has a similar method, called `counting`, shown in Example 3-40.

*Example 3-40. Counting the elements using Collectors.counting*

```
count = Stream.of(3, 1, 4, 1, 5, 9, 2, 6, 5)
    .collect(Collectors.counting());
System.out.printf("There are %d elements in the stream%n", count);
```

The result is the same. The question is, why do this? Why not use the `count` method on `Stream` instead?

You can, of course, and arguably should. Where this becomes useful, however, is as a *downstream collector*, discussed more extensively in Recipe 4.6. As a spoiler, consider Example 3-41.

*Example 3-41. Counting string partitioned by length*

```
Map<Boolean, Long> numberLengthMap = strings.stream()
    .collect(Collectors.partitioningBy(
        s -> s.length() % 2 == 0, ❶
        Collectors.counting()));  ❷

numberLengthMap.forEach((k,v) -> System.out.printf("%5s: %d%n", k, v));
//
// false: 4
//  true: 8
```

❶ Predicate

❷ Downstream collector

The first argument to `partitioningBy` is a `Predicate`, used to separate the strings into two categories: those that satisfy the predicate, and those that do not. If that was the only argument to `partitioningBy`, the result would be a `Map<Boolean, List<String>>`, where the keys would be the values `true` and `false`, and the values would be lists of even- and odd-length strings.

The two-argument overload of `partitioningBy` used here takes a `Predicate` followed by a `Collector`, called a downstream collector, which postprocesses each list of strings returned. This is the use case for the `Collectors.counting` method. The output now is a `Map<Boolean, Long>` where the values are the number of even- and odd-length strings in the stream.

Several other methods in `Stream` have analogs in `Collectors` methods, which are discussed in that section. In each case, if you are working directly with a stream, use the `Stream` methods. The `Collectors` methods are intended for downstream post-processing of a `partitioningBy` or `groupingBy` operation.

## See Also

Downstream collectors are discussed in Recipe 4.6. Collectors in general are discussed in several recipes included in Chapter 4. Counting is a built-in reduction operation, as discussed in Recipe 3.3.

# 3.8 Summary Statistics

## Problem

You want the count, sum, min, max, and average of a stream of numerical values.

## Solution

Use the `summaryStatistics` method in `IntStream`, `DoubleStream`, and `LongStream`.

## Discussion

The primitive streams `IntStream`, `DoubleStream`, and `LongStream` add methods to the `Stream` interface that work for primitive types. One of those methods is `summaryStatistics`, shown in Example 3-42.

*Example 3-42. SummaryStatistics*

```
DoubleSummaryStatistics stats = DoubleStream.generate(Math::random)
    .limit(1_000_000)
    .summaryStatistics();

System.out.println(stats);  ❶

System.out.println("count: " + stats.getCount());
System.out.println("min  : " + stats.getMin());
System.out.println("max  : " + stats.getMax());
System.out.println("sum  : " + stats.getSum());
System.out.println("ave  : " + stats.getAverage());
```

❶ Print using the `toString` method

Java 7 added the capability to use underscores in numerical literals, as in 1_000_000.

A typical run yields:

```
DoubleSummaryStatistics{count=1000000, sum=499608.317465, min=0.000001,
    average=0.499608, max=0.999999}
count: 1000000
min  : 1.3938598313334438E-6
max  : 0.9999988915490642
sum  : 499608.31746475823
ave  : 0.49960831746475826
```

The `toString` implementation of `DoubleSummaryStatistics` shows all the values, but the class also has getter methods for the individual quantities: `getCount`, `getSum`, `getMax`, `getMin`, and `getAverage`. With one million doubles, it's not surprising that the minimum is close to zero, the maximum is close to 1, the sum is approximately 500,000, and the average is nearly 0.5.

There are two other interesting methods in the `DoubleSummaryStatistics` class:

```
void accept(double value)
void combine(DoubleSummaryStatistics other)
```

The `accept` method records another value into the summary information. The `combine` method combines two `DoubleSummaryStatistics` objects into one. They are used when adding data to an instance of the class before computing the results.

As an example, the website Spotrac (*http://www.spotrac.com*) keeps track of payroll statistics for various sports teams. In the source code for this book you will find a file holding the team salary payroll for all 30 teams in Major League Baseball for the 2017 season, taken from this site.[4]

The source code in Example 3-43 defines a class called `Team` that contains an `id`, a team `name`, and a total `salary`.

*Example 3-43. Team class contains id, name, and salary*

```
public class Team {
    private static final NumberFormat nf = NumberFormat.getCurrencyInstance();

    private int id;
    private String name;
```

4 Source: *http://www.spotrac.com/mlb/payroll/*, where you can specify a year or other information.

```
    private double salary;

    // ... constructors, getters and setters ...

    @Override
    public String toString() {
        return "Team{" +
                "id=" + id +
                ", name='" + name + '\'' +
                ", salary=" + nf.format(salary) +
                '}';
    }
}
```

After parsing the team salary file, the results are:

```
Team{id=1, name='Los Angeles Dodgers', salary=$245,269,535.00}
Team{id=2, name='Boston Red Sox', salary=$202,135,939.00}
Team{id=3, name='New York Yankees', salary=$202,095,552.00}
...
Team{id=28, name='San Diego Padres', salary=$73,754,027.00}
Team{id=29, name='Tampa Bay Rays', salary=$73,102,766.00}
Team{id=30, name='Milwaukee Brewers', salary=$62,094,433.00}
```

There are now two ways to compute the summary statistics on the collection of teams. The first is to use the three-argument `collect` method as in Example 3-44.

*Example 3-44. Collect with a Supplier, accumulator, and combiner*

```
DoubleSummaryStatistics teamStats = teams.stream()
        .mapToDouble(Team::getSalary)
        .collect(DoubleSummaryStatistics::new,
                 DoubleSummaryStatistics::accept,
                 DoubleSummaryStatistics::combine);
```

This version of the `collect` method is discussed in Recipe 4.9. Here it relies on a constructor reference to supply an instance of `DoubleSummaryStatistics`, the `accept` method to add another value to an existing `DoubleSummaryStatistics` object, and the `combine` method to combine two separate `DoubleSummaryStatistics` objects into one.

The results are (formatted for easy reading):

```
30 teams
  sum = $4,232,271,100.00
  min =     $62,094,433.00
  max =   $245,269,535.00
  ave =   $141,075,703.33
```

The recipe on downstream collectors (Recipe 4.6) shows an alternative way to compute the same data. In this case, the summary is computed as in Example 3-45.

*Example 3-45. Collect using summarizingDouble*

```
teamStats = teams.stream()
        .collect(Collectors.summarizingDouble(Team::getSalary));
```

The argument to the `Collectors.summarizingDouble` method is the salary for each team. Either way, the result is the same.

The summary statistics classes are essentially a "poor developer's" approach to statistics. They're limited to only the properties shown (count, max, min, sum, and average), but if those are all you need, it's nice to know the library provides them automatically.[5]

## See Also

Summary statistics is a special form of a reduction operation. Others appear in Recipe 3.3. Downstream collectors are covered in Recipe 4.6. The multi-argument `collect` method is discussed in Recipe 4.9.

# 3.9 Finding the First Element in a Stream

## Problem

You wish to find the first element in a stream that satisfies a particular condition.

## Solution

Use the `findFirst` or `findAny` method after applying a filter.

## Discussion

The `findFirst` and `findAny` methods in `java.util.stream.Stream` return an `Optional` describing the first element of a stream. Neither takes an argument, implying that any mapping or filtering operations have already been done.

For example, given a list of integers, to find the first even number, apply an even-number filter and then use `findFirst`, as in Example 3-46.

*Example 3-46. Finding the first even integer*

```
Optional<Integer> firstEven = Stream.of(3, 1, 4, 1, 5, 9, 2, 6, 5)
    .filter(n -> n % 2 == 0)
```

5 Of course, another lesson of this recipe is that if you can find a way to play Major League Baseball, you probably ought to consider it, even if only for a short time. Java will still be here when you're done.

```
    .findFirst();

System.out.println(firstEven); ❶
```

❶ Prints `Optional[4]`

If the stream is empty, the return value is an empty `Optional` (see Example 3-47).

*Example 3-47. Using findFirst on an empty stream*

```
Optional<Integer> firstEvenGT10 = Stream.of(3, 1, 4, 1, 5, 9, 2, 6, 5)
    .filter(n -> n > 10)
    .filter(n -> n % 2 == 0)
    .findFirst();

System.out.println(firstEvenGT10); ❶
```

❶ Prints `Optional.empty`

Since the code returns the first element after applying the filter, you might think that it involves a lot of wasted work. Why apply a modulus operation to all the elements and then pick just the first one? Stream elements are actually processed one by one, so this isn't a problem. This is discussed in Recipe 3.13.

If the stream has no encounter order, then any element may be returned. In the current example, the stream does have an encounter order, so the "first" even number (in the original example) is always 4, *whether we do the search using a sequential or a parallel stream.* See Example 3-48.

*Example 3-48. Using firstEven in parallel*

```
firstEven = Stream.of(3, 1, 4, 1, 5, 9, 2, 6, 5)
    .parallel()
    .filter(n -> n % 2 == 0)
    .findFirst();

System.out.println(firstEven); ❶
```

❶ Always prints `Optional[4]`

That feels bizarre at first. Why would you get the same value back even though several numbers are being processed at the same time? The answer lies in the notion of *encounter order*.

The API defines encounter order as the order in which the source of data makes its elements available. A `List` and an array both have an encounter order, but a `Set` does not.

There is also a method called `unordered` in `BaseStream` (which `Stream` extends) that (optionally!) returns an unordered stream as an intermediate operation, though it may not.

## Sets and Encounter Order

`HashSet` instances have no defined encounter order, but if you initialize one with the same data repeatedly (in Java 8) you will get the same order of elements each time. That means using `findFirst` will give the same result each time as well. The method documentation says that `findFirst` *may* give a different result on unordered streams, but the current implementation doesn't change its behavior just because the stream is unordered.

To get a `Set` with a different encounter order, you can add and remove enough elements to force a rehash. For example:

```
List<String> wordList = Arrays.asList(
    "this", "is", "a", "stream", "of", "strings");
Set<String> words = new HashSet<>(wordList);
Set<String> words2 = new HashSet<>(words);

// Now add and remove enough elements to force a rehash
IntStream.rangeClosed(0, 50).forEachOrdered(i ->
  words2.add(String.valueOf(i)));
words2.retainAll(wordList);

// The sets are equal, but have different element ordering
System.out.println(words.equals(words2));
System.out.println("Before: " + words);
System.out.println("After : " + words2);
```

The outputs will be something like:

```
true
Before: [a, strings, stream, of, this, is]
After : [this, is, strings, stream, of, a]
```

The ordering is different, so the result of `findFirst` will be different.

In Java 9, the new immutable sets (and maps) are randomized, so their iteration orders will change from run to run, even if they are initialized the same way every time.[6]

The `findAny` method returns an `Optional` describing some element of the stream, or an empty `Optional` if the stream is empty. In this case, the behavior of the operation

6 Thanks to Stuart Marks for this explanation.

is *explicitly nondeterministic*, meaning it is free to select any element of the stream. This allows optimization in parallel operations.

To demonstrate this, consider returning any element from an unordered, parallel stream of integers. Example 3-49 introduces an artificial delay by mapping each element to itself after a random delay of up to 100 milliseconds.

*Example 3-49. Using findAny in parallel after a random delay*

```
public Integer delay(Integer n) {
    try {
        Thread.sleep((long) (Math.random() * 100));
    } catch (InterruptedException ignored) { ❶
    }
    return n;
}

// ...

Optional<Integer> any = Stream.of(3, 1, 4, 1, 5, 9, 2, 6, 5)
    .unordered()        ❷
    .parallel()         ❸
    .map(this::delay)   ❹
    .findAny();         ❺

System.out.println("Any: " + any);
```

❶ The only exception in Java that it is OK to catch and ignore[7]

❷ We don't care about order

❸ Use the common fork-join pool in parallel

❹ Introduce a random delay

❺ Return the first element, regardless of encounter order

The output now could be any of the given numbers, depending on which thread gets there first.

Both `findFirst` and `findAny` are *short-circuiting*, *terminal* operations. A short-circuiting operation may produce a finite stream when presented with an infinite one. A terminal operation is short-circuiting if it may terminate in finite time even when presented with infinite input.

---

7 To be serious for a moment, it's not a good idea to catch and ignore any exception. It's just fairly common to do so with `InterruptedException`. That doesn't make it a great idea, though.

Note that the examples used in this recipe demonstrate that sometimes parallelization can hurt rather than help performance. Streams are lazy, meaning they will only process as many elements as are necessary to satisfy the pipeline. In this case, since the requirement is simply to return the first element, firing up a fork-join pool is overkill. See Example 3-50.

*Example 3-50. Using findAny on sequential and parallel streams*

```
Optional<Integer> any = Stream.of(3, 1, 4, 1, 5, 9, 2, 6, 5)
    .unordered()
    .map(this::delay)
    .findAny(); ❶

System.out.println("Sequential Any: " + any);

any = Stream.of(3, 1, 4, 1, 5, 9, 2, 6, 5)
    .unordered()
    .parallel()
    .map(this::delay)
    .findAny(); ❷

System.out.println("Parallel Any: " + any);
```

❶ Sequential stream (by default)

❷ Parallel stream

Typical output looks like the following (on an eight-core machine, which therefore uses a fork-join pool with eight threads by default).[8]

For sequential processing:

```
main // sequential, so only one thread
Sequential Any: Optional[3]
```

For parallel processing:

```
ForkJoinPool.commonPool-worker-1
ForkJoinPool.commonPool-worker-5
ForkJoinPool.commonPool-worker-3
ForkJoinPool.commonPool-worker-6
ForkJoinPool.commonPool-worker-7
main
ForkJoinPool.commonPool-worker-2
ForkJoinPool.commonPool-worker-4
Parallel Any: Optional[1]
```

8 This demo assumes that the delay method has been modified to print the name of the current thread along with the value it is processing.

The sequential stream only needs to access one element, which it then returns, short-circuiting the process. The parallel stream fires up eight different threads, finds one element, and shuts them all down. The parallel stream therefore accesses many values it doesn't need.

Again, the key concept is that of encounter order with streams. If the stream has an encounter order, then `findFirst` will always return the same value. The `findAny` method is allowed to return any element, making it more appropriate for parallel operations.

## See Also

Lazy streams are discussed in Recipe 3.13. Parallel streams are in Chapter 9.

# 3.10 Using anyMatch, allMatch, and noneMatch

## Problem

You wish to determine if any elements in a stream match a `Predicate`, or if all match, or if none match.

## Solution

Use the methods `anyMatch`, `allMatch`, and `noneMatch` on the `Stream` interface, each of which returns a boolean.

## Discussion

The signatures of the `anyMatch`, `allMatch`, and `noneMatch` methods on `Stream` are:

```
boolean anyMatch(Predicate<? super T> predicate)
boolean allMatch(Predicate<? super T> predicate)
boolean noneMatch(Predicate<? super T> predicate)
```

Each does exactly what it sounds like. As an example, consider a prime number calculator. A number is prime if none of the integers from 2 up to the value minus 1 evenly divide into it.

A trivial way to check if a number is prime is to compute the modulus of the number from every number from 2 up to its square root, rounded up, as in Example 3-51.

*Example 3-51. Prime number check*

```
public boolean isPrime(int num) {
    int limit = (int) (Math.sqrt(num) + 1);          ❶
    return num == 2 || num > 1 && IntStream.range(2, limit)
```

```java
        .noneMatch(divisor -> num % divisor == 0); ❷
}
```

❶ Upper limit for check

❷ Using `noneMatch`

The `noneMatch` method makes the calculation particularly simple.

> **BigInteger and Primes**
>
> Interestingly, the `java.math.BigInteger` class has the method `isProbablyPrime`, which has the following signature:
>
> ```java
> boolean isProbablyPrime(int certainty)
> ```
>
> If the method returns `false`, the value is definitely composite. For `true`, however, the `certainty` argument comes into play.
>
> The value of `certainty` represents the amount of uncertainty that the caller is willing to tolerate. If the method returns `true`, the probability that the number is actually prime exceeds `1 - 1/2^{certainty}`, so a `certainty` of 2 implies a probability of 0.5, a `certainty` of 3 implies 0.75, 4 implies 0.875, 5 implies 0.9375, and so on.
>
> Asking for greater values of `certainty` makes the algorithm take longer.

Two ways to test the calculation are shown in Example 3-52.

*Example 3-52. Tests for the prime calculation*

```java
private Primes calculator = new Primes();

@Test ❶
public void testIsPrimeUsingAllMatch() throws Exception {
    assertTrue(IntStream.of(2, 3, 5, 7, 11, 13, 17, 19)
        .allMatch(calculator::isPrime));
}

@Test ❷
public void testIsPrimeWithComposites() throws Exception {
    assertFalse(Stream.of(4, 6, 8, 9, 10, 12, 14, 15, 16, 18, 20)
        .anyMatch(calculator::isPrime));
}
```

❶ Use `allMatch` for simplicity

❷ Test with composites

The first test invokes the `allMatch` method, whose argument is a `Predicate`, on a stream of known primes and returns `true` only if all the values are prime.

The second test uses `anyMatch` with a collection of composite (nonprime) numbers, and asserts that none of them satisfy the predicate.

The `anyMatch`, `allMatch`, and `noneMatch` methods are convenient ways to check a stream of values against a particular condition.

You need to be aware of one problematic edge condition. The `anyMatch`, `allMatch`, and `noneMatch` methods don't necessarily behave intuitively on empty streams, as the tests in Example 3-53 show.

*Example 3-53. Testing empty streams*

```
@Test
public void emptyStreamsDanger() throws Exception {
    assertTrue(Stream.empty().allMatch(e -> false));
    assertTrue(Stream.empty().noneMatch(e -> true));
    assertFalse(Stream.empty().anyMatch(e -> true));
}
```

For both `allMatch` and `noneMatch`, the Javadocs say, "if the stream is empty then `true` is returned and the predicate is not evaluated," so in both of these cases the predicate can be anything. For `anyMatch`, the method returns `false` on an empty stream. That can lead to very difficult-to-diagnose errors, so be careful.

The `allMatch` and `noneMatch` methods return `true` and the `anyMatch` method returns false on an empty stream regardless of the supplied predicate. Any supplied predicate is not evaluated when the stream is empty.

## See Also

Predicates are discussed in Recipe 2.3.

# 3.11 Stream flatMap Versus map

## Problem

You have a stream and you need to transform the elements in some way, but you're not sure whether to use `map` or `flatMap`.

## Solution

Use `map` if each element is transformed into a single value. Use `flatMap` if each element will be transformed to multiple values and the resulting stream needs to be "flattened."

## Discussion

Both the `map` and the `flatMap` methods on `Stream` take a `Function` as an argument. The signature for `map` is:

```
<R> Stream<R> map(Function<? super T,? extends R> mapper)
```

A `Function` takes a single input and transforms it into a single output. In the case of `map`, a single input of type `T` is transformed into a single output of type `R`.

Consider a `Customer` class, where a customer has a name and a collection of `Order`. To keep things simple, the `Order` class just has an integer ID. Both classes are shown in Example 3-54.

*Example 3-54. A one-to-many relationship*

```
public class Customer {
    private String name;
    private List<Order> orders = new ArrayList<>();

    public Customer(String name) {
        this.name = name;
    }

    public String getName() { return name; }
    public List<Order> getOrders() { return orders; }

    public Customer addOrder(Order order) {
        orders.add(order);
        return this;
    }
}

public class Order {
    private int id;

    public Order(int id) {
        this.id = id;
    }

    public int getId() { return id; }
}
```

Now create a few customers and add some orders, as in Example 3-55.

*Example 3-55. Sample customers with orders*

```
Customer sheridan = new Customer("Sheridan");
Customer ivanova = new Customer("Ivanova");
Customer garibaldi = new Customer("Garibaldi");

sheridan.addOrder(new Order(1))
        .addOrder(new Order(2))
        .addOrder(new Order(3));
ivanova.addOrder(new Order(4))
        .addOrder(new Order(5));

List<Customer> customers = Arrays.asList(sheridan, ivanova, garibaldi);
```

A map operation is done when there is a one-to-one relationship between the input parameter and the output type. In this case, you can map the customers to names and print them, as in Example 3-56.

*Example 3-56. Using map on Customer to name*

```
customers.stream()                     ❶
        .map(Customer::getName)        ❷
        .forEach(System.out::println); ❸
```

❶ Stream<Customer>

❷ Stream<String>

❸ Sheridan, Ivanova, Garibaldi

If instead of mapping customers to name, you map them to orders, you get a collection of collections, as in Example 3-57.

*Example 3-57. Using map on Customer to orders*

```
customers.stream()
        .map(Customer::getOrders)                                  ❶
        .forEach(System.out::println);                             ❷

customers.stream()
        .map(customer -> customer.getOrders().stream()) ❸
        .forEach(System.out::println);
```

❶ Stream<List<Order>>

❷ [Order{id=1}, Order{id=2}, Order{id=3}], [Order{id=4}, Order{id=5}], []

❸ Stream<Stream<Order>>

The mapping operation results in a Stream<List<Order>>, where the last list is empty. If you invoke the stream method on the lists of orders, you get a Stream<Stream<Order>>, where the last inner stream is an empty stream.

This is where the flatMap method comes in. The flatMap method has the following signature:

```
<R> Stream<R> flatMap(Function<? super T,? extends Stream<? extends R>> mapper)
```

For each generic argument T, the function produces a Stream<R> rather than just an R. The flatMap method then "flattens" the resulting stream by removing each element from the individual streams and adding them to the output.

The Function argument to flatMap takes a generic input argument, but produces a Stream of output types.

The code in Example 3-58 demonstrates flatMap.

*Example 3-58. Using flatMap on Customer orders*

```
customers.stream()                                          ❶
        .flatMap(customer -> customer.getOrders().stream()) ❷
        .forEach(System.out::println);                      ❸
```

❶ Stream<Customer>

❷ Stream<Order>

❸ Order{id=1}, Order{id=2}, Order{id=3}, Order{id=4}, Order{id=5}

The result of the flatMap operation is to produce a Stream<Order>, which has been flattened so you don't need to worry about the nested streams any more.

The two key concepts for flatMap are:

- The Function argument to flatMap produces a Stream of output values.
- The resulting stream of streams is flattened into a single stream of results.

If you keep those ideas in mind, you should find the flatMap method quite helpful.

As a final note, the `Optional` class also has a `map` method and a `flatMap` method. See Recipes 6.4 and 6.5 for details.

## See Also

The `flatMap` method is also demonstrated in Recipe 6.5. `flatMap` in `Optional` is discussed in Recipe 6.4.

# 3.12 Concatenating Streams

## Problem

You want to combine two or more streams into a single one.

## Solution

The `concat` method on `Stream` combines two streams, which works if the number of streams is small. Otherwise use `flatMap`.

## Discussion

Say you acquire data from several locations, and you want to process every element in all of them using streams. One mechanism you can use is the `concat` method in `Stream`, whose signature is:

```
static <T> Stream<T> concat(Stream<? extends T> a, Stream<? extends T> b)
```

This method creates a lazily concatenated stream that accesses all the elements of the first stream, followed by all the elements of the second stream. As the Javadocs say, the resulting stream is ordered if the input streams are ordered, and the resulting stream is parallel if *either* of the input streams are parallel. Closing the returned stream also closes the underlying input streams.

Both input streams must hold elements of the same type.

As a simple example of concatenating streams, see Example 3-59.

*Example 3-59. Concatenating two streams*

```
@Test
public void concat() throws Exception {
    Stream<String> first = Stream.of("a", "b", "c").parallel();
```

```
    Stream<String> second = Stream.of("X", "Y", "Z");
    List<String> strings = Stream.concat(first, second) ❶
            .collect(Collectors.toList());
    List<String> stringList = Arrays.asList("a", "b", "c", "X", "Y", "Z");
    assertEquals(stringList, strings);
}
```

❶ First elements followed by second elements

If you want to add a third stream to the mix, you can nest the concatenations, Example 3-60.

*Example 3-60. Concatenating multiple streams*

```
@Test
public void concatThree() throws Exception {
    Stream<String> first = Stream.of("a", "b", "c").parallel();
    Stream<String> second = Stream.of("X", "Y", "Z");
    Stream<String> third = Stream.of("alpha", "beta", "gamma");

    List<String> strings = Stream.concat(Stream.concat(first, second), third)
            .collect(Collectors.toList());
    List<String> stringList = Arrays.asList("a", "b", "c",
        "X", "Y", "Z", "alpha", "beta", "gamma");
    assertEquals(stringList, strings);
}
```

This nesting approach works, but the Javadocs contain a note about this:

> Use caution when constructing streams from repeated concatenation. Accessing an element of a deeply concatenated stream can result in deep call chains, or even `StackOverflowException`

The idea is that the `concat` method essentially builds a binary tree of streams, which can grow unwieldy if too many are used.

An alternative approach is to use the `reduce` method to perform multiple concatenations, as in Example 3-61.

*Example 3-61. Concatenating with reduce*

```
@Test
public void reduce() throws Exception {
    Stream<String> first = Stream.of("a", "b", "c").parallel();
    Stream<String> second = Stream.of("X", "Y", "Z");
    Stream<String> third = Stream.of("alpha", "beta", "gamma");
    Stream<String> fourth = Stream.empty();

    List<String> strings = Stream.of(first, second, third, fourth)
            .reduce(Stream.empty(), Stream::concat) ❶
```

```
            .collect(Collectors.toList());

    List<String> stringList = Arrays.asList("a", "b", "c",
        "X", "Y", "Z", "alpha", "beta", "gamma");
    assertEquals(stringList, strings);
}
```

❶ Using reduce with an empty stream and a binary operator

This works because the `concat` method when used as a method reference is a binary operator. Note this is simpler code, but doesn't fix the potential stack overflow problem.

Instead, when combining streams, the `flatMap` method is a natural solution, as in Example 3-62.

*Example 3-62. Using flatMap to concatenate streams*

```
@Test
public void flatMap() throws Exception {
    Stream<String> first = Stream.of("a", "b", "c").parallel();
    Stream<String> second = Stream.of("X", "Y", "Z");
    Stream<String> third = Stream.of("alpha", "beta", "gamma");
    Stream<String> fourth = Stream.empty();

    List<String> strings = Stream.of(first, second, third, fourth)
            .flatMap(Function.identity())
            .collect(Collectors.toList());
    List<String> stringList = Arrays.asList("a", "b", "c",
        "X", "Y", "Z", "alpha", "beta", "gamma");
    assertEquals(stringList, strings);
}
```

This approach works, but also has its quirks. Using `concat` creates a parallel stream if any of the input streams are parallel, but `flatMap` does not (Example 3-63).

*Example 3-63. Parallel or not?*

```
@Test
public void concatParallel() throws Exception {
    Stream<String> first = Stream.of("a", "b", "c").parallel();
    Stream<String> second = Stream.of("X", "Y", "Z");
    Stream<String> third = Stream.of("alpha", "beta", "gamma");

    Stream<String> total = Stream.concat(Stream.concat(first, second), third);

    assertTrue(total.isParallel());
}

@Test
```

```
public void flatMapNotParallel() throws Exception {
    Stream<String> first = Stream.of("a", "b", "c").parallel();
    Stream<String> second = Stream.of("X", "Y", "Z");
    Stream<String> third = Stream.of("alpha", "beta", "gamma");
    Stream<String> fourth = Stream.empty();

    Stream<String> total = Stream.of(first, second, third, fourth)
            .flatMap(Function.identity());
    assertFalse(total.isParallel());
}
```

Still, you can always make the stream parallel if you want by calling the `parallel` method, as long as you have not yet processed the data (Example 3-64).

*Example 3-64. Making a flatMap stream parallel*

```
@Test
public void flatMapParallel() throws Exception {
    Stream<String> first = Stream.of("a", "b", "c").parallel();
    Stream<String> second = Stream.of("X", "Y", "Z");
    Stream<String> third = Stream.of("alpha", "beta", "gamma");
    Stream<String> fourth = Stream.empty();

    Stream<String> total = Stream.of(first, second, third, fourth)
            .flatMap(Function.identity());
    assertFalse(total.isParallel());

    total = total.parallel();
    assertTrue(total.isParallel());
}
```

Since `flatMap` is an intermediate operation, the stream can still be modified using the `parallel` method, as shown.

In short, the `concat` method is effective for two streams, and can be used as part of a general reduction operation, but `flatMap` is a natural alternative.

## See Also

See the excellent blog post online at *http://bit.ly/efficient-multistream-concatentation* for details, performance considerations, and more.

The `flatMap` method on `Stream` is discussed in Recipe 3.11.

# 3.13 Lazy Streams

## Problem

You want to process the minimum number of stream elements necessary to satisfy a condition.

## Solution

Streams are already lazy and do not process elements until a terminal condition is reached. Then each element is processed individually. If there is a short-circuiting operation at the end, the stream processing will terminate whenever all the conditions are satisfied.

## Discussion

When you first encounter stream processing, it's tempting to think that much more effort is being expended than necessary. For example, consider taking a range of numbers between 100 and 200, doubling each of them, and then finding the first value that is evenly divisible by three, as in Example 3-65.[9]

*Example 3-65. First double between 200 and 400 divisible by 3*

```
OptionalInt firstEvenDoubleDivBy3 = IntStream.range(100, 200)
    .map(n -> n * 2)
    .filter(n -> n % 3 == 0)
    .findFirst();
System.out.println(firstEvenDoubleDivBy3); ❶
```

❶ Prints `Optional[204]`

If you didn't know better, you might think a lot of wasted effort was expended:

- The range of numbers from 100 to 199 is created (100 operations)
- Each number is doubled (100 operations)
- Each number is checked for divisibility (100 operations)
- The first element of the resulting stream is returned (1 operation)

Since the first value that satisfies the stream requirements is 204, why process all the other numbers?

9 Thanks to the inimitable Venkat Subramaniam for the basis of this example.

Fortunately, stream processing doesn't work that way. Streams are *lazy*, in that no work is done until the terminal condition is reached, and then each element is processed through the pipeline individually. To demonstrate this, Example 3-66 shows the same code, but refactored to show each element as it passes through the pipeline.

*Example 3-66. Explicit processing of each stream element*

```
public int multByTwo(int n) {        ❶
    System.out.printf("Inside multByTwo with arg %d%n", n);
    return n * 2;
}

public boolean divByThree(int n) { ❷
    System.out.printf("Inside divByThree with arg %d%n", n);
    return n % 3 == 0;
}

// ...

firstEvenDoubleDivBy3 = IntStream.range(100, 200)
    .map(this::multByTwo)             ❶
    .filter(this::divByThree)         ❷
    .findFirst();
```

❶ Method reference for multiply by two, with print

❷ Method reference for modulus 3, with print

The output this time is:

```
Inside multByTwo with arg 100
Inside divByThree with arg 200
Inside multByTwo with arg 101
Inside divByThree with arg 202
Inside multByTwo with arg 102
Inside divByThree with arg 204
First even divisible by 3 is Optional[204]
```

The value 100 goes through the `map` to produce 200, but does not pass the filter, so the stream moves to the value 101. That is mapped to 202, which also doesn't pass the filter. Then the next value, 102, is mapped to 204, but that is divisible by 3, so it passes. The stream processing terminates *after processing only three values*, using six operations.

This is one of the great advantages of stream processing over working with collections directly. With a collection, all of the operations would have to be performed before moving to the next step. With streams, the intermediate operations form a pipeline, but nothing happens until the terminal operation is reached. Then the stream processes only as many values as are necessary.

This isn't always relevant—if any of the operations are stateful, like sorting or adding them all together, then all the values are going to have to be processed anyway. But when you have stateless operations followed by a short-circuiting, terminal operation, the advantage is clear.

## See Also

The differences between `findFirst` and `findAny` are discussed in Recipe 3.9.

# CHAPTER 4

# Comparators and Collectors

Java 8 enhances the `Comparator` interface with several static and default methods that make sorting operations much simpler. It's now possible to sort a collection of POJOs by one property, then equal first properties by a second, then by a third, and so on, just with a series of library calls.

Java 8 also adds a new utility class called `java.util.stream.Collectors`, which provides static methods to convert from streams back into various types of collections. The collectors can also be applied "downstream," meaning that they can postprocess a grouping or partitioning operation.

The recipes in this chapter illustrate all these concepts.

## 4.1 Sorting Using a Comparator

### Problem

You want to sort objects.

### Solution

Use the `sorted` method on `Stream` with a `Comparator`, either implemented with a lambda expression or generated by one of the static `compare` methods on the `Comparator` interface.

### Discussion

The `sorted` method on `Stream` produces a new, sorted stream using the natural ordering for the class. The natural ordering is specified by implementing the `java.util.Comparable` interface.

For example, consider sorting a collection of strings, as shown in Example 4-1.

*Example 4-1. Sorting strings lexicographically*

```
private List<String> sampleStrings =
    Arrays.asList("this", "is", "a", "list", "of", "strings");

public List<String> defaultSort() {
    Collections.sort(sampleStrings);  ❶
    return sampleStrings;
}

public List<String> defaultSortUsingStreams() {
    return sampleStrings.stream()
        .sorted()                     ❷
        .collect(Collectors.toList());
}
```

❶ Default sort from Java 7 and below

❷ Default sort from Java 8 and above

Java has had a utility class called `Collections` ever since the collections framework was added back in version 1.2. The static `sort` method on `Collections` takes a `List` as an argument, but returns `void`. The sort is destructive, modifying the supplied collection. This approach does not follow the functional principles supported by Java 8, which emphasize immutability.

Java 8 uses the `sorted` method on streams to do the same sorting, but produces a new stream rather than modifying the original collection. In this example, after sorting the collection, the returned list is sorted according to the natural ordering of the class. For strings, the natural ordering is lexicographical, which reduces to alphabetical when all the strings are lowercase, as in this example.

If you want to sort the strings in a different way, then there is an overloaded `sorted` method that takes a `Comparator` as an argument.

Example 4-2 shows a length sort for strings in two different ways.

*Example 4-2. Sorting strings by length*

```
public List<String> lengthSortUsingSorted() {
    return sampleStrings.stream()
        .sorted((s1, s2) -> s1.length() - s2.length()) ❶
        .collect(toList());
}

public List<String> lengthSortUsingComparator() {
```

```
    return sampleStrings.stream()
        .sorted(Comparator.comparingInt(String::length)) ❷
        .collect(toList());
}
```

❶ Using a lambda for the `Comparator` to sort by length

❷ Using a `Comparator` using the `comparingInt` method

The argument to the `sorted` method is a `java.util.Comparator`, which is a functional interface. In `lengthSortUsingSorted`, a lambda expression is provided to implement the `compare` method in `Comparator`. In Java 7 and earlier, the implementation would normally be provided by an anonymous inner class, but here a lambda expression is all that is required.

Java 8 added `sort(Comparator)` as a `default` instance method on `List`, equivalent to the `static void sort(List, Comparator)` method on `Collections`. Both are destructive sorts that return `void`, so the `sorted(Comparator)` approach on streams discussed here (which returns a new, sorted stream) is still preferred.

The second method, `lengthSortUsingComparator`, takes advantage of one of the static methods added to the `Comparator` interface. The `comparingInt` method takes an argument of type `ToIntFunction` that transforms the string into an int, called a `keyExtractor` in the docs, and generates a `Comparator` that sorts the collection using that key.

The added default methods in `Comparator` are extremely useful. While you can write a `Comparator` that sorts by length pretty easily, when you want to sort by more than one field that can get complicated. Consider sorting the strings by length, then equal-length strings alphabetically. Using the default and static methods in `Comparator`, that becomes almost trivial, as shown in Example 4-3.

*Example 4-3. Sorting by length, then equal lengths lexicographically*

```
public List<String> lengthSortThenAlphaSort() {
    return sampleStrings.stream()
        .sorted(comparing(String::length)           ❶
                    .thenComparing(naturalOrder()))
        .collect(toList());
}
```

❶ Sort by length, then equal-length strings alphabetically

Comparator provides a default method called thenComparing. Just like comparing, it also takes a Function as an argument, again known as a keyExtractor. Chaining this to the comparing method returns a Comparator that compares by the first quantity, then equal first by the second, and so on.

Static imports often make the code easier to read. Once you get used to the static methods in both Comparator and Collectors, this becomes an easy way to simplify the code. In this case, the comparing and naturalOrder methods have been statically imported.

This approach works on any class, even if it does not implement Comparable. Consider the Golfer class shown in Example 4-4.

*Example 4-4. A class for golfers*

```
public class Golfer {
    private String first;
    private String last;
    private int score;

    // ... other methods ...
}
```

To create a leader board at a tournament, it makes sense to sort by score, then by last name, and then by first name. Example 4-5 shows how to do that.

*Example 4-5. Sorting golfers*

```
private List<Golfer> golfers = Arrays.asList(
    new Golfer("Jack", "Nicklaus", 68),
    new Golfer("Tiger", "Woods", 70),
    new Golfer("Tom", "Watson", 70),
    new Golfer("Ty", "Webb", 68),
    new Golfer("Bubba", "Watson", 70)
);

public List<Golfer> sortByScoreThenLastThenFirst() {
    return golfers.stream()
        .sorted(comparingInt(Golfer::getScore)
                    .thenComparing(Golfer::getLast)
                    .thenComparing(Golfer::getFirst))
        .collect(toList());
}
```

The output from calling sortByScoreThenLastThenFirst is shown in Example 4-6.

*Example 4-6. Sorted golfers*

```
Golfer{first='Jack', last='Nicklaus', score=68}
Golfer{first='Ty', last='Webb', score=68}
Golfer{first='Bubba', last='Watson', score=70}
Golfer{first='Tom', last='Watson', score=70}
Golfer{first='Tiger', last='Woods', score=70}
```

The golfers are sorted by score, so Nicklaus and Webb come before Woods and both Watsons.[1] Then equal scores are sorted by last name, putting Nicklaus before Webb and Watson before Woods. Finally, equal scores and last names are sorted by first name, putting Bubba Watson before Tom Watson.

The default and static methods in `Comparator`, along with the new `sorted` method on `Stream`, makes generating complex sorts easy.

# 4.2 Converting a Stream into a Collection

## Problem

After stream processing, you want to convert to a `List`, `Set`, or other linear collection.

## Solution

Use the `toList`, `toSet`, or `toCollection` methods in the `Collectors` utility class.

## Discussion

Idiomatic Java 8 often involves passing elements of a stream through a pipeline of intermediate operations, finishing with a terminal operation. One terminal operation is the `collect` method, which is used to convert a `Stream` into a collection.

The `collect` method in `Stream` has two overloaded versions, as shown in Example 4-7.

*Example 4-7. The collect method in Stream<T>*

```
<R,A> R collect(Collector<? super T,A,R> collector)
<R>   R collect(Supplier<R> supplier,
                BiConsumer<R,? super T> accumulator,
                BiConsumer<R,R> combiner)
```

1 Ty Webb, of course, is from the movie *Caddyshack*. Judge Smails: "Ty, what did you shoot today?" Ty Webb: "Oh, Judge, I don't keep score." Smails: "Then how do you measure yourself with other golfers?" Webb: "By height." Adding a sort by height is left to the reader as an easy exercise.

This recipe deals with the first version, which takes a `Collector` as an argument. Collectors perform a "mutable reduction operation" that accumulates elements into a result container. Here the result will be a collection.

`Collector` is an interface, so it can't be instantiated. The interface contains a static `of` method for producing them, but there is often a better, or at least easier, way.

The Java 8 API frequently uses a static method called `of` as a factory method.

Here, the static methods in the `Collectors` class will be used to produce `Collector` instances, which are used as the argument to `Stream.collect` to populate a collection.

A simple example that creates a `List` is shown in Example 4-8.[2]

*Example 4-8. Creating a List*

```
List<String> superHeroes =
    Stream.of("Mr. Furious", "The Blue Raja", "The Shoveler",
              "The Bowler", "Invisible Boy", "The Spleen", "The Sphinx")
          .collect(Collectors.toList());
```

This method creates and populates an `ArrayList` with the given stream elements. Creating a `Set` is just as easy, as in Example 4-9.

*Example 4-9. Creating a Set*

```
Set<String> villains =
    Stream.of("Casanova Frankenstein", "The Disco Boys",
              "The Not-So-Goodie Mob", "The Suits", "The Suzies",
              "The Furriers", "The Furriers") ❶
          .collect(Collectors.toSet());
}
```

❶ Duplicate name, removed when converting to a `Set`

2 The names in this recipe come from *Mystery Men*, one of the great overlooked movies of the '90s. (Mr. Furious: "Lance Hunt *is* Captain Amazing." The Shoveler: "Lance Hunt wears glasses. Captain Amazing *doesn't* wear glasses." Mr. Furious: "He takes them off when he transforms." The Shoveler: "That doesn't make any sense! He wouldn't be able to *see*!")

This method creates an instance of HashSet and populates it, leaving out any duplicates.

Both of these examples used the default data structures—ArrayList for List, and HashSet for Set. If you wish to specify a particular data structure, you should use the Collectors.toCollection method, which takes a Supplier as an argument. Example 4-10 shows the sample code.

*Example 4-10. Creating a linked list*

```
List<String> actors =
    Stream.of("Hank Azaria", "Janeane Garofalo", "William H. Macy",
              "Paul Reubens", "Ben Stiller", "Kel Mitchell", "Wes Studi")
          .collect(Collectors.toCollection(LinkedList::new));
}
```

The argument to the toCollection method is a collection Supplier, so the constructor reference to LinkedList is provided here. The collect method instantiates a LinkedList and then populates it with the given names.

The Collectors class also contains a method to create an array of objects. There are two overloads of the toArray method:

```
        Object[] toArray();
    <A> A[]      toArray(IntFunction<A[]> generator);
```

The former returns an array containing the elements of this stream, but without specifying the type. The latter takes a function that produces a new array of desired type with length equal to the size of the stream, and is easiest to use with an array constructor reference as shown in Example 4-11.

*Example 4-11. Creating an array*

```
String[] wannabes =
    Stream.of("The Waffler", "Reverse Psychologist", "PMS Avenger")
          .toArray(String[]::new); ❶
}
```

❶ Array constructor reference as a Supplier

The returned array is of the specified type, whose length matches the number of elements in the stream.

To transform into a Map, the Collectors.toMap method requires two Function instances—one for the keys and one for the values.

Consider an Actor POJO, which wraps a name and a role. If you have a Set of Actor instances from a given movie, the code in Example 4-12 creates a Map from them.

*Example 4-12. Creating a Map*

```
Set<Actor> actors = mysteryMen.getActors();

Map<String, String> actorMap = actors.stream()
    .collect(Collectors.toMap(Actor::getName, Actor::getRole)); ❶

actorMap.forEach((key,value) ->
    System.out.printf("%s played %s%n", key, value));
```

❶ Functions to produce keys and values

The output is

```
Janeane Garofalo played The Bowler
Greg Kinnear played Captain Amazing
William H. Macy played The Shoveler
Paul Reubens played The Spleen
Wes Studi played The Sphinx
Kel Mitchell played Invisible Boy
Geoffrey Rush played Casanova Frankenstein
Ben Stiller played Mr. Furious
Hank Azaria played The Blue Raja
```

Similar code works for `ConcurrentMap` using the `toConcurrentMap` method.

## See Also

`Suppliers` are discussed in Recipe 2.2. Constructor references are in Recipe 1.3. The `toMap` method is also demonstrated in Recipe 4.3.

# 4.3 Adding a Linear Collection to a Map

## Problem

You want to add a collection of objects to a `Map`, where the key is one of the object properties and the value is the object itself.

## Solution

Use the `toMap` method of `Collectors`, along with `Function.identity`.

## Discussion

This is a short, very focused use case, but when it comes up in practice the solution here can be quite convenient.

Say you had a List of Book instances, where Book is a simple POJO that has an ID, a name, and a price. An abbreviated form of the Book class is shown in Example 4-13.

*Example 4-13. A simple POJO representing a book*

```
public class Book {
    private int id;
    private String name;
    private double price;

    // ... other methods ...
}
```

Now assume you have a collection of Book instances, as shown in Example 4-14.

*Example 4-14. A collection of books*

```
List<Book> books = Arrays.asList(
    new Book(1, "Modern Java Recipes", 49.99),
    new Book(2, "Java 8 in Action", 49.99),
    new Book(3, "Java SE8 for the Really Impatient", 39.99),
    new Book(4, "Functional Programming in Java", 27.64),
    new Book(5, "Making Java Groovy", 45.99)
    new Book(6, "Gradle Recipes for Android", 23.76)
);
```

In many situations, instead of a List you might want a Map, where the keys are the book IDs and the values are the books themselves. This is really easy to accomplish using the toMap method in Collectors, as shown two different ways in Example 4-15.

*Example 4-15. Adding the books to a Map*

```
Map<Integer, Book> bookMap = books.stream()
    .collect(Collectors.toMap(Book::getId, b -> b));              ❶

bookMap = books.stream()
    .collect(Collectors.toMap(Book::getId, Function.identity())); ❷
```

❶ Identity lambda: given an element, return it

❷ Static identity method in Function does the same thing

The toMap method in Collectors takes two Function instances as arguments, the first of which generates a key and the second of which generates the value from the provided object. In this case, the key is mapped by the getId method in Book, and the value is the book itself.

The first toMap in Example 4-15 uses the getId method to map to the key and an explicit lambda expression that simply returns its parameter. The second example uses the static identity method in Function to do the same thing.

### The Two Static Identity Methods

The static identity method in Function has the signature

```
static <T> Function<T,T>        identity()
```

The implementation in the standard library is shown in Example 4-16.

*Example 4-16. The static identity method in Function*

```
static <T> Function<T, T> identity() {
    return t -> t;
}
```

The UnaryOperator class extends Function, but you can't override a static method. In the Javadocs, it also declares a static identity method:

```
static <T> UnaryOperator<T>     identity()
```

Its implementation in the standard library is essentially the same, as shown in Example 4-17.

*Example 4-17. The static identity method in UnaryOperator*

```
static <T> UnaryOperator<T> identity() {
    return t -> t;
}
```

The differences are only in the way you call them (from the two interface names) and the corresponding return types. In this case, it doesn't matter which one you use, but it's interesting to see that they're both there.

Whether you decide to supply an explicit lambda or use the static method is merely a matter of style. Either way, it is easy to add collection values to a Map where the key is a property of the object and the value is the object itself.

## See Also

Functions are covered in Recipe 2.4, which also discusses unary and binary operators.

# 4.4 Sorting Maps

## Problem

You want to sort a `Map` by key or by value.

## Solution

Use the new static methods in the `Map.Entry` interface.

## Discussion

The `Map` interface has always contained a public, static, inner interface called `Map.Entry`, which represents a key-value pair. The `Map.entrySet` method returns a `Set` of `Map.Entry` elements. Prior to Java 8, the primary methods used in this interface were `getKey` and `getValue`, which do what you'd expect.

In Java 8, the static methods in Table 4-1 have been added.

*Table 4-1. Static methods in Map.Entry (from Java 8 docs)*

| Method | Description |
| --- | --- |
| `comparingByKey()` | Returns a comparator that compares `Map.Entry` in natural order on key |
| `comparingByKey(Comparator<? super K> cmp)` | Returns a comparator that compares `Map.Entry` by key using the given `Comparator` |
| `comparingByValue()` | Returns a comparator that compares `Map.Entry` in natural order on value |
| `comparingByValue(Comparator<? super V> cmp)` | Returns a comparator that compares `Map.Entry` by value using the given `Comparator` |

To demonstrate how to use them, Example 4-18 generates a `Map` of word lengths to number of words in a dictionary. Every Unix system contains a file in the *usr/share/dict/words* directory holding the contents of Webster's 2nd edition dictionary, with one word per line. The `Files.lines` method can be used to read a file and produce a stream of strings containing those lines. In this case, the stream will contain each word from the dictionary.

*Example 4-18. Reading the dictionary file into a Map*

```
System.out.println("\nNumber of words of each length:");
try (Stream<String> lines = Files.lines(dictionary)) {
    lines.filter(s -> s.length() > 20)
        .collect(Collectors.groupingBy(
            String::length, Collectors.counting()))
```

```
        .forEach((len, num) -> System.out.printf("%d: %d%n", len, num));
} catch (IOException e) {
    e.printStackTrace();
}
```

This example is discussed in Recipe 7.1, but to summarize:

- The file is read inside a `try-with-resources` block. `Stream` implements `AutoCloseable`, so when the try block exits, Java calls the `close` method on `Stream`, which then calls the `close` method on `File`.
- The filter restricts further processing to only words of at least 20 characters in length.
- The `groupingBy` method of `Collectors` takes a `Function` as the first argument, representing the classifier. Here, the classifier is the length of each string. If you only provide one argument, the result is a `Map` where the keys are the values of the classifier and the values are lists of elements that match the classifier. In the case we're currently examining, `groupingBy(String::length)` would have produced a `Map<Integer,List<String>>` where the keys are the word lengths and the values are lists of words of that length.
- In this case, the two-argument version of `groupingBy` lets you supply another `Collector`, called a *downstream* collector, that postprocesses the lists of words. In this case, the return type is `Map<Integer,Long>`, where the keys are the word lengths and the values are the number of words of that length in the dictionary.

The result is:

```
Number of words of each length:
21: 82
22: 41
23: 17
24: 5
```

In other words, there are 82 words of length 21, 41 words of length 22, 17 words of length 23, and 5 words of length 24.[3]

The results show that the map is printed in ascending order of word length. In order to see it in descending order, use `Map.Entry.comparingByKey` as in Example 4-19.

3 For the record, those five longest words are formaldehydesulphoxylate, pathologicopsychological, scientificophilosophical, tetraiodophenolphthalein, and thyroparathyroidectomize. Good luck with that, spell checker.

*Example 4-19. Sorting the map by key*

```
System.out.println("\nNumber of words of each length (desc order):");
try (Stream<String> lines = Files.lines(dictionary)) {
    Map<Integer, Long> map = lines.filter(s -> s.length() > 20)
        .collect(Collectors.groupingBy(
            String::length, Collectors.counting()));

    map.entrySet().stream()
        .sorted(Map.Entry.comparingByKey(Comparator.reverseOrder()))
        .forEach(e -> System.out.printf("Length %d: %2d words%n",
            e.getKey(), e.getValue()));
} catch (IOException e) {
    e.printStackTrace();
}
```

After computing the `Map<Integer,Long>`, this operation extracts the `entrySet` and produces a stream. The `sorted` method on `Stream` is used to produce a sorted stream using the provided comparator.

In this case, `Map.Entry.comparingByKey` generates a comparator that sorts by the keys, and using the overload that takes a comparator allows the code to specify that we want it in reverse order.

The `sorted` method on `Stream` produces a new, sorted stream that does not modify the source. The original `Map` is unaffected.

The result is:

```
Number of words of each length (desc order):
Length 24:  5 words
Length 23: 17 words
Length 22: 41 words
Length 21: 82 words
```

The other sorting methods listed in Table 4-1 are used similarly.

## See Also

An additional example of sorting a `Map` by keys or values is shown in Appendix A. Downstream collectors are discussed in Recipe 4.6. File operations on the dictionary is part of Recipe 7.1.

# 4.5 Partitioning and Grouping

## Problem

You want to divide a collection of elements into categories.

## Solution

The `Collectors.partitioningBy` method splits elements into those that satisfy a `Predicate` and those that do not. The `Collectors.groupingBy` method produces a `Map` of categories, where the values are the elements in each category.

## Discussion

Say you have a collection of strings. If you want to split them into those with even lengths and those with odd lengths, you can use `Collectors.partitioningBy`, as in Example 4-20.

*Example 4-20. Partitioning strings by even or odd lengths*

```
List<String> strings = Arrays.asList("this", "is", "a", "long", "list", "of",
        "strings", "to", "use", "as", "a", "demo");

Map<Boolean, List<String>> lengthMap = strings.stream()
    .collect(Collectors.partitioningBy(s -> s.length() % 2 == 0)); ❶

lengthMap.forEach((key,value) -> System.out.printf("%5s: %s%n", key, value));
//
// false: [a, strings, use, a]
//  true: [this, is, long, list, of, to, as, demo]
```

❶ Partitioning by even or odd length

The signature of the two `partitioningBy` methods are:

```
static <T> Collector<T,?,Map<Boolean,List<T>>> partitioningBy(
    Predicate<? super T> predicate)
static <T,D,A> Collector<T,?,Map<Boolean,D>> partitioningBy(
    Predicate<? super T> predicate, Collector<? super T,A,D> downstream)
```

The return types look rather nasty due to the generics, but you rarely have to deal with them in practice. Instead, the result of either operation becomes the argument to the `collect` method, which uses the generated collector to create the output map defined by the third generic argument.

The first `partitioningBy` method takes a single `Predicate` as an argument. It divides the elements into those that satisfy the `Predicate` and those that do not. You will always get a Map as a result that has exactly two entries: a list of values that satisfy the Predicate, and a list of values that do not.

The overloaded version of the method takes a second argument of type Collector, called a *downstream collector*. This allows you to postprocess the lists returned by the partition, and is discussed in Recipe 4.6.

The groupingBy method performs an operation like a "group by" statement in SQL. It returns a Map where the keys are the groups and the values are lists of elements in each group.

If you are getting your data from a database, by all means do any grouping operations there. The new API methods are convenience methods for data in memory.

The signature for the groupingBy method is:

```
static <T,K> Collector<T,?,Map<K,List<T>>>      groupingBy(
    Function<? super T,? extends K> classifier)
```

The Function argument takes each element of the stream and extracts a property to group by. This time, rather than simply partition the strings into two categories, consider separating them by length, as in Example 4-21.

*Example 4-21. Grouping strings by length*

```
List<String> strings = Arrays.asList("this", "is", "a", "long", "list", "of",
        "strings", "to", "use", "as", "a", "demo");

Map<Integer, List<String>> lengthMap = strings.stream()
    .collect(Collectors.groupingBy(String::length)); ❶

lengthMap.forEach((k,v) -> System.out.printf("%d: %s%n", k, v));
//
// 1: [a, a]
// 2: [is, of, to, as]
// 3: [use]
// 4: [this, long, list, demo]
// 7: [strings]
```

❶ Grouping strings by length

The keys in the resulting map are the lengths of the strings (1, 2, 3, 4, and 7) and the values are lists of strings of each length.

## See Also

An extension of the recipe we just looked at, Recipe 4.6 shows how to postprocess the lists returned by a `groupingBy` or `partitioningBy` operation.

# 4.6 Downstream Collectors

## Problem

You want to postprocess the collections returned by a `groupingBy` or `partitioningBy` operation.

## Solution

Use one of the static utility methods from the `java.util.stream.Collectors` class.

## Discussion

In Recipe 4.5, we looked at how to separate elements into multiple categories. The `partitioningBy` and `groupingBy` methods return a `Map` where the keys were the categories (booleans `true` and `false` for `partitioningBy`, objects for `groupingBy`) and the values were lists of elements that satisfied each category. Recall the example partitioning strings by even and odd lengths, shown in Example 4-20 but repeated in Example 4-22 for convenience.

*Example 4-22. Partitioning strings by even or odd lengths*

```
List<String> strings = Arrays.asList("this", "is", "a", "long", "list", "of",
        "strings", "to", "use", "as", "a", "demo");

Map<Boolean, List<String>> lengthMap = strings.stream()
    .collect(Collectors.partitioningBy(s -> s.length() % 2 == 0));

lengthMap.forEach((key,value) -> System.out.printf("%5s: %s%n", key, value));
//
// false: [a, strings, use, a]
//  true: [this, is, long, list, of, to, as, demo]
```

Rather than the actual lists, you may be interested in how many elements fall into each category. In other words, instead of producing a `Map` whose values are `List<String>`, you might want just the number of elements in each of the lists. The `partitioningBy` method has an overloaded version whose second argument is of type `Collector`:

```
static <T,D,A> Collector<T,?,Map<Boolean,D>>    partitioningBy(
    Predicate<? super T> predicate, Collector<? super T,A,D> downstream)
```

This is where the static `Collectors.counting` method becomes useful. Example 4-23 shows how it works.

*Example 4-23. Counting the partitioned strings*

```
Map<Boolean, Long> numberLengthMap = strings.stream()
    .collect(Collectors.partitioningBy(s -> s.length() % 2 == 0,
                Collectors.counting()));  ❶

numberLengthMap.forEach((k,v) -> System.out.printf("%5s: %d%n", k, v));
//
// false: 4
//  true: 8
```

❶ Downstream collector

This is called a *downstream collector*, because it is postprocessing the resulting lists downstream (i.e., after the partitioning operation is completed).

The `groupingBy` method also has an overload that takes a downstream collector:

```
/**
* @param <T> the type of the input elements
* @param <K> the type of the keys
* @param <A> the intermediate accumulation type of the downstream collector
* @param <D> the result type of the downstream reduction
* @param classifier a classifier function mapping input elements to keys
* @param downstream a {@code Collector} implementing the downstream reduction
* @return a {@code Collector} implementing the cascaded group-by operation
*/
static <T,K,A,D> Collector<T,?,Map<K,D>>        groupingBy(
    Function<? super T,? extends K> classifier,
    Collector<? super T,A,D> downstream)
```

A portion of the Javadoc comment from the source code is included in the signature, which shows that `T` is the type of the element in the collection, `K` is the key type for the resulting map, `A` is an accumulator, and `D` is the type of the downstream collector. The ? represents "unknown." See Appendix A for more details on generics in Java 8.

Several methods in `Stream` have analogs in the `Collectors` class. Table 4-2 shows how they align. <<<

*Table 4-2. Collectors methods similar to Stream methods*

| Stream | Collectors |
|---|---|
| `count` | `counting` |
| `map` | `mapping` |
| `min` | `minBy` |

| Stream | Collectors |
|---|---|
| `max` | `maxBy` |
| `IntStream.sum` | `summingInt` |
| `DoubleStream.sum` | `summingDouble` |
| `LongStream.sum` | `summingLong` |
| `IntStream.summarizing` | `summarizingInt` |
| `DoubleStream.summarizing` | `summarizingDouble` |
| `LongStream.summarizing` | `summarizingLong` |

Again, the purpose of a downstream collector is to postprocess the collection of objects produced by an upstream operation, like partitioning or grouping.

## See Also

Recipe 7.1 shows an example of a downstream collector when determining the longest words in a dictionary. Recipe 4.5 discusses the `partitionBy` and `groupingBy` methods in more detail. The whole issue of generics is covered in Appendix A.

# 4.7 Finding Max and Min Values

## Problem

You want to determine the maximum or minimum value in a stream.

## Solution

You have several choices: the `maxBy` and `minBy` methods on `BinaryOperator`, the `max` and `min` methods on `Stream`, or the `maxBy` and `minBy` utility methods on `Collectors`.

## Discussion

A `BinaryOperator` is one of the functional interfaces in the `java.util.function` package. It extends `BiFunction` and applies when both arguments to the function and the return value are all from the same class.

The `BinaryOperator` interface adds two static methods:

```
static <T> BinaryOperator<T> maxBy(Comparator<? super T> comparator)
static <T> BinaryOperator<T> minBy(Comparator<? super T> comparator)
```

Each of these returns a `BinaryOperator` that uses the supplied `Comparator`.

To demonstrate the various ways to get the maximum value from a stream, consider a POJO called `Employee` that holds three attributes: `name`, `salary`, and `department`, as in Example 4-24.

*Example 4-24. Employee POJO*

```
public class Employee {
    private String name;
    private Integer salary;
    private String department;

    // ... other methods ...
}

List<Employee> employees = Arrays.asList(                        ❶
        new Employee("Cersei",     250_000, "Lannister"),
        new Employee("Jamie",      150_000, "Lannister"),
        new Employee("Tyrion",       1_000, "Lannister"),
        new Employee("Tywin",    1_000_000, "Lannister"),
        new Employee("Jon Snow",    75_000, "Stark"),
        new Employee("Robb",       120_000, "Stark"),
        new Employee("Eddard",     125_000, "Stark"),
        new Employee("Sansa",            0, "Stark"),
        new Employee("Arya",         1_000, "Stark"));

Employee defaultEmployee =                                       ❷
    new Employee("A man (or woman) has no name", 0, "Black and White");
```

❶ Collection of employees

❷ Default for when the stream is empty

Given a collection of employees, you can use the `reduce` method on `Stream`, which takes a `BinaryOperator` as an argument. The snippet in Example 4-25 shows how to get the employee with the largest salary.

*Example 4-25. Using BinaryOperator.maxBy*

```
Optional<Employee> optionalEmp = employees.stream()
    .reduce(BinaryOperator.maxBy(Comparator.comparingInt(Employee::getSalary)));

System.out.println("Emp with max salary: " +
    optionalEmp.orElse(defaultEmployee));
```

The `reduce` method requires a `BinaryOperator`. The static `maxBy` method produces that `BinaryOperator` based on the supplied `Comparator`, which in this case compares employees by salary.

This works, but there's actually a convenience method called `max` that can be applied directly to the stream:

```
Optional<T> max(Comparator<? super T> comparator)
```

Using that method directly is shown in Example 4-26.

*Example 4-26. Using Stream.max*

```
optionalEmp = employees.stream()
        .max(Comparator.comparingInt(Employee::getSalary));
```

The result is the same.

Note that there is also a method called `max` on the primitive streams (`IntStream`, `LongStream`, and `DoubleStream`) that takes no arguments. Example 4-27 shows that method in action.

*Example 4-27. Finding the highest salary*

```
OptionalInt maxSalary = employees.stream()
        .mapToInt(Employee::getSalary)
        .max();
System.out.println("The max salary is " + maxSalary);
```

In this case, the `mapToInt` method is used to convert the stream of employees into a stream of integers by invoking the `getSalary` method, and the returned stream is an `IntStream`. The `max` method then returns an `OptionalInt`.

There is also a static method called `maxBy` in the `Collectors` utility class. You can use it directly here, as in Example 4-28.

*Example 4-28. Using Collectors.maxBy*

```
optionalEmp = employees.stream()
    .collect(Collectors.maxBy(Comparator.comparingInt(Employee::getSalary)));
```

This is awkward, however, and can be replaced by the `max` method on `Stream`, as shown in the preceding example. The `maxBy` method on `Collectors` is helpful when used as a downstream collector (i.e., when postprocessing a grouping or partitioning operation). The code in Example 4-29 uses `groupingBy` on `Stream` to create a `Map` of departments to lists of employees, but then determines the employee with the greatest salary in each department.

*Example 4-29. Using Collectors.maxBy as a downstream collector*

```
Map<String, Optional<Employee>> map = employees.stream()
    .collect(Collectors.groupingBy(
                Employee::getDepartment,
                Collectors.maxBy(
                    Comparator.comparingInt(Employee::getSalary))));

map.forEach((house, emp) ->
        System.out.println(house + ": " + emp.orElse(defaultEmployee)));
```

The `minBy` method in each of these classes works the same way.

## See Also

Functions are discussed in Recipe 2.4. Downstream collectors are in Recipe 4.6.

# 4.8 Creating Immutable Collections

## Problem

You want to create an immutable list, set, or map using the `Stream` API.

## Solution

Use the new static method `collectingAndThen` in the `Collectors` class.

## Discussion

With its focus on parallelization and clarity, functional programming favors using immutable objects wherever possible. The Collections framework, added in Java 1.2, has always had methods to create immutable collections from existing ones, though in a somewhat awkward fashion.

The `Collections` utility class has methods `unmodifiableList`, `unmodifiableSet`, and `unmodifiableMap` (along with a few other methods with the same `unmodifiable` prefix), as shown in Example 4-30.

*Example 4-30. Unmodifiable methods in the Collections class*

```
static <T> List<T>    unmodifiableList(List<? extends T> list)
static <T> Set<T>     unmodifiableSet(Set<? extends T> s)
static <K,V> Map<K,V> unmodifiableMap(Map<? extends K,? extends V> m)
```

In each case, the argument to the method is an existing list, set, or map, and the resulting list, set, or map has the same elements as the argument, but with an important difference: all the methods that could modify the collection, like `add` or `remove`, now throw an `UnsupportedOperationException`.

Prior to Java 8, if you received the individual values as an argument, using a variable argument list, you produced an unmodifiable list or set as shown in Example 4-31.

*Example 4-31. Creating unmodifiable lists or sets prior to Java 8*

```
@SafeVarargs  ❶
public final <T> List<T> createImmutableListJava7(T... elements) {
    return Collections.unmodifiableList(Arrays.asList(elements));
}

@SafeVarargs  ❶
public final <T> Set<T> createImmutableSetJava7(T... elements) {
    return Collections.unmodifiableSet(new HashSet<>(Arrays.asList(elements)));
}
```

❶ You promise not to corrupt the input array type. See Appendix A for details.

The idea in each case is to start by taking the incoming values and converting them into a `List`. You can wrap the resulting list using `unmodifiableList`, or, in the case of a `Set`, use the list as the argument to a set constructor before using `unmodifiableSet`.

In Java 8, with the new `Stream` API, you can instead take advantage of the static `Collectors.collectingAndThen` method, as in Example 4-32.

*Example 4-32. Creating unmodifiable lists or sets in Java 8*

```
import static java.util.stream.Collectors.collectingAndThen;
import static java.util.stream.Collectors.toList;
import static java.util.stream.Collectors.toSet;

// ... define a class with the following methods ...

@SafeVarargs
public final <T> List<T> createImmutableList(T... elements) {
    return Arrays.stream(elements)
        .collect(collectingAndThen(toList(),
                    Collections::unmodifiableList));  ❶
}

@SafeVarargs
public final <T> Set<T> createImmutableSet(T... elements) {
    return Arrays.stream(elements)
        .collect(collectingAndThen(toSet(),
                    Collections::unmodifiableSet));  ❶
}
```

❶ "Finisher" wraps the generated collections

The `Collectors.collectingAndThen` method takes two arguments: a downstream `Collector` and a `Function` called a *finisher*. The idea is to stream the input elements and then collect them into a `List` or `Set`, and then the unmodifiable function wraps the resulting collection.

Converting a series of input elements into an unmodifiable `Map` isn't as clear, partly because it's not obvious which of the input elements would be assumed to be keys and which would be values. The code shown in Example 4-33[4] creates an immutable `Map` in a very awkward way, using an instance initializer.

*Example 4-33. Creating an immutable Map*

```
Map<String, Integer> map = Collections.unmodifiableMap(
  new HashMap<String, Integer>() {{
    put("have", 1);
    put("the", 2);
    put("high", 3);
    put("ground", 4);
}});
```

Readers who are familiar with Java 9, however, already know that this entire recipe can be replaced with a very simple set of factory methods: `List.of`, `Set.of`, and `Map.of`.

## See Also

Recipe 10.3 shows the new factory methods in Java 9 that automatically create immutable collections.

# 4.9 Implementing the Collector Interface

## Problem

You need to implement `java.util.stream.Collector` manually, because none of the factory methods in the `java.util.stream.Collectors` class give you exactly what you need.

4 From Carl Martensen's blog post "Java 9's Immutable Collections Are Easier To Create But Use With Caution" (*http://carlmartensen.com/immutability-made-easy-in-java-9*).

## Solution

Provide lambda expressions or method references for the `Supplier`, accumulator, combiner, and finisher functions used by the `Collector.of` factory methods, along with any desired characteristics.

## Discussion

The utility class `java.util.stream.Collectors` has several convenient static methods whose return type is `Collector`. Examples are `toList`, `toSet`, `toMap`, and even `toCollection`, each of which is illustrated elsewhere in this book. Instances of classes that implement `Collector` are sent as arguments to the `collect` method on `Stream`. For instance, in Example 4-34, the method accepts string arguments and returns a `List` containing only those whose length is even.

*Example 4-34. Using collect to return a List*

```
public List<String> evenLengthStrings(String... strings) {
    return Stream.of(strings)
        .filter(s -> s.length() % 2 == 0)
        .collect(Collectors.toList()); ❶
}
```

❶ Collect even-length strings into a `List`

If you need to write your own collectors, however, the procedure is a bit more complicated. Collectors use five functions that work together to accumulate entries into a mutable container and optionally transform the result. The five functions are called `supplier`, `accumulator`, `combiner`, `finisher`, and `characteristics`.

Taking the `characteristics` function first, it represents an immutable `Set` of elements of an `enum` type `Collector.Characteristics`. The three possible values are `CONCURRENT`, `IDENTITY_FINISH`, and `UNORDERED`. `CONCURRENT` means that the result container can support the accumulator function being called concurrently on the result container from multiple threads. `UNORDERED` says that the collection operation does not need to preserve the encounter order of the elements. `IDENTITY_FINISH` means that the finishing function returns its argument without any changes.

Note that you don't have to provide any characteristics if the defaults are what you want.

The purpose of each of the required methods is:

`supplier()`
: Create the accumulator container using a `Supplier<A>`

`accumulator()`
: Add a single new data element to the accumulator container using a `BiConsumer<A,T>`

`combiner()`
: Merge two accumulator containers using a `BinaryOperator<A>`

`finisher()`
: Transform the accumulator container into the result container using a `Function<A,R>`

`characteristics()`
: A `Set<Collector.Characteristics>` chosen from the enum values

As usual, an understanding of the functional interfaces defined in the `java.util.function` package makes everything clearer. A `Supplier` is used to create the container where temporary results are accumulated. A `BiConsumer` adds a single element to the accumulator. A `BinaryOperator` means that both input types and the output type are the same, so here the idea is to combine two accumulators into one. A `Function` finally transforms the accumulator into the desired result container.

Each of these methods is invoked during the collection process, which is triggered by (for example) the `collect` method on `Stream`. Conceptually, the collection process is equivalent to the (generic) code shown in Example 4-35, taken from the Javadocs.

*Example 4-35. How the Collector methods are used*

```
R container = collector.supplier.get();             ❶
for (T t : data) {
    collector.accumulator().accept(container, t); ❷
}
return collector.finisher().apply(container);      ❸
```

❶ Create the accumulator container

❷ Add each element to the accumulator container

❸ Convert the accumulator container to the result container using the finisher

Conspicuous by its absence is any mention of the `combiner` function. If your stream is sequential, you don't need it—the algorithm proceeds as described. If, however, you are operating on a parallel stream, then the work is divided into multiple regions, each of which produces its own accumulator container. The combiner is then used during the join process to merge the accumulator containers together into a single one before applying the finisher function.

A code sample, similar to that shown in Example 4-34, is given in Example 4-36.

*Example 4-36. Using collect to return an unmodifiable SortedSet*

```
public SortedSet<String> oddLengthStringSet(String... strings) {
        Collector<String, ?, SortedSet<String>> intoSet =
                Collector.of(TreeSet<String>::new,          ❶
                        SortedSet::add,                     ❷
                        (left, right) -> {                  ❸
                              left.addAll(right);
                              return left;
                        },
                        Collections::unmodifiableSortedSet); ❹
        return Stream.of(strings)
                .filter(s -> s.length() % 2 != 0)
                .collect(intoSet);
    }
```

❶ `Supplier` to create a new `TreeSet`

❷ `BiConsumer` to add each string to the `TreeSet`

❸ `BinaryOperator` to combine two `SortedSet` instances into one

❹ `finisher` function to create an unmodifiable set

The result will be a sorted, unmodifiable set of strings, ordered lexicographically.

This example used one of the two overloaded versions of the `static` `of` method for producing collectors, whose signatures are:

```
static <T,A,R> Collector<T,A,R> of(Supplier<A> supplier,
    BiConsumer<A,T> accumulator,
    BinaryOperator<A> combiner,
    Function<A,R> finisher,
    Collector.Characteristics... characteristics)
static <T,R> Collector<T,R,R>   of(Supplier<R> supplier,
    BiConsumer<R,T> accumulator,
    BinaryOperator<R> combiner,
    Collector.Characteristics... characteristics)
```

Given the convenience methods in the `Collectors` class that produce collectors for you, you rarely need to make one of your own this way. Still, it's a useful skill to have, and once again illustrates how the functional interfaces in the `java.util.function` package come together to create interesting objects.

## See Also

The `finisher` function is an example of a downstream collector, discussed further in Recipe 4.6. The `Supplier`, `Function`, and `BinaryOperator` functional interfaces are discussed in various recipes in Chapter 2. The static utility methods in `Collectors` are discussed in Recipe 4.2.

CHAPTER 5

# Issues with Streams, Lambdas, and Method References

Now that you know the basics of lambdas and method references and how they are used in streams, there are several topics that arise from the combination. For example, now that interfaces can have default methods, what happens when a class implements multiple interfaces that have the same default method signature but different implementations? As another example, what happens when you are writing code in a lambda expression and try to access or modify a variable defined outside it? Also, what about exceptions? How are they handled in lambda expressions, where you have no method signature on which to add a `throws` clause?

This chapter deals with all these issues and more.

## 5.1 The java.util.Objects Class

### Problem

You wish to use static utility methods for null checking, comparisons, and more.

### Solution

Use the `java.util.Objects` class, added in Java 7, but helpful during stream processing.

### Discussion

One of the lesser-known classes added in Java 7 is the `java.util.Objects` class, which contains static methods for a variety of tasks. These methods include:

`static boolean deepEquals(Object a, Object b)`
: Checks for "deep" equality, which is particularly useful when comparing arrays.

`static boolean equals(Object a, Object b)`
: Uses the `equals` method from the first argument, but is null safe.

`static int hash(Object... values)`
: Generates a hash code for a sequence of input values.

`static String toString(Object o)`
: Returns the result of calling `toString` on the argument if not null, and returns `null` otherwise.

`static String toString(Object o, String nullDefault)`
: Returns the result of calling `toString` on the first argument, and returns the second argument if the first argument is null.

There are also a few overloads of a method useful for validation of arguments:

`static <T> T requireNotNull(T obj)`
: Returns `T` if not null and throws a `NullPointerException` (NPE) otherwise.

`static <T> T requireNotNull(T obj, String message)`
: Same as previous method, but the NPE resulting from a null argument has the specified message.

`static <T> T requireNotNull(T obj, Supplier<String> messageSupplier)`
: Same as previous method, but invokes the given `Supplier` to generate a message for the NPE if the first argument is null.

That last method takes a `Supplier<String>` as an argument, which finally gives a reason for including this class in a book focused on Java 8 and above. An arguably better reason, however, is given by the `isNull` and `nonNull` methods. Each of those returns a `boolean`:

`static boolean isNull(Object obj)`
: Returns `true` if the provided reference is null and `false` otherwise.

`static boolean nonNull(Object obj)`
: Returns `true` if the provided reference is not null and `false` otherwise.

The beauty of these methods is that they can be used as `Predicate` instances in a filter.

For example, say you have a class that returns a collection. Example 5-1 has a method to return the complete collection, whatever it may be, and a method to return the collection without any nulls.

*Example 5-1. Returning a collection and filtering out nulls*

```
List<String> strings = Arrays.asList(
    "this", null, "is", "a", null, "list", "of", "strings", null);

List<String> nonNullStrings = strings.stream()
    .filter(Objects::nonNull)       ❶
    .collect(Collectors.toList());
```

❶ Filter out null elements

You can use the `Objects.deepEquals` method to test this, as in Example 5-2.

*Example 5-2. Testing the filter*

```
@Test
public void testNonNulls() throws Exception {
    List<String> strings =
        Arrays.asList("this", "is", "a", "list", "of", "strings");
    assertTrue(Objects.deepEquals(strings, nonNullStrings);
}
```

This process can be generalized so that it doesn't just apply to strings. The code in Example 5-3 filters nulls out of any list.

*Example 5-3. Filtering nulls from a generic list*

```
public <T> List<T> getNonNullElements(List<T> list) {
    return list.stream()
            .filter(Objects::nonNull)
            .collect(Collectors.toList());
}
```

Now a method that produces a `List` with multiple elements being null can be filtered with ease.

# 5.2 Lambdas and Effectively Final

## Problem

Inside a lambda expression you want to access a variable defined outside it.

## Solution

Local variables accessed inside lambda expressions must be final or "effectively final." Attributes can be both accessed and modified.

## Discussion

Back in the late '90s, when Java was still shiny and new, occasionally developers would write client-side Java applications using the Swing user interface library. Like all GUI libraries, Swing components are event-driven: components generate events and listeners react to them.

Since it was considered a good practice to write separate listeners for each component, listeners were often implemented as anonymous inner classes. This kept them modular, but using inner classes had an added benefit: code in inner classes can access and modify the private attributes of the outer class. For example, a `JButton` instance generates an `ActionEvent`, and a `ActionEventListener` interface contains a single method called `actionPerformed` that is invoked once an implementation is registered as a listener. See Example 5-4 for a sample.

*Example 5-4. A trivial Swing user interface*

```
public class MyGUI extends JFrame {
    private JTextField name = new JTextField("Please enter your name");
    private JTextField response = new JTextField("Greeting");
    private JButton button = new JButton("Say Hi");

    public MyGUI() {
        // ... unrelated GUI setup code ...
        String greeting = "Hello, %s!";                          ❶
        button.addActionListener(new ActionListener() {
           @Override
           public void actionPerformed(ActionEvent e) {
              response.setText(
                  String.format(greeting, name.getText());      ❷
              // greeting = "Anything else";                     ❸
           }
        });
    }
}
```

❶ Local variable

❷ Access local variable and attributes

❸ Modify local variable (will not compile)

The `greeting` string is a local variable defined inside the constructor. The `name` and `response` variables are attributes of the class. The `ActionListener` interface is implemented as an anonymous inner class, whose one method is `actionPerformed`. Inside the inner class, code can:

- Access attributes like `name` and `response`
- Modify attributes (though that's not shown here)
- Access the local variable `greeting`
- *Cannot* modify the local variable

In fact, prior to Java 8, the compiler would have required the `greeting` variable to be declared `final`. In Java 8, the variable doesn't have to be declared final, but it must be *effectively final.* In other words, any code that tries to change the value of a local variable will not compile.

Of course, in Java 8, the anonymous inner class would be replaced by a lambda expression, as in Example 5-5.

*Example 5-5. Lambda expression for the listener*

```
String greeting = "Hello, %s!";
button.addActionListener(e ->
    response.setText(String.format(greeting,name.getText())));
```

The same rules apply. The `greeting` variable doesn't have to be declared to be `final`, but it must be effectively final or the code will not compile.

If Swing isn't to your liking, here's another way to approach this problem. Say you want to sum values in a given `List`, as in Example 5-6.

*Example 5-6. Sum the values in a List*

```
List<Integer> nums = Arrays.asList(3, 1, 4, 1, 5, 9);

int total = 0;                                  ❶
for (int n : nums) {                            ❷
    total += n;
}

total = 0;
nums.forEach(n -> total += n);                  ❸

total = nums.stream()                           ❹
            .mapToInt(Integer::valueOf)
            .sum()
```

❶ Local variable `total`

❷ Traditional for-each loop

❸ Modify local variable in a lambda: WILL NOT COMPILE

❹ Convert stream to `IntStream` and call `sum`

The code declares a local variable called `total`. Summing the values using a traditional for-each loop works just fine.

The `forEach` method defined on `Iterable` takes a `Consumer` as an argument, but if the consumer tries to modify the `total` variable, the code will not compile.

Of course, the right way to solve the problem is to convert the stream into an `IntStream`, which then has a `sum` method—no local variables involved at all.

Technically, a function along with the accessible variables defined in its environment is called a *closure*. By that definition, Java is in somewhat of a gray area—local variables are accessible but cannot be modified. You could argue that Java 8 lambdas are actually closures, in that they are closed over values rather than variables.[1]

## See Also

Other languages have different rules for closure variables. For example, Groovy allows you to modify them, though that is not considered a good practice.

# 5.3 Streams of Random Numbers

## Problem

You want a stream of random integers, longs, or doubles, within a given set of bounds.

## Solution

Use the static `ints`, `longs`, and `doubles` methods in `java.util.Random`.

1 Why, then, aren't Java 8 lambdas actually called closures? According to Bruce Eckel, the term "closure" is so heavily overloaded it leads to arguments. "When someone says *real closures*, it too often means, *what closure meant in the first language I encountered with something called closures*." For more information, see his blog post "Are Java 8 Lamdas Closures?". (*http://bit.ly/eckel-java-8-lambdas*)

## Discussion

If all you need is a single random double, the static Math.random method is convenient. It returns a double value between 0.0 and 1.0.[2] The process is equivalent to instantiating the java.util.Random class and invoking the nextDouble method.

The Random class provides a constructor that lets you specify a seed. If you specify the same seed, you get the same resulting sequence of random numbers, which can be useful in testing.

If you want a sequential stream of random numbers, however, Java 8 added several methods to the Random class that return them. The methods are ints, longs, and doubles, whose signatures are (without the various overloads):

```
IntStream    ints()
LongStream   longs()
DoubleStream doubles()
```

The overloaded versions of each allow you to specify the size of the resulting stream and the min and max values for the generated numbers. For example:

```
DoubleStream doubles(long streamSize, double randomNumberOrigin,
    double randomNumberBound)
```

The returned stream produces the given streamSize number of pseudorandom double values, each of which is greater than or equal to the randomNumberOrigin and strictly less than the randomNumberBound.

Variants that don't specify streamSize return an "effectively unlimited" stream of values.

If you don't specify the min or max, they default to zero and one for doubles, the complete range of Integer for ints, and (effectively) the complete range of Long for longs. In each case, the result is like repeatedly invoking nextDouble, nextInt, or nextLong, respectively.

Example 5-7 shows the sample code.

*Example 5-7. Generating streams of random numbers*

```
Random r = new Random();
r.ints(5)                          ❶
 .sorted()
 .forEach(System.out::println);
```

2 The Javadocs say the returned values are chosen "pseudorandomly with (approximately) uniform distribution" from that range, which shows the sort of hedging you have to do when discussing random number generators.

```
r.doubles(5, 0, 0.5)                       ❷
 .sorted()
 .forEach(System.out::println);

List<Long> longs = r.longs(5)
                   .boxed()          ❸
                   .collect(Collectors.toList());
System.out.println(longs);

List<Integer> listOfInts = r.ints(5, 10, 20)
    .collect(LinkedList::new, LinkedList::add, LinkedList::addAll); ❹
System.out.println(listOfInts);
```

❶ Five random integers

❷ Five random doubles between 0 (inclusive) and 0.5 (exclusive)

❸ Boxing `long` to `Long` so they can be collected

❹ Alternative form of `collect` instead of calling `boxed`

The latter two examples deal with the minor annoyance that occurs when you want to create a collection of primitives. You can't invoke `collect(Collectors.toList())` on a collection of primitives, as discussed in Recipe 3.2. As suggested in that recipe, you can either use the `boxed` method to convert the `long` values to instances of `Long`, or you can use the three-argument version of `collect` and specify the `Supplier`, accumulator, and combiner yourself, as shown.

It's worth noting that `SecureRandom` is a subclass of `Random`. It provides a cryptographically strong random number generator. All the same methods (`ints`, `longs`, `doubles`, and their overloads) also work on `SecureRandom`, just with a different generator.

## See Also

The `boxed` method in `Stream` is discussed in Recipe 3.2.

# 5.4 Default Methods in Map

## Problem

You want to add or replace elements in a `Map` only if they already exist or are absent, or other related operations.

## Solution

Use one of the many new default methods in the `java.util.Map` interface, like `computeIfAbsent`, `computeIfPresent`, `replace`, `merge`, and so on.

## Discussion

The `Map` interface has been in Java since the rest of the collections framework was added way back in version 1.2. Java 8 introduced default methods in interfaces, and several new methods have been added to `Map` as a result.

Table 5-1 shows the new methods.

*Table 5-1. Default methods in Map*

| Method | Purpose |
| --- | --- |
| `compute` | Compute a new value based on the existing key and value |
| `computeIfAbsent` | Return the value for the given key if it exists, or use the supplied function to compute and store it if not |
| `computeIfPresent` | Compute a new value to replace an existing value |
| `forEach` | Iterate over a `Map`, passing each key and value to the consumer |
| `getOrDefault` | If the key exists in the `Map`, return its value; otherwise return the default |
| `merge` | If the key is not in the `Map`, return the supplied value; otherwise compute a new value |
| `putIfAbsent` | If the key isn't in the `Map`, associate it with the given value |
| `remove` | Remove the entry for this key only if it matches the given value |
| `replace` | Replace the existing key with the new value |
| `replaceAll` | Replace each entry in the `Map` with the result of applying the given function to the current entry |

That's a lot of new methods for an interface we've been using for over a decade. Some of them are really convenient, however.

### computeIfAbsent

The complete signature for the `computIfAbsent` method is:

```
V computeIfAbsent(K key, Function<? super K, ? extends V> mappingFunction)
```

This method is particularly useful when creating a cache of the results of method calls. For example, consider the classic recursive calculation of Fibonacci numbers.

The value of any Fibonacci number greater than 1 is equal to the sum of the previous two Fibonacci numbers,[3] as in Example 5-8.

*Example 5-8. Recursive calculation of Fibonacci numbers*

```
long fib(long i) {
    if (i == 0) return 0;
    if (i == 1) return 1;
    return fib(i - 1) + fib(i - 2);  ❶
}
```

❶ Highly inefficient

The problem is that `fib(5) = fib(4) + fib(3) = fib(3) + fib(2) + fib(2) + fib(1) = ...` and there are many, many repeated calculations. The way to fix this is to use a cache, a technique known as *memoization* in functional programming. The result, modified to store `BigInteger` instances, is shown in Example 5-9.

*Example 5-9. Fibonacci calculation with a cache*

```
private Map<Long, BigInteger> cache = new HashMap<>();

public BigInteger fib(long i) {
    if (i == 0) return BigInteger.ZERO;
    if (i == 1) return BigInteger.ONE;

    return cache.computeIfAbsent(i, n -> fib(n - 2).add(fib(n - 1))); ❶
}
```

❶ Cache returns value if it exists, or computes and stores it if not

The calculation uses a cache where the keys are the supplied numbers and the values are the corresponding Fibonacci numbers. The `computeIfAbsent` method looks in the cache for a given number. If it exists, it returns the value. Otherwise it uses the supplied `Function` to compute the new value, store it in the cache, and return it. That's quite an improvement for a single method.

### computeIfPresent

The complete signature of the `computeIfPresent` method is:

```
V computeIfPresent(K key,
    BiFunction<? super K, ? super V, ? extends V> remappingFunction)
```

3 In the wildly unlikely event that you haven't already heard this joke: "Rumor has it that this year's Fibonacci conference is going to be as good as the last two combined."

The `computeIfPresent` method only updates a value if its associated key is already in the map. Consider the case where you are parsing text and making a count of how many times each word appears. Such a calculation, known as a concordance, is not uncommon. If, however, you only care about certain specific keywords, you can use `computeIfPresent` to update those. See Example 5-10.

*Example 5-10. Update the word counts only for specific words*

```
public Map<String,Integer> countWords(String passage, String... strings) {
    Map<String, Integer> wordCounts = new HashMap<>();

    Arrays.stream(strings).forEach(s -> wordCounts.put(s, 0)); ❶

    Arrays.stream(passage.split(" ")).forEach(word ->          ❷
        wordCounts.computeIfPresent(word, (key, val) -> val + 1));

    return wordCounts;
}
```

❶ Put the words we care about in the map with a count of zero

❷ Read the passage, updating the counts only for the words we care about

By putting the words you care about into the map initially with a count of zero, the `computeIfPresent` method will only update those values.

If you run this with a passage of text and a comma-separated list of words, as in Example 5-11, you get the results you're looking for.

*Example 5-11. Calling the countWords method*

```
String passage = "NSA agent walks into a bar. Bartender says, " +
    "'Hey, I have a new joke for you.' Agent says, 'heard it'.";

Map<String, Integer> counts = demo.countWords(passage, "NSA", "agent", "joke");
counts.forEach((word, count) -> System.out.println(word + "=" + count));

// Output is agent=1, NSA=2, joke=1
```

Only the desired words are keys in the map, so only those have their counts updated. As usual, printing the values takes advantage of the default `forEach` method in `Map`, which takes a `BiConsumer`, whose arguments are the keys and the values.

### Other methods

The `replace` method works like the `put` method, but only if the key already exists. If not, the `replace` method does nothing, while `put` adds a null key, which may not be what you want.

There are two overloads of the `replace` method:

```
V replace(K key, V value)
boolean replace(K key, V oldValue, V newValue)
```

The first one replaces the value of the key if it exists in the map at all. The second only does the replacement if the current value is the one specified.

The `getOrDefault` method solves the occasionally annoying fact that calling `get` on a `Map` with a key that doesn't exist returns null. That's helpful, but the method only returns the default, it doesn't also add it to the map.

The signature of `getOrDefault` is:

```
V getOrDefault(Object key, V defaultValue)
```

The `getOrDefault` method returns the default if the key does not exist in the map, but it does not add the key to the map.

The `merge` method is very helpful. Its complete signature is:

```
V merge(K key, V value,
            BiFunction<? super V, ? super V, ? extends V> remappingFunction)
```

Say you want the complete word count map for a given passage of text, rather than just the counts for specific words. Normally you would have two conditions: if the word is already in the map, update the count; otherwise put it in the map with a count of one. With `merge` the process simplifies, as in Example 5-12.

*Example 5-12. Using the merge method*

```
public Map<String, Integer> fullWordCounts(String passage) {
    Map<String, Integer> wordCounts = new HashMap<>();
    String testString = passage.toLowerCase().replaceAll("\\W"," "); ❶

    Arrays.stream(testString.split("\\s+")).forEach(word ->
        wordCounts.merge(word, 1, Integer::sum));                    ❷

    return wordCounts;
}
```

❶ Remove case sensitivity and punctuation

❷ Add or update the count for a given word

The `merge` method takes the key and default value, which is inserted if the key doesn't already exist in the map. Otherwise `merge` uses the `BinaryOperator` (here the `sum` method in `Integer`) to compute the new value based on the old value.

Hopefully this recipe makes it clear that the new default methods on `Map` provide several convenient techniques for your coding.

# 5.5 Default Method Conflict

## Problem

You have a class that implements two interfaces, each of which contains the same default method with different implementations.

## Solution

Implement the method in your class. Your implementation can still use the provided defaults from the interfaces through the `super` keyword.

## Discussion

Java 8 supports both static and default methods in interfaces. Default methods provide an implementation, which is then inherited by the class. This allows interfaces to add new methods without breaking existing class implementations.

Since classes can implement multiple interfaces, a class may inherit default methods that have the same signature but are implemented differently, or it may already contain its own version of a default method.

There are three possibilities when this occurs:

- In any conflict between a method in a class and a default method in an interface, the class always wins.
- If the conflict comes between two interfaces where one is a descendant of the other, then the descendant wins, the same way they do in classes.
- If there is no inheritance relationship between the two defaults, the class will not compile.

In the last case, simply implement the method in the class and everything will work again. This reduces the third case to the first one.

As an example, consider the `Company` interface shown in Example 5-13 and the `Employee` interface shown in Example 5-14.

*Example 5-13. The Company interface with a default method*

```
public interface Company {
    default String getName() {
        return "Initech";
    }

    // other methods
}
```

The `default` keyword indicates that the `getName` method is a default method, which provides an implementation that returns the company name.

*Example 5-14. The Employee interface with a default method*

```
public interface Employee {
    String getFirst();

    String getLast();

    void convertCaffeineToCodeForMoney();

    default String getName() {
        return String.format("%s %s", getFirst(), getLast());
    }
}
```

The `Employee` interface also contains a default method called `getName` with the same signature as the one in `Company`, but with a different implementation. The `Company Employee` class shown in Example 5-15 implements both interfaces, causing a conflict.

*Example 5-15. First attempt at CompanyEmployee (WON'T COMPILE)*

```
public class CompanyEmployee implements Company, Employee {
    private String first;
    private String last;

    @Override
    public void convertCaffeineToCodeForMoney() {
        System.out.println("Coding...");
    }

    @Override
    public String getFirst() {
        return first;
    }
```

```
    @Override
    public String getLast() {
        return last;
    }
}
```

Since `CompanyEmployee` inherits unrelated defaults for `getName`, the class won't compile. To fix this, you need to add your own version of `getName` to the class, which will then override both the defaults.

You can still use the provided defaults, however, using the `super` keyword, as shown in Example 5-16.

*Example 5-16. Fixed version of CompanyEmployee*

```
public class CompanyEmployee implements Company, Employee {

    @Override
    public String getName() {                                          ❶
        return String.format("%s working for %s",
            Employee.super.getName(), Company.super.getName()); ❷
    }

    // ... rest as before ...
}
```

❶ Implement `getName`

❷ Access default implementations using `super`

In this version, the `getName` method in the class builds a `String` from the default versions provided by both `Company` and `Employee`.

The best news of all is that this is as complicated as default methods ever get. You now know everything there is to know about them.

Actually, there's one edge case to consider. If the `Company` interface contained `getName` but was not marked `default` (and didn't have an implementation, making it abstract), would that still cause a conflict because `Employee` also had the same method? The answer is yes, interestingly enough, and you still need to provide an implementation in the `CompanyEmployee` class.

Of course, if the same method appears in both interfaces and neither is a default, then this is the pre-Java 8 situation. There's no conflict, but the class must provide an implementation.

## See Also

Default methods in interfaces are discussed in Recipe 1.5.

# 5.6 Iterating Over Collections and Maps

## Problem

You want to iterate over a collection or map.

## Solution

Use the `forEach` method, which was added as a default method to both `Iterable` and `Map`.

## Discussion

Rather than using a loop to iterate over a linear collection (i.e., a class that implements `Collection` or one of its descendants), you can use the new `forEach` method that has been added to `Iterable` as a default method.

From the Javadocs, its signature is:

```
default void forEach(Consumer<? super T> action)
```

The argument to `forEach` is of type `Consumer`, one of the functional interfaces added to the `java.util.function` package. A `Consumer` represents an operation that takes a single generic parameter and returns no result. As the docs say, "unlike most other functional interfaces, `Consumer` is expected to operate via side effects."

A *pure* function operates without side effects, so applying the function with the same parameters always gives the same result. In functional programming, this is known as *referential transparency*, where a function can be replaced by its corresponding value.

Since `java.util.Collection` is a subinterface of `Iterable`, the `forEach` method is available on all linear collections, from `ArrayList` to `LinkedHashSet`. Iterating over each is therefore simple, as Example 5-17 shows.

*Example 5-17. Iterating over a linear collection*

```
List<Integer> integers = Arrays.asList(3, 1, 4, 1, 5, 9);

integers.forEach(new Consumer<Integer>() {     ❶
    @Override
```

```
    public void accept(Integer integer) {
        System.out.println(integer);
    }
});

integers.forEach((Integer n) -> {                ❷
    System.out.println(n);
});

integers.forEach(n -> System.out.println(n)); ❸

integers.forEach(System.out::println);           ❹
}
```

❶ Anonymous inner class implementation

❷ Full verbose form of a block lambda

❸ Expression lambda

❹ Method reference

The anonymous inner class version is shown simply as a reminder of the signature of the `accept` method in the `Consumer` interface. As the inner class shows, the `accept` method takes a single argument and returns `void`. The lambda versions shown are compatible with this. Since each of the lambda versions consists of a single call to the `println` method on `System.out`, that method can be used as a method reference, as shown in the last version.

The `Map` interface also has a `forEach` method, added as a default. In this case, the signature takes a `BiConsumer`:

```
default void forEach(BiConsumer<? super K, ? super V> action)
```

`BiConsumer` is another of the new interfaces in the `java.util.function` package. It represents a function that takes two generic arguments and returns `void`. When implemented in the `forEach` method in `Map`, the arguments become the keys and values from the `Map.Entry` instances in the `entrySet`.

That means iterating over a `Map` is now as easy as iterating over a `List`, `Set`, or any other linear collection. Example 5-18 shows the sample code.

*Example 5-18. Iterating over a Map*

```
Map<Long, String> map = new HashMap<>();
map.put(86L, "Don Adams (Maxwell Smart)");
map.put(99L, "Barbara Feldon");
map.put(13L, "David Ketchum");
```

```
map.forEach((num, agent) ->
    System.out.printf("Agent %d, played by %s%n", num, agent));
```

The output from the iteration is shown in Example 5-19.[4]

*Example 5-19. Map iteration output*

```
Agent 99, played by Barbara Feldon
Agent 86, played by Don Adams (Maxwell Smart)
Agent 13, played by David Ketchum
```

Prior to Java 8, to iterate over a `Map` you needed to first use the `keySet` or `entrySet` methods to acquire the `Set` of keys or `Map.Entry` instances and then iterate over that. With the new default `forEach` method, iteration is much simpler.

Keep in mind that there is no easy way to break out of `forEach`. Consider rewriting your stream processing code as a `filter` and/or `sorted` instead, followed by a `findFirst`.

## See Also

The functional interfaces `Consumer` and `BiConsumer` are discussed in Recipe 2.1.

# 5.7 Logging with a Supplier

## Problem

You want to create a log message, but only if the log level ensures it will be seen.

## Solution

Use the new logging overloads in the `Logger` class that take a `Supplier`.

## Discussion

The logging methods in `java.util.logging.Logger`, like `info`, `warning`, or `severe`, now have two overloaded versions: one that takes a single `String` as an argument, and one that takes a `Supplier<String>`.

---

4 These examples are taken from the now ancient TV series *Get Smart*, which ran from 1965 to 1970. Maxwell Smart is essentially a bumbling combination of James Bond and Inspector Clouseau, created by producers Mel Brooks and Buck Henry.

For instance, Example 5-20 shows the signatures of the various logging methods.[5]

*Example 5-20. Overloaded logging methods java.util.logging.Logger*

```
void config(String msg)
void config(Supplier<String> msgSupplier)

void fine(String msg)
void fine(Supplier<String> msgSupplier)

void finer(String msg)
void finer(Supplier<String> msgSupplier)

void finest(String msg)
void finest(Supplier<String> msgSupplier)

void info(String msg)
void info(Supplier<String> msgSupplier)

void warning(String msg)
void warning(Supplier<String> msgSupplier)

void severe(String msg)
void severe(Supplier<String> msgSupplier)
```

For each method, the version that takes a `String` was part of the original API that appeared in Java 1.4. The `Supplier` version is new to Java 8. If you look at the implementation of the `Supplier` version in the standard library, you see the code shown in Example 5-21.

*Example 5-21. Implementation details of the Logger class*

```
public void info(Supplier<String> msgSupplier) {
    log(Level.INFO, msgSupplier);
}

public void log(Level level, Supplier<String> msgSupplier) {
    if (!isLoggable(level)) {                              ❶
        return;
    }
    LogRecord lr = new LogRecord(level, msgSupplier.get()); ❷
    doLog(lr);
}
```

5 You may be wondering why the designers of the Java logging framework didn't use the same log levels (trace, debug, info, warn, error, and fatal) that every other logging API uses. That's an excellent question. If you ever find out, please let me know, too.

❶ Return if the message will not be shown

❷ Retrieve the message from the `Supplier` by calling `get`

Rather than construct a message that will never be shown, the implementation checks to see if the message will be "loggable." If the message was provided as a simple string, it would be evaluated whether it was logged or not. The version that uses a `Supplier` allows the developer to put empty parentheses and an arrow in front of the message, converting it into a `Supplier`, which will only be invoked if the log level is appropriate. Example 5-22 shows how to use both overloads of `info`.

*Example 5-22. Using a Supplier in the info method*

```
private Logger logger = Logger.getLogger(this.getClass().getName());
private List<String> data = new ArrayList<>();

// ... populate list with data ...

logger.info("The data is " + data.toString());        ❶
logger.info(() -> "The data is " + data.toString()); ❷
```

❶ Argument always constructed

❷ Argument only constructed if log level shows info messages

In this example, the message invokes the `toString` method on every object in the list. In the first case, the resulting string will be formed whether the program shows info messages or not. Converting the log argument to a `Supplier` by simply adding `() ->` in front of it means that the `get` method on the `Supplier` will only be invoked if the message will be used.

The technique of replacing an argument with a `Supplier` of the same type is known as *deferred execution*, and can be used in any context where object creation might be expensive.

## See Also

Deferred execution is one of the primary use cases for `Supplier`. `Suppliers` are discussed in Recipe 2.2.

# 5.8 Closure Composition

## Problem

You want to apply a series of small, independent functions consecutively.

## Solution

Use the composition methods defined as defaults in the `Function`, `Consumer`, and `Predicate` interfaces.

## Discussion

One of the benefits of functional programming is that you can create a set of small, reusable functions that you can combine to solve larger problems. To support this, the functional interfaces in the `java.util.function` package include methods to make composition easy.

For example, the `Function` interface has two default methods with the signatures shown in Example 5-23.

*Example 5-23. Composition methods in java.util.function.Function*

```
default <V> Function<V,R>      compose(Function<? super V,? extends T> before)
default <V> Function<T,V>      andThen(Function<? super R,? extends V> after)
```

The dummy arguments' names in the Javadocs indicate what each method does. The `compose` method applies its argument *before* the original function, while the `andThen` method applies its argument *after* the original function.

To demonstrate this, consider the trivial example shown in Example 5-24.

*Example 5-24. Using the compose and andThen methods*

```
Function<Integer, Integer> add2  = x -> x + 2;
Function<Integer, Integer> mult3 = x -> x * 3;

Function<Integer, Integer> mult3add2  = add2.compose(mult3); ❶
Function<Integer, Integer> add2mmult3 = add2.andThen(mult3); ❷

System.out.println("mult3add2(1): " + mult3add2.apply(1));
System.out.println("add2mult3(1): " + add2mult3.apply(1));
```

❶ First `mult3`, then `add2`

❷ First `add2`, then `mult3`

The `add2` function adds 2 to its argument. The `mult3` function multiplies its argument by 3. Since `mult3add2` is made using `compose`, first the `mult3` function is applied and then the `add2` function, whereas for `add2mult3` using the `andThen` function does the opposite.

The results of applying each composite function gives:

```
mult3add2(1): 5  // because (1 * 3) + 2 == 5
add2mult3(1): 9  // because (1 + 2) * 3 == 9
```

The result of the composition is a function, so this process creates new operations that can be used later. Say, for example, you receive data as part of an HTTP request, which means it is transmitted in string form. You already have a method to operate on the data, but only if it's already a number. If this happens frequently, you can compose a function that parses the string data before applying the numerical operation. For instance, see Example 5-25.

*Example 5-25. Parse an integer from a string, then add 2*

```
Function<Integer, Integer> add2 = x -> x + 2;
Function<String, Integer> parseThenAdd2 = add2.compose(Integer::parseInt);
System.out.println(parseThenAdd2.apply("1"));
// prints 3
```

The new function, `parseThenAdd2`, invokes the static `Integer.parseInt` method before adding 2 to the result. Going the other way, you can define a function that invokes a `toString` method after a numerical operation, as in Example 5-26.

*Example 5-26. Add a number, then convert to a string*

```
Function<Integer, Integer> add2 = x -> x + 2;
Function<Integer, String> plus2toString = add2.andThen(Object::toString);
System.out.println(plus2toString.apply(1));
// prints "3"
```

This operation returns a function that takes an `Integer` argument and returns a `String`.

The `Consumer` interface also has a method used for closure composition, as shown in Example 5-27.

*Example 5-27. Closure composition with consumers*

```
default Consumer<T> andThen(Consumer<? super T> after)
```

The Javadocs for `Consumer` explain that the `andThen` method returns a composed `Consumer` that performs the original operation followed by the `Consumer` argument. If either operation throws an exception, it is thrown to the caller of the composed operation.

See the sample code in Example 5-28.

*Example 5-28. Composed consumer for printing and logging*

```
Logger log = Logger.getLogger(...);
Consumer<String> printer = System.out::println;
Consumer<String> logger = log::info;

Consumer<String> printThenLog = printer.andThen(logger);
Stream.of("this", "is", "a", "stream", "of", "strings").forEach(printThenLog);
```

The example code creates two consumers—one for printing to the console, and one for logging. The composed consumer does both printing and logging for each element of the stream.

The `Predicate` interface has three methods that can be used to compose predicates, as shown in Example 5-29.

*Example 5-29. Composition methods in the Predicate interface*

```
default Predicate<T>    and(Predicate<? super T> other)
default Predicate<T>    negate()
default Predicate<T>    or(Predicate<? super T> other)
```

As you might expect the `and`, `or`, and `negate` methods are used to compose predicates using logical and, logical or, and logical not operations. Each returns a composed predicate.

To give a moderately interesting example, consider properties of integers. A perfect square is a number whose square root is also an integer. A triangle number counts the objects that can form an equilateral triangle.[6]

The code in Example 5-30 shows methods for computing perfect squares and triangle numbers, and how you can use the `and` method to find numbers that are both.

*Example 5-30. Triangle numbers that are perfect squares*

```
public static boolean isPerfect(int x) {        ❶
    return Math.sqrt(x) % 1 == 0;
}

public static boolean isTriangular(int x) {     ❷
    double val = (Math.sqrt(8 * x + 1) - 1) / 2;
    return val % 1 == 0;
}

// ...
```

6 See *https://en.wikipedia.org/wiki/Triangular_number* for details. Triangle numbers are the number of handshakes needed if each person in a room shakes hands with every other person exactly once.

```
IntPredicate triangular = CompositionDemo::isTriangular;
IntPredicate perfect = CompositionDemo::isPerfect;
IntPredicate both = triangular.and(perfect);

IntStream.rangeClosed(1, 10_000)
        .filter(both)
        .forEach(System.out::println);        ❸
```

❶ Examples: 1, 4, 9, 16, 25, 36, 49, 64, 81, ...

❷ Examples: 1, 3, 6, 10, 15, 21, 28, 36, 45, ...

❸ Both (between 1 and 10,000): 1, 36, 1225

The composition approach can be used to build up complex operations from a small library of simple functions.[7]

## See Also

Functions are discussed in Recipe 2.4, consumers in Recipe 2.1, and predicates in Recipe 2.3.

# 5.9 Using an Extracted Method for Exception Handling

## Problem

Code in a lambda expression needs to throw an exception, but you do not want to clutter a block lambda with exception handling code.

## Solution

Create a separate method that does the operation, handle the exception there, and invoke the extracted method in your lambda expression.

## Discussion

A lambda expression is effectively the implementation of the single abstract method in a functional interface. As with anonymous inner classes, lambda expressions can only throw exceptions declared in the abstract method signature.

7 The Unix operating system is based on this idea, with similar advantages.

If the required exception is unchecked, the situation is relatively easy. The ancestor of all unchecked exceptions is `java.lang.RuntimeException`.[8] Like any Java code, a lambda expression can throw a runtime exception without declaring it or wrapping the code in a try/catch block. The exception is then propagated to the caller.

Consider, for instance, a method that divides all elements of a collection by a constant value, as shown in Example 5-31.

*Example 5-31. A lambda expression that may throw an unchecked exception*

```
public List<Integer> div(List<Integer> values, Integer factor) {
    return values.stream()
        .map(n -> n / factor)  ❶
        .collect(Collectors.toList());
}
```

❶ Can throw an `ArithmeticException`

Integer division will throw an `ArithmeticException` (an unchecked exception) if the denominator is zero.[9] This will be propagated to the caller, as shown in Example 5-32.

*Example 5-32. Client code*

```
List<Integer> values = Arrays.asList(30, 10, 40, 10, 50, 90);
List<Integer> scaled = demo.div(values, 10);
System.out.println(scaled);
// prints: [3, 1, 4, 1, 5, 9]

scaled = demo.div(values, 0);
System.out.println(scaled);
// throws ArithmeticException: / by zero
```

The client code invokes the `div` method, and if the divisor is zero, the lambda expression throws an `ArithmeticException`. The client can add a try/catch block inside the `map` method in order to handle the exception, but that leads to some seriously ugly code (see Example 5-33).

---

8 Isn't that just about the worst-named class in the entire Java API? All exceptions are thrown at runtime; otherwise they're compiler errors. Shouldn't that class have been called `UncheckedException` all along? To emphasize how silly the situation can get, Java 8 also adds a new class called `java.io.UncheckedIOException` just to avoid some of the issues discussed in this recipe.

9 Interestingly enough, if the values and the divisor are changed to `Double` instead of `Integer`, you don't get an exception at all, even if the divisor is 0.0. Instead you get a result where all the elements are "Infinity." This, believe it or not, is the correct behavior according to the IEEE 754 specification for handling floating-point values in a binary computer (and caused me massive headaches back when I used to program in—ugh—Fortran; the nightmares have gone away, but it took a while).

*Example 5-33. Lambda expression with try/catch*

```
public List<Integer> div(List<Integer> values, Integer factor) {
    return values.stream()
        .map( n -> {
            try {
                return n / factor;
            } catch (ArithmeticException e) {
                e.printStackTrace();
            }
        })
        .collect(Collectors.toList());
}
```

This same process works even for checked exceptions, as long as the checked exception is declared in the functional interface.

It's generally a good idea to keep stream processing code as simple as possible, with the goal of writing one line per intermediate operation. In this case, you can simplify the code by extracting the function inside `map` into a method, and the stream processing could be done by calling it, as in Example 5-34.

*Example 5-34. Extracting a lambda into a method*

```
private Integer divide(Integer value, Integer factor) {
    try {
        return value / factor;
    } catch (ArithmeticException e) { ❶
        e.printStackTrace();
    }
}

public List<Integer> divUsingMethod(List<Integer> values, Integer factor) {
    return values.stream()
        .map(n -> divide(n, factor)) ❷
        .collect(Collectors.toList());
}
```

❶ Handle the exception here

❷ Stream code is simplified

As an aside, if the extracted method had not needed the `factor` value, the argument to `map` could have been simplified to a method reference.

The technique of extracting the lambda to a separate method has benefits as well. You can write tests for the extracted method (using reflection if the method is private), set break points in it, or any other mechanism normally associated with methods.

## See Also

Lambda expressions with checked exceptions are discussed in Recipe 5.10. Using a generic wrapper method for exceptions is in Recipe 5.11.

# 5.10 Checked Exceptions and Lambdas

## Problem

You have a lambda expression that throws a checked exception, and the abstract method in the functional interface you are implementing does not declare that exception.

## Solution

Add a try/catch block to the lambda expression, or delegate to an extracted method to handle it.

## Discussion

A lambda expression is effectively the implementation of the single abstract method in a functional interface. A lambda expression can therefore only throw checked exceptions declared in the signature of the abstract method.

Say you are planning to invoke a service using a URL and you need to form a query string from a collection of string parameters. The parameters need to be encoded in a way that allows them to be used in a URL. Java provides a class for this purpose called, naturally enough, `java.net.URLEncoder`, which has a static `encode` method that takes a `String` and encodes it according to a specified encoding scheme.

In this case, what you would like to write is code like Example 5-35.

*Example 5-35. URL encoding a collection of strings (NOTE: DOES NOT COMPILE)*

```
public List<String> encodeValues(String... values) {
    return Arrays.stream(values)
        .map(s -> URLEncoder.encode(s, "UTF-8")))  ❶
        .collect(Collectors.toList());
}
```

❶ Throws `UnsupportedEncodingException`, which must be handled

The method takes a variable argument list of strings and tries to run each of them through the `UREncoder.encode` method under the recommended `UTF-8` encoding. Unfortunately, the code does not compile because that method throws a (checked) `UnsupportedEncodingException`.

You might be tempted to simply declare that the encodeValues method throws that exception, but that doesn't work (see Example 5-36).

*Example 5-36. Declaring the exception (ALSO DOES NOT COMPILE)*

```
public List<String> encodeValues(String... values)
    throws UnsupportedEncodingException {  ❶
        return Arrays.stream(values)
            .map(s -> URLEncoder.encode(s, "UTF-8")))
            .collect(Collectors.toList());
}
```

❶ Throwing the exception from the surrounding method also DOES NOT COMPILE

The problem is that throwing an exception from a lambda is like building an entirely separate class with a method and throwing the exception from there. It helps to think of the lambda as the implementation of an anonymous inner class, because then it becomes clear that throwing the exception in the inner object still needs to be handled or declared there, not in the surrounding object. Code like that is shown in Example 5-37, which shows both the anonymous inner class version and the lambda expression version.

*Example 5-37. URL encoding using try/catch (CORRECT)*

```
public List<String> encodeValuesAnonInnerClass(String... values) {
    return Arrays.stream(values)
        .map(new Function<String, String>() {           ❶
            @Override
            public String apply(String s) {             ❷
                try {
                    return URLEncoder.encode(s, "UTF-8");
                } catch (UnsupportedEncodingException e) {
                    e.printStackTrace();
                    return "";
                }
            }
        })
        .collect(Collectors.toList());
}

public List<String> encodeValues(String... values) {  ❸
    return Arrays.stream(values)
        .map(s -> {
            try {
                return URLEncoder.encode(s, "UTF-8");
            } catch (UnsupportedEncodingException e) {
                e.printStackTrace();
                return "";
```

```
            }
        })
        .collect(Collectors.toList());
}
```

❶ Anonymous inner class

❷ Contains code that will throw a checked exception

❸ Lambda expression version

Since the `apply` method (the single abstract method from `Function`) does not declare any checked exceptions, you must add a try/catch block inside any lambda expression that is implementing it. If you use a lambda expression as shown, you don't even see the `apply` method signature at all, even if you wanted to modify it (which isn't allowed anyway).

Example 5-38 shows a version that uses an extracted method for the encoding.

*Example 5-38. URL encoding delegating to a method*

```
private String encodeString(String s) { ❶
    try {
        return URLEncoder.encode(s, "UTF-8");
    } catch (UnsupportedEncodingException e) {
        throw new RuntimeException(e);
    }
}

public List<String> encodeValuesUsingMethod(String... values) {
    return Arrays.stream(values)
        .map(this::encodeString)       ❷
        .collect(Collectors.toList());
}
```

❶ Extracted method for exception handling

❷ Method reference to the extracted method

This works, and is simple to implement. It also gives you a method that you can test and/or debug separately. The only downside is that you need to extract a method for each operation that may throw an exception. As mentioned in the previous recipe, however, it often allows for easier testing of the component parts of the stream processing.

## See Also

Using an extracted method to handle exceptions in lambdas is covered in Recipe 5.9. Using a generic wrapper for exceptions is discussed in Recipe 5.11.

# 5.11 Using a Generic Exception Wrapper

## Problem

You have a lambda expression that throws an exception, but you wish to use a generic wrapper that catches all checked exceptions and rethrows them as unchecked.

## Solution

Create special exception classes and add a generic method to accept them and return lambdas without exceptions.

## Discussion

Both Recipes 5.9 and 5.10 show how to delegate to a separate method to handle exceptions thrown from lambda expressions. Unfortunately, you need to define a private method for each operation that may throw an exception. This can be made more versatile using a *generic wrapper*.

For this approach, define a separate functional interface with a method that declares it throws `Exception`, and use a wrapper method to connect it to your code.

For example, the `map` method on `Stream` requires a `Function`, but the `apply` method in `Function` does not declare any checked exceptions. If you want to use a lambda expression in `map` that may throw a checked exception, start by creating a separate functional interface that declares that it throws `Exception`, as in Example 5-39.

*Example 5-39. A functional interface based on Function that throws Exception*

```
@FunctionalInterface
public interface FunctionWithException<T, R, E extends Exception> {
    R apply(T t) throws E;
}
```

Now you can add a wrapper method that takes a `FunctionWithException` and returns a `Function` by wrapping the `apply` method in a try/catch block, as shown in Example 5-40.

*Example 5-40. A wrapper method to deal with exceptions*

```
private static <T, R, E extends Exception>
    Function<T, R> wrapper(FunctionWithException<T, R, E> fe) {
        return arg -> {
            try {
                return fe.apply(arg);
            } catch (Exception e) {
                throw new RuntimeException(e);
            }
        };
}
```

The `wrapper` method accepts code that throws any `Exception` and builds in the necessary try/catch block, while delegating to the `apply` method. In this case the `wrapper` method was made `static`, but that isn't required. The result is that you can invoke the wrapper with any `Function` that throws an exception, as in Example 5-41.

*Example 5-41. Using a generic static wrapper method*

```
public List<String> encodeValuesWithWrapper(String... values) {
    return Arrays.stream(values)
        .map(wrapper(s -> URLEncoder.encode(s, "UTF-8"))) ❶
        .collect(Collectors.toList());
}
```

❶ Using the `wrapper` method

Now you can write code in your `map` operation that throws any exception, and the `wrapper` method will rethrow it as unchecked. The downside to this approach is that a separate generic wrapper, like `ConsumerWithException`, `SupplierWithException`, and so on, is needed for each functional interface you plan to use.

It's complications like this that make it clear why some Java frameworks (like Spring and Hibernate), and even entire languages (like Groovy and Kotlin), catch all checked exceptions and rethrow them as unchecked.

## See Also

Lambda expressions with checked exceptions are discussed in Recipe 5.10. Extracting to a method is covered in Recipe 5.9.

# CHAPTER 6
# The Optional Type

> *Sigh, why does everything related to Optional have to take 300 messages?*
>
> —*Brian Goetz, lambda-libs-spec-experts mailing list (October 23, 2013)*

The Java 8 API introduced a new class called `java.util.Optional<T>`. While many developers assume that the goal of `Optional` is to remove `NullPointerExceptions` from your code, that's not its real purpose. Instead, `Optional` is designed to communicate to the user when a returned value may legitimately be null. This situation can arise whenever a stream of values is filtered by some condition that happens to leave no elements remaining.

In the `Stream` API, the following methods return an `Optional` if no elements remain in the stream: `reduce`, `min`, `max`, `findFirst`, `findAny`.

An instance of `Optional` can be in one of two states: a reference to an instance of type `T`, or empty. The former case is called *present*, and the latter is known as *empty* (as opposed to `null`).

While `Optional` is a reference type, it should never be assigned a value of `null`. Doing so is a serious error.

This chapter looks at the idiomatic ways to use `Optional`. While the proper use of `Optional` is likely to be a lively source of discussions in your company,[1] the good

1 I'm being diplomatic here.

news is that there are standard recommendations for its proper use. Following these principles should help keep your intentions clear and maintainable.

# 6.1 Creating an Optional

## Problem

You need to return an `Optional` from an existing value.

## Solution

Use `Optional.of`, `Optional.ofNullable`, or `Optional.empty`.

## Discussion

Like many other new classes in the Java 8 API, instances of `Optional` are immutable. The API refers to `Optional` as a *value-based class*, meaning instances:

- Are final and immutable (though they may contain references to mutable objects)[2]
- Have no public constructors, and thus must be instantiated by factory methods
- Have implementations of `equals`, `hashCode`, and `toString` that are based only on their state

### Optional and Immutability

Instances of `Optional` are immutable, but the objects they wrap may not be. If you create an `Optional` that contains an instance of a mutable object, you can still modify the instance. See, for instance, Example 6-1.

*Example 6-1. Are Optionals immutable?*

```
AtomicInteger counter = new AtomicInteger();
Optional<AtomicInteger> opt = Optional.ofNullable(counter);

System.out.println(optional);                        // Optional[0]

counter.incrementAndGet();                           ❶
System.out.println(optional);                        // Optional[1]

optional.get().incrementAndGet();                    ❷
```

2 See the sidebar about immutability.

```
System.out.println(optional);                          // Optional[2]

optional = Optional.ofNullable(new AtomicInteger()); ❸
```

❶ Increment using counter directly

❷ Retrieve contained value and increment

❸ `Optional` reference can be reassigned

You can modify the contained value either with the original reference, or one retrieved by calling `get` on the `Optional`. You can even reassign the reference itself, which basically says that immutable is not the same thing as `final`. What you can't do is modify the `Optional` instance itself, because there are no methods available to do so.

This idea of the word "immutable" being something of a gray area is pretty common in Java, which doesn't have a good, built-in way of creating classes that only produce objects that can't be changed.

The static factory methods to create an `Optional` are `empty`, `of`, and `ofNullable`, whose signatures are:

```
static <T> Optional<T>  empty()
static <T> Optional<T>  of(T value)
static <T> Optional<T>  ofNullable(T value)
```

The `empty` method returns, naturally enough, an empty `Optional`. The `of` method returns an `Optional` that wraps the specified value or throws an exception if the argument is `null`. The expected way to use it is as shown in Example 6-2.

*Example 6-2. Creating an Optional with "of"*

```
public static <T> Optional<T> createOptionalTheHardWay(T value) {
    return value == null ? Optional.empty() : Optional.of(value);
}
```

The description of the method in Example 6-2 is called "The Hard Way" not because it's particularly difficult, but because an easier way is to use the `ofNullable` method, as in Example 6-3.

*Example 6-3. Creating an Optional with "ofNullable"*

```
public static <T> Optional<T> createOptionalTheEasyWay(T value) {
    return Optional.ofNullable(value);
}
```

In fact, the implementation of `ofNullable` in the reference implementation of Java 8 is the line shown in `createOptionalTheHardWay`: check if the contained value is null, and if it is return an empty `Optional`, otherwise use `Optional.of` to wrap it.

Incidentally, the classes `OptionalInt`, `OptionalLong`, and `OptionalDouble` wrap primitives that can never be null, so they only have an `of` method:

```
static OptionalInt    of(int value)
static OptionalLong   of(long value)
static OptionalDouble of(double value)
```

Instead of `get`, the getter methods on those classes are `getAsInt`, `getAsLong`, and `getAsDouble`.

## See Also

Other recipes in this chapter, like Recipes 6.4 and 6.5, also create `Optional` values, but from provided collections. Recipe 6.3 uses the methods in this recipe to wrap provided values.

# 6.2 Retrieving Values from an Optional

## Problem

You want to extract a contained value from an `Optional`.

## Solution

Use the `get` method, but only if you're sure a value exists inside the `Optional`. Otherwise use one of the variations of `orElse`. You can also use `ifPresent` if you only want to execute a `Consumer` when a value is present.

## Discussion

If you invoke a method that returns an `Optional`, you can retrieve the value contained inside by invoking the `get` method. If the `Optional` is empty, however, then the `get` method throws a `NoSuchElementException`.

Consider a method that returns the first even-length string from a stream of them, as shown in Example 6-4.

*Example 6-4. Retrieving the first even-length string*

```
Optional<String> firstEven =
    Stream.of("five", "even", "length", "string", "values")
```

```
        .filter(s -> s.length() % 2 == 0)
        .findFirst();
```

The `findFirst` method returns an `Optional<String>`, because it's possible that none of the strings in the stream will pass the filter. You could print the returned value by calling `get` on the `Optional`:

```
System.out.println(firstEven.get())  // Don't do this, even if it works
```

The problem is that while this will work here, you should never call `get` on an `Optional` unless you're sure it contains a value or you risk throwing the exception, as in Example 6-5.

*Example 6-5. Retrieving the first odd-length string*

```
Optional<String> firstOdd =
    Stream.of("five", "even", "length", "string", "values")
        .filter(s -> s.length() % 2 != 0)
        .findFirst();

System.out.println(firstOdd.get()); // throws NoSuchElementException
```

How do you get around this? You have several options. The first is to check that the `Optional` contains a value before retrieving it, as in Example 6-6.

*Example 6-6. Retrieving the first even-length string with a protected get*

```
Optional<String> firstEven =                                        ❶
    Stream.of("five", "even", "length", "string", "values")
          .filter(s -> s.length() % 2 == 0)
          .findFirst();

System.out.println(
    first.isPresent() ? first.get() : "No even length strings");  ❷
```

❶ Same as before

❷ Only call `get` if `isPresent` returns true

While this works, you've only traded null checking for `isPresent` checking, which doesn't feel like much of an improvement.

Fortunately, there's a good alternative, which is to use the very convenient `orElse` method, as shown in Example 6-7.

*Example 6-7. Using orElse*

```
Optional<String> firstOdd =
    Stream.of("five", "even", "length", "string", "values")
        .filter(s -> s.length() % 2 != 0)
        .findFirst();

System.out.println(firstOdd.orElse("No odd length strings"));
```

The `orElse` method returns the contained value if one is present, or a supplied default otherwise. It's therefore a convenient method to use if you have a fallback value in mind.

There are a few variations of `orElse`:

- `orElse(T other)` returns the value if present, otherwise it returns the default value, `other`
- `orElseGet(Supplier<? extends T> other)` returns the value if present, otherwise it invokes the `Supplier` and returns the result
- `orElseThrow(Supplier<? extends X> exceptionSupplier)` returns the value if present, otherwise throws the exception created by the `Supplier`

The difference between `orElse` and `orElseGet` is that the former returns a string that is always created, whether the value exists in the `Optional` or not, while the latter uses a `Supplier`, which is only executed if the `Optional` is empty.

In this case, the value is a simple string, so the difference is pretty minimal. If, however, the argument to `orElse` is a complex object, `orElseGet` with a `Supplier` ensures the object is only created when needed, as in Example 6-8.

*Example 6-8. Using a Supplier in orElseGet*

```
Optional<ComplexObject> val = values.stream.findFirst()

val.orElse(new ComplexObject());          ❶
val.orElseGet(() -> new ComplexObject()) ❷
```

❶ Always creates the new object

❷ Only creates object if necessary

Using a `Supplier` as a method argument is an example of *deferred* or *lazy execution*. It allows you to avoid invoking the `get` method on the `Supplier` until necessary.[3]

The implementation of `orElseGet` in the library is shown in Example 6-9.

*Example 6-9. Implementation of Optional.orElseGet in the JDK*

```
public T orElseGet(Supplier<? extends T> other) {
    return value != null ? value : other.get();  ❶
}
```

❶ `value` is a final attribute of type `T` in `Optional`

The `orElseThrow` method also takes a `Supplier`. From the API, the method signature is:

```
<X extends Throwable> T orElseThrow(Supplier<? extends X> exceptionSupplier)
```

Therefore, in Example 6-10, the constructor reference used as the `Supplier` argument isn't executed when the `Optional` contains a value.

*Example 6-10. Using orElseThrow as a Supplier*

```
Optional<String> first =
    Stream.of("five", "even", "length", "string", "values")
        .filter(s -> s.length() % 2 == 0)
        .findFirst();

System.out.println(first.orElseThrow(NoSuchElementException::new));
```

Finally, the `ifPresent` method allows you to provide a `Consumer` that is only executed when the `Optional` contains a value, as in Example 6-11.

*Example 6-11. Using the ifPresent method*

```
Optional<String> first =
    Stream.of("five", "even", "length", "string", "values")
        .filter(s -> s.length() % 2 == 0)
        .findFirst();

first.ifPresent(val -> System.out.println("Found an even-length string"));
```

3 See Chapter 6 of Venkat Subramaniam's book *Functional Programming in Java* (Pragmatic Programmers, 2014) for a detailed explanation.

```
first = Stream.of("five", "even", "length", "string", "values")
    .filter(s -> s.length() % 2 != 0)
    .findFirst();

first.ifPresent(val -> System.out.println("Found an odd-length string"));
```

In this case, only the message "Found an even-length string" will be printed.

## See Also

`Suppliers` are discussed in Recipe 2.2. Constructor references are in Recipe 1.3. The `findAny` and `findFirst` methods in `Stream` that return an `Optional` are covered in Recipe 3.9.

# 6.3 Optional in Getters and Setters

## Problem

You wish to use `Optional` in accessors and mutators.

## Solution

Wrap the result of getter methods in `Optionals`, but do not do the same for setters, and especially not for attributes.

## Discussion

The `Optional` data type communicates to a user that the result of an operation may legitimately be null, without throwing a `NullPointerException`. The `Optional` class, however, was deliberately designed *not* to be serializable, so you don't want to use it to wrap fields in a class.

Consequently, the preferred mechanism for adding `Optionals` in getters and setters is to wrap nullable attributes in them when returned from getter methods, but not to do the same in setters, as in Example 6-12.

*Example 6-12. Using Optional in a DAO layer*

```
public class Department {
    private Manager boss;

    public Optional<Manager> getBoss() {
        return Optional.ofNullable(boss);
    }

    public void setBoss(Manager boss) {
```

```
        this.boss = boss;
    }
}
```

In `Department`, the `Manager` attribute `boss` is considered nullable.[4] You might be tempted to make the attribute of type `Optional<Manager>`, but because `Optional` is not serializable, neither would be `Department`.

The approach here is not to require the user to wrap a value in an `Optional` in order to call a setter method, which is what would be necessary if the `setBoss` method took an `Optional<Manager>` as an argument. The purpose of an `Optional` is to indicate a value that may legitimately be null, and the client already knows whether or not the value is null, and the internal implementation here doesn't care.

Finally, returning an `Optional<Manager>` in the getter method accomplishes the goal of telling the caller that the department may or may not have a boss at the moment and that's OK.

The downside to this approach is that for years the "JavaBeans" convention defined getters and setters in parallel, based on the attribute. In fact, the definition of a *property* in Java (as opposed to simply an attribute) is that you have getters and setters that follow the standard pattern. The approach in this recipe violates that pattern. The getter and the setter are no longer symmetrical.

It's (partly) for this reason that some developers say that `Optional` should not appear in your getters and setters at all. Instead, they treat it as an internal implementation detail that shouldn't be exposed to the client.

The approach used here is popular among open source developers who use Object-Relational Mapping (ORM) tools like Hibernate, however. The overriding consideration there is communicating to the client that you've got a nullable database column backing this particular field, without forcing the client to wrap a reference in the setter as well.

That seems a reasonable compromise, but, as they say, your mileage may vary.

## See Also

Recipe 6.5 uses this DAO example to convert a collection of IDs into a collection of employees. Recipe 6.1 discusses wrapping values in an `Optional`.

---

4 Perhaps this is just wishful thinking, but an appealing idea, nonetheless.

# 6.4 Optional flatMap Versus map

## Problem

You want to avoid wrapping an `Optional` inside another `Optional`.

## Solution

Use the `flatMap` method in `Optional`.

## Discussion

The `map` and `flatMap` methods in `Stream` are discussed in Recipe 3.11. The concept of `flatMap` is a general one, however, and can also be applied to `Optional`.

The signature of the `flatMap` method in `Optional` is:

```
<U> Optional<U> flatMap(Function<? super T, Optional<U>> mapper)
```

This is similar to `map` from `Stream`, in that the `Function` argument is applied to each element and produces a single result, in this case of type `Optional<U>`. More specifically, if the argument `T` exists, `flatMap` applies the function to it and returns an `Optional` wrapping the contained value. If the argument is not present, the method returns an empty `Optional`.

As discussed in Recipe 6.3, a Data Access Object (DAO) is often written with getter methods that return `Optionals` (if the property can be null), but the setter methods do not wrap their arguments in `Optionals`. Consider a `Manager` class that has a non-null string called `name`, and a `Department` class that has a nullable `Manager` called `boss`, as shown in Example 6-13.

*Example 6-13. Part of a DAO layer with Optionals*

```
public class Manager {
    private String name;                    ❶

    public Manager(String name) {
        this.name = name;
    }

    public String getName() {
        return name;
    }
}

public class Department {
    private Manager boss;                   ❷
```

```
    public Optional<Manager> getBoss() {  ❷
        return Optional.ofNullable(boss);
    }

    public void setBoss(Manager boss) {
        this.boss = boss;
    }
}
```

❶ Assumed not null, so no need for `Optional`s

❷ Might be null, so wrap getter return in an `Optional`, but not setter

If the client calls the `getBoss` method on `Department`, the result is wrapped in an `Optional`. See Example 6-14.

*Example 6-14. Returning an Optional*

```
Manager mrSlate = new Manager("Mr. Slate");

Department d = new Department();
d.setBoss(mrSlate);                             ❶
System.out.println("Boss: " + d.getBoss());     ❷


Department d1 = new Department();               ❸
System.out.println("Boss: " + d1.getBoss());    ❹
```

❶ Department with a nonnull manager

❷ Prints `Boss: Optional[Manager{name='Mr. Slate'}]`

❸ Department without a manager

❹ Prints `Boss: Optional.empty`

So far, so good. If the `Department` has a `Manager`, the getter method returns it wrapped in an `Optional`. If not, the method returns an empty `Optional`.

The problem is, if you want the name of the `Manager`, you can't call `getName` on an `Optional`. You either have to get the contained value out of the `Optional`, or use the `map` method (Example 6-15).

*Example 6-15. Extract a name from an Optional manager*

```
System.out.println("Name: " +
        d.getBoss().orElse(new Manager("Unknown")).getName());      ❶
```

```
System.out.println("Name: " +
        d1.getBoss().orElse(new Manager("Unknown")).getName());

System.out.println("Name: " + d.getBoss().map(Manager::getName)); ❷
System.out.println("Name: " + d1.getBoss().map(Manager::getName));
```

❶ Extract boss from `Optional` before calling `getName`

❷ Use `Optional.map` to apply `getName` to contained `Manager`

The `map` method (discussed further in Recipe 6.5) applies the given function only if the `Optional` it's called on is not empty, so that's the simpler approach here.

Life gets more complicated if the `Optionals` might be chained. Say a `Company` might have a `Department` (only one, just to keep the code simple), as in Example 6-16.

*Example 6-16. A company may have a department (only one, for simplicity)*

```
public class Company {
    private Department department;

    public Optional<Department> getDepartment() {
        return Optional.ofNullable(department);
    }

    public void setDepartment(Department department) {
        this.department = department;
    }
}
```

If you call `getDepartment` on a `Company`, the result is wrapped in an `Optional`. If you then want the manager, the solution would appear to be to use the `map` method as in Example 6-15. But that leads to a problem, because the result is an `Optional` wrapped inside an `Optional` (Example 6-17).

*Example 6-17. An Optional wrapped inside an Optional*

```
Company co = new Company();
co.setDepartment(d);

System.out.println("Company Dept: " + co.getDepartment());           ❶

System.out.println("Company Dept Manager: " + co.getDepartment()
    .map(Department::getBoss));                                      ❷
```

❶ Prints `Company Dept: Optional[Department{boss=Manager{name='Mr. Slate'}}]`

❷ Prints `Company Dept Manager: Optional[Optional[Manager{name='Mr. Slate'}]]`

This is where `flatMap` on `Optional` comes in. Using `flatMap` flattens the structure, so that you only get a single `Optional`. See Example 6-18, which assumes the company was created as in the previous example.

*Example 6-18. Using flatMap on a company*

```
System.out.println(
    co.getDepartment()                   ❶
        .flatMap(Department::getBoss)    ❷
        .map(Manager::getName));         ❸
```

❶ `Optional<Department>`

❷ `Optional<Manager>`

❸ `Optional<String>`

Now wrap the company in an `Optional` as well, as in Example 6-19.

*Example 6-19. Using flatMap on an optional company*

```
Optional<Company> company = Optional.of(co);

System.out.println(
    company                                 ❶
        .flatMap(Company::getDepartment)    ❷
        .flatMap(Department::getBoss)       ❸
        .map(Manager::getName)              ❹
);
```

❶ `Optional<Company>`

❷ `Optional<Department>`

❸ `Optional<Manager>`

❹ `Optional<String>`

Whew! As the example shows, you can even wrap the company in an `Optional`, then just use `Optional.flatMap` repeatedly to get to whatever property you want, finishing with an `Optional.map` operation.

## See Also

Wrapping a value inside an `Optional` is discussed in Recipe 6.1. The `flatMap` method in `Stream` is discussed in Recipe 3.11. Using `Optional` in a DAO layer is in Recipe 6.3. The `map` method in `Optional` is in Recipe 6.5.

# 6.5 Mapping Optionals

## Problem

You want to apply a function to a collection of `Optional` instances, but only if they contain a value.

## Solution

Use the `map` method in `Optional`.

## Discussion

Say you have a list of employee ID values and you want to retrieve a collection of the corresponding employee instances. If the `findEmployeeById` method has the signature

```
public Optional<Employee> findEmployeeById(int id)
```

then searching for all the employees will return a collection of `Optional` instances, some of which may be empty. You can then filter out the empty `Optional`s, as shown in Example 6-20.

*Example 6-20. Finding Employees by ID*

```
public List<Employee> findEmployeesByIds(List<Integer> ids) {
    return ids.stream()
        .map(this::findEmployeeById)         ❶
        .filter(Optional::isPresent))        ❷
        .map(Optional::get)                  ❸
        .collect(Collectors.toList());
}
```

❶ `Stream<Optional<Employee>>`

❷ Remove empty `Optional`s

❸ Retrieve values you know exist

The result of the first map operation is a stream of Optionals, each of which either contains an employee or is empty. To extract the contained value, the natural idea is to invoke the get method, but you're never supposed to call get unless you're sure a value is present. Instead use the filter method with Optional::isPresent as a predicate to remove all the empty Optionals. Then you can map the Optionals to their contained values by mapping them using Optional::get.

This example used the map method on Stream. For a different approach, there is also a map method on Optional, whose signature is:

```
<U> Optional<U> map(Function<? super T,? extends U> mapper)
```

The map method in Optional takes a Function as an argument. If the Optional is not empty, the map method extracts the contained value, applies the function to it, and returns an Optional containing the result. Otherwise it returns an empty Optional.

The finder operation in Example 6-20 can be rewritten using this method to the version in Example 6-21.

*Example 6-21. Using Optional.map*

```
public List<Employee> findEmployeesByIds(List<Integer> ids) {
    return ids.stream()
        .map(this::findEmployeeById)                    ❶
        .flatMap(optional ->
            optional.map(Stream::of)                    ❷
                    .orElseGet(Stream::empty))          ❸
        .collect(Collectors.toList());
}
```

❶ Stream<Optional<Employee>>

❷ Turns nonempty Optional<Employee> into Optional<Stream<Employee>>

❸ Extracts the Stream<Employee> from the Optional

The idea is that if the optional containing an employee is not empty, invoke the Stream::of method *on the contained value*, which turns it into a one-element stream of that value, which is then wrapped in an Optional. Otherwise return an empty optional.

Say an employee was found by ID. The findEmployeeById method returns an Optional<Employee> for that value. The optional.map(Stream::of) method then returns an Optional containing a one-element stream holding that employee, so we have Optional<Stream<Employee>>. Then the orElseGet method extracts the contained value, yielding Stream<Employee>.

If the `findEmployeeById` method returned an empty `Optional`, then `optional.map(Stream::of)` returns an empty `Optional` as well, and the `orElseGet(Stream::empty)` method returns an empty stream.

The result is that you get a combination of `Stream<Employee>` elements and empty streams, and that's exactly what the `flatMap` method in `Stream` was designed to handle. It reduces everything down to a `Stream<Employee>` for only the nonempty streams, so the `collect` method can return them as a `List` of employees.

The process is illustrated in Figure 6-1.

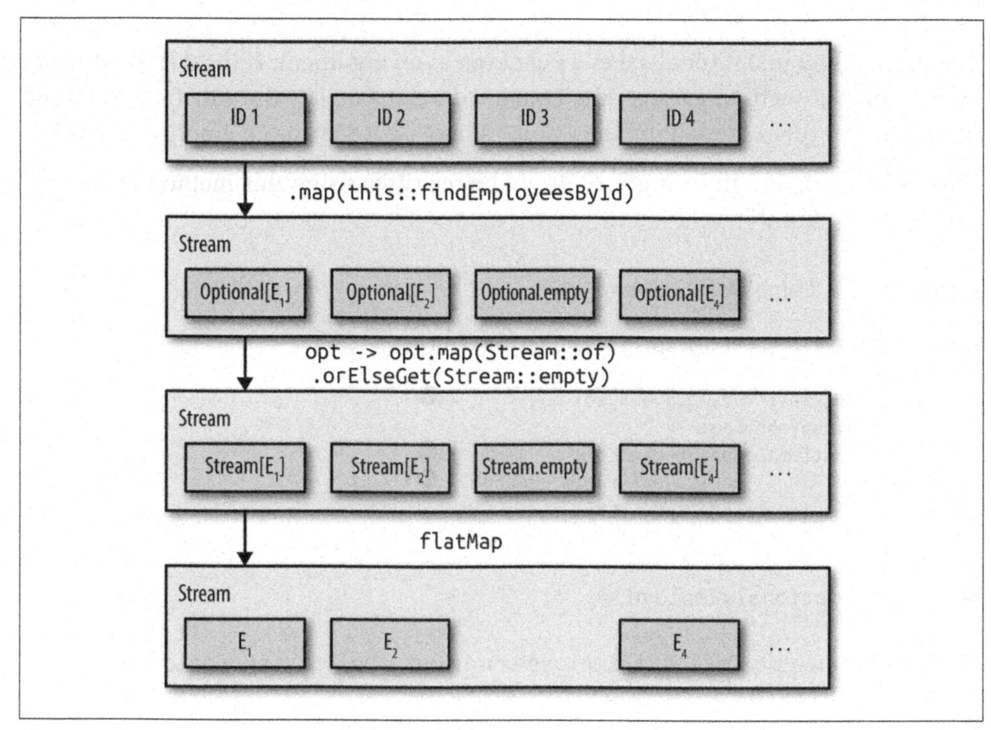


*Figure 6-1. Optional map and flatMap*

The `Optional.map` method is a convenience[5] method for (hopefully) simplifying stream processing code. The filter/map approach discussed earlier is certainly more intuitive, especially for developers unaccustomed to `flatMap` operations, but the result is the same.

5 At least, that's the idea.

Of course, you can use any function you wish inside the `Optional.map` method. The Javadocs illustrate converting names into file input streams. A different example is shown in Recipe 6.4.

Incidentally, Java 9 adds a `stream` method to `Optional`. If the `Optional` is not empty, it returns a one-element stream wrapping the contained value. Otherwise it returns an empty stream. See Recipe 10.6 for details.

## See Also

Recipe 6.3 illustrates how to use `Optional` in a DAO (data access object) layer. Recipe 3.11 discusses the `flatMap` method on streams, while Recipe 6.4 discusses the `flatMap` method on `Optionals`. Recipe 10.6 talks about the new methods added to `Optional` in Java 9.

# CHAPTER 7
# File I/O

The nonblocking (or "new") input/output package, referred to as NIO, was added in J2SE 1.4.[1] The NIO.2 extension, added in Java 7, brought in new classes for manipulating files and directories. The additions included the `java.nio.file` package, which is the subject of this chapter. Several of the new classes in that package, like `java.nio.files.File`, have been enhanced in Java 8 with methods that use streams.

Unfortunately, here is where the stream metaphor from functional programming conflicts with the same term from input/output, leading to potential confusion. For example, the `java.nio.file.DirectoryStream` interface has nothing to do with functional streams. It is implemented by classes that iterate over a directory tree using the traditional for-each construct.[2]

This chapter focuses on capabilities in I/O that support functional streams. In Java 8, several methods were added to the `java.nio.file.Files` class to support functional streams. Those methods are shown in Table 7-1. Note that all the methods in the `Files` class are static.

1 Most Java developers are astonished to learn that NIO was added that early.

2 Even more confusing, the interface `DirectoryStream.Filter` is actually a functional interface, though again it has nothing to do with functional streams. It's used to approve only selected entries in a directory tree.

*Table 7-1. Methods in java.nio.files.Files that return streams*

| Method | Return type |
|---|---|
| `lines` | `Stream<String>` |
| `list` | `Stream<Path>` |
| `walk` | `Stream<Path>` |
| `find` | `Stream<Path>` |

The recipes in this chapter deal with each of these methods.

# 7.1 Process Files

## Problem

You want to process the contents of a text file using streams.

## Solution

Use the static `lines` method in either `java.io.BufferedReader` or `java.nio.file.Files` to return the contents of a file as a stream.

## Discussion

All FreeBSD-based Unix systems (including macOS) include a version of Webster's Second International Dictionary in the */usr/share/dict/* folder. The file *web2* includes approximately 230,000 words. Each word appears on its own line.

Say you wanted to find the 10 longest words in that dictionary. You can use the `Files.lines` method to retrieve the words as a stream of strings, and then do normal stream processing like `map` and `filter`. An example is shown in Example 7-1.

*Example 7-1. Finding the 10 longest words in the web2 dictionary*

```
try (Stream<String> lines = Files.lines(Paths.get("/usr/share/dict/web2")) {
    lines.filter(s -> s.length() > 20)
         .sorted(Comparator.comparingInt(String::length).reversed())
         .limit(10)
         .forEach(w -> System.out.printf("%s (%d)%n", w, w.length()));
} catch (IOException e) {
    e.printStackTrace();
}
```

The predicate in the `filter` passes only words longer than 20 characters. The `sorted` method then sorts the words by length in descending order. The `limit` method terminates after the first 10 words, which are then printed. By opening the stream in a `try-with-resources` block, the system will automatically close it, and the dictionary file, when the try block completes.

### Streams and AutoCloseable

The `Stream` interface extends `BaseStream`, which is a subinterface of `AutoCloseable`. Streams can therefore be used inside the Java 7 `try-with-resources` block. When exiting the block, the system will automatically invoke the `close` method, which will not only close the stream, it will also call any close handlers from the stream pipeline to release any resources.

So far in this book the `try-with-resources` wrapper has not been needed, because the streams were generated from collections or otherwise in memory. In this recipe, however, the stream is based on a file, so `try-with-resources` ensures that the dictionary file is also closed.

The results from executing the code in Example 7-1 is shown in Example 7-2.

*Example 7-2. Longest words in dictionary*

```
formaldehydesulphoxylate (24)
pathologicopsychological (24)
scientificophilosophical (24)
tetraiodophenolphthalein (24)
thyroparathyroidectomize (24)
anthropomorphologically (23)
blepharosphincterectomy (23)
epididymodeferentectomy (23)
formaldehydesulphoxylic (23)
gastroenteroanastomosis (23)
```

There are five words in the dictionary that are 24 characters in length. The results show them in alphabetical order, only because the original file was in alphabetical order. If you add a `thenComparing` clause to the `Comparator` argument to `sorted`, you can choose how you want the equal-length words to be sorted.

Following the list of 24-character words are five 23-character words, many of which are from the medical field.[3]

By applying `Collectors.counting` as a downstream collector, you can determine how many words of each length exist in the dictionary, as shown in Example 7-3.

3 Fortunately, the word *blepharosphincterectomy* doesn't mean what it sounds like. It has to do with relieving pressure of the eyelid on the cornea, which is bad enough, but it could have been worse.

*Example 7-3. Determining number of words of each length*

```
try (Stream<String> lines = Files.lines(Paths.get("/usr/share/dict/web2"))) {
    lines.filter(s -> s.length() > 20)
        .collect(Collectors.groupingBy(String::length, Collectors.counting()))
        .forEach((len, num) -> System.out.println(len + ": " + num));
}
```

This snippet used the `groupingBy` collector to create a `Map` where the keys are the word lengths and values are the number of words of each length. The result is:

```
21: 82
22: 41
23: 17
24: 5
```

The output has the information, but isn't terribly informative. It's also sorted in ascending order, which may not be what you want.

As an alternative, the `Map.Entry` interface now has static methods `comparingByKey` and `comparingByValue`, each of which also takes an optional `Comparator`, as discussed in Recipe 4.4. In this case, sorting by the `reverseOrder` comparator gives the reverse of the natural order. See Example 7-4.

*Example 7-4. Number of words of each length, in descending order*

```
try (Stream<String> lines = Files.lines(Paths.get("/usr/share/dict/web2"))) {
    Map<Integer, Long> map = lines.filter(s -> s.length() > 20)
        .collect(Collectors.groupingBy(String::length, Collectors.counting()));

    map.entrySet().stream()
       .sorted(Map.Entry.comparingByKey(Comparator.reverseOrder()))
       .forEach(e -> System.out.printf("Length %d: %d words%n",
           e.getKey(), e.getValue()));
}
```

The result now is:

```
Length 24: 5 words
Length 23: 17 words
Length 22: 41 words
Length 21: 82 words
```

If your source of data is not a `File`, the `BufferedReader` class also has a `lines` method, though in this case it is an instance method. The equivalent version of Example 7-4 using `BufferedReader` is shown in Example 7-5.

*Example 7-5. Using BufferedReader.lines method*

```
try (Stream<String> lines =
        new BufferedReader(
            new FileReader("/usr/share/dict/words")).lines()) {

    // ... same as previous example ...
}
```

Again, since `Stream` implements `AutoCloseable`, when the `try-with-resources` block closes the stream, it will then close the underlying `BufferedReader`.

### See Also

Sorting maps is discussed in Recipe 4.4.

## 7.2 Retrieving Files as a Stream

### Problem

You want to process all the files in a directory as a `Stream`.

### Solution

Use the static `Files.list` method.

### Discussion

The static `list` method in the `java.nio.file.Files` class takes a `Path` as an argument and returns a `Stream` that wraps a `DirectoryStream`.[4] The `DirectoryStream` interface extends `AutoCloseable`, so using the `list` method is best done using a try-with-resources construct, as in Example 7-6.

*Example 7-6. Using Files.list(path)*

```
try (Stream<Path> list = Files.list(Paths.get("src/main/java"))) {
    list.forEach(System.out::println);
} catch (IOException e) {
    e.printStackTrace();
}
```

Assuming this is executed in the root of a project that has the standard Maven or Gradle structure, this will print the names of all files and folders in the *src/main/java*

4 That's an I/O stream, not a functional one.

directory. Using the `try-with-resources` block means that when the try block completes, the system will invoke `close` on the stream, which will then invoke `close` on the underlying `DirectoryStream`. The listing is not recursive.

When run on the source code for this book, the result includes both directories and individual files:

```
src/main/java/collectors
src/main/java/concurrency
src/main/java/datetime
...
src/main/java/Summarizing.java
src/main/java/tasks
src/main/java/UseFilenameFilter.java
```

The signature for the `list` method shows that the return type is a `Stream<Path>` and its argument a directory:

```
public static Stream<Path> list(Path dir) throws IOException
```

Executing the method on a non-directory resource results in a `NotDirectoryException`.

The Javadocs make a point of saying that the resulting stream is *weakly consistent*, meaning "it is thread safe but does not freeze the directory while iterating, so it may (or may not) reflect updates to the directory that occur after returning from this method."

## See Also

To navigate a filesystem using a depth-first search, see Recipe 7.3.

# 7.3 Walking the Filesystem

## Problem

You need to perform a depth-first traversal of the filesystem.

## Solution

Use the static `Files.walk` method.

## Discussion

The signature of the static `Files.walk` method in the `java.nio.file` package is:

```
public static Stream<Path> walk(Path start,
                                FileVisitOption... options)
                        throws IOException
```

The arguments are the starting Path and a variable argument list of FileVisitOption values. The return type is a lazily populated Stream of Path instances obtained by walking the filesystem from the starting path, performing a depth-first traversal.

The returned Stream encapsulates a DirectoryStream, so again it is recommended that you invoke the method using a try-with-resources block, as in Example 7-7.

*Example 7-7. Walking the tree*

```
try (Stream<Path> paths = Files.walk(Paths.get("src/main/java"))) {
    paths.forEach(System.out::println);
} catch (IOException e) {
    e.printStackTrace();
}
```

The walk method takes zero or more FileVisitOption values as the second and subsequent arguments. This example didn't use any. FileVisitOption is an enum, added in Java 1.7, whose only defined value is FileVisitOption.FOLLOW_LINKS. Following links means that, at least in principle, the tree can involve a cycle, so the stream keeps track of files visited. If a cycle is detected, a FileSystemLoopException is thrown.

The results of this example on the book source code is similar to:

```
src/main/java
src/main/java/collectors
src/main/java/collectors/Actor.java
src/main/java/collectors/AddCollectionToMap.java
src/main/java/collectors/Book.java
src/main/java/collectors/CollectorsDemo.java
src/main/java/collectors/ImmutableCollections.java
src/main/java/collectors/Movie.java
src/main/java/collectors/MysteryMen.java
src/main/java/concurrency
src/main/java/concurrency/CommonPoolSize.java
src/main/java/concurrency/CompletableFutureDemos.java
src/main/java/concurrency/FutureDemo.java
src/main/java/concurrency/ParallelDemo.java
src/main/java/concurrency/SequentialToParallel.java
src/main/java/concurrency/Timer.java
src/main/java/datetime
...
```

The paths are traversed lazily. The resulting stream is guaranteed to have at least one element—the starting argument. As each path is encountered, the system determines if it is a directory, at which point it is traversed before moving on to the next sibling. The result is a depth-first traversal. Each directory is closed after all of its entries have been visited.

There is also an overload of this method available:

```
public static Stream<Path> walk(Path start,
                                int maxDepth,
                                FileVisitOption... options)
                         throws IOException
```

The `maxDepth` argument is the maximum number of levels of directories to visit. Zero means only use the starting level. The version of this method without a `maxDepth` parameter uses a value of `Integer.MAX_VALUE`, meaning all levels should be visited.

## See Also

Listing files in a single directory is shown in Recipe 7.2. Searching for files is done using Recipe 7.4.

# 7.4 Searching the Filesystem

## Problem

You want to find files in a file tree that satisfy given properties.

## Solution

Use the static `Files.find` method in the `java.nio.file` package.

## Discussion

The signature of the `Files.find` method is:

```
public static Stream<Path> find(Path start,
                                int maxDepth,
                                BiPredicate<Path, BasicFileAttributes> matcher,
                                FileVisitOption... options)
                         throws IOException
```

This is similar to the `walk` method, but with an added `BiPredicate` to determine whether or not a particular `Path` should be returned. The `find` method starts at a given path and performs a depth-first search, up to the `maxDepth` number of levels, evaluating each path against the `BiPredicate`, following links if specified as the value of the `FileVisitOption` enum.

The `BiPredicate` matcher needs to return a boolean based on each path element, along with its associated `BasicFileAttributes` object. For instance, Example 7-8 returns the paths for nondirectory files in the `fileio` package in the book's source code.

*Example 7-8. Finding the nondirectory files in the fileio package*

```
try (Stream<Path> paths =
    Files.find(Paths.get("src/main/java"), Integer.MAX_VALUE,
        (path, attributes) ->
            !attributes.isDirectory() && path.toString().contains("fileio"))) {
    paths.forEach(System.out::println);
} catch (IOException e) {
    e.printStackTrace();
}
```

The result is:

```
src/main/java/fileio/FileList.java
src/main/java/fileio/ProcessDictionary.java
src/main/java/fileio/SearchForFiles.java
src/main/java/fileio/WalkTheTree.java
```

For each file encountered while walking the tree, the method evaluates it against the given `BiPredicate`. This is just like calling the `walk` method with a filter, but the Javadocs claim this approach may be more efficient by avoiding redundant retrieval of the `BasicFileAttributes` objects.

As usual, the resulting `Stream` encapsulates a `DirectoryStream`, so closing the stream closes the underlying source. Using the method in a `try-with-resources` block, as shown, is therefore the preferred approach.

## See Also

Walking the filesystem is discussed in Recipe 7.3.

CHAPTER 8

# The java.time Package

*Friends don't let friends use java.util.Date.*
*—Tim Yates*

From the beginning of the language, the standard edition library has included two classes for handling dates and times: `java.util.Date` and `java.util.Calendar`. The former is a classic example of how *not* to design a class. If you check the public API, practically all the methods are deprecated, and have been since Java 1.1 (roughly 1997). The deprecations recommend using `Calendar` instead, which isn't much fun either.

Both predate[1] the addition of enums into the language, so they use integer constants for fields like months. Both are mutable, and therefore not thread safe. To handle some issues, the library later added the `java.sql.Date` class as a subclass of the version in `java.util`, but that didn't really address the fundamental problems.

Finally, in Java SE 8, a completely new package has been added that addressed everything. The `java.time` package is based on the Joda-Time library (*http://www.joda.org/joda-time/*), which has been used as a free, open source alternative for years. In fact, the designers of Joda-Time helped design and build the new package, and recommend that future development take advantage of it.

The new package was developed under JSR-310: Date and Time API, and supports the ISO 8601 standard. It correctly adjusts for leap years and daylight savings rules in individual regions.

1 No pun intended.

This chapter contains recipes that illustrate the usefulness of the `java.time` package. Hopefully they will address basic questions you may have, and point you to further information wherever needed.

As a reference, the Java Tutorial online has an excellent section on the Date-Time library. See *https://docs.oracle.com/javase/tutorial/datetime/TOC.html* for details.

## 8.1 Using the Basic Date-Time Classes

### Problem

You want to use the new date and time classes in the `java.time` package.

### Solution

Work with the factory methods in classes like `Instant`, `Duration`, `Period`, `LocalDate`, `LocalTime`, `LocalDateTime`, `ZonedDateTime`, and others.

### Discussion

The classes in Date-Time all produce immutable instances, so they are thread safe. They also do not have public constructors, so each is instantiated using factory methods.

Two static factory methods are of particular note: `now` and `of`. The `now` method is used to create an instance based on the current date or time. Example 8-1 shows the sample code.

*Example 8-1. The now factory method*

```
System.out.println("Instant.now():       " + Instant.now());
System.out.println("LocalDate.now():     " + LocalDate.now());
System.out.println("LocalTime.now():     " + LocalTime.now());
System.out.println("LocalDateTime.now(): " + LocalDateTime.now());
System.out.println("ZonedDateTime.now(): " + ZonedDateTime.now());
```

A sample set of results are shown in Example 8-2.

*Example 8-2. The results of calling the now method*

```
Instant.now():       2017-06-20T17:27:08.184Z
LocalDate.now():     2017-06-20
LocalTime.now():     13:27:08.318
LocalDateTime.now(): 2017-06-20T13:27:08.319
ZonedDateTime.now(): 2017-06-20T13:27:08.319-04:00[America/New_York]
```

All output values are using the ISO 8601 standard formatting. For dates, the basic format is `yyyy-MM-dd`. For times, the format is `hh:mm:ss.sss`. The format for `LocalDateTime` combines the two, using a capital `T` as a separator. Date/times with a time zone append a numerical offset (here, `-04:00`) using UTC as a base, as well as a so-called *region name* (here, `America/New_York`). The output of the `toString` method in `Instant` shows the time to nanosecond precision, in Zulu time.

The `now` method also appears in the classes `Year`, `YearMonth`, and `ZoneId`.

The static `of` factory method is used to produce new values. For `LocalDate`, the arguments are the year, month (either the enum or an int), and the day of month.

The month field in all the `of` methods is overloaded to accept a `Month` enum, like `Month.JANUARY`, or an integer that starts at 1. Since integer constants in `Calendar` start at 0 (that is, `Calendar.JANUARY` is 0), watch out for off-by-one errors. Use the `Month` enum wherever possible.

For `LocalTime`, there are several overloads, depending on how many values of the set of hour, minute, second, and nanosecond are available. The `of` method on `LocalDateTime` combines the others. Some examples are shown in Example 8-3.

*Example 8-3. The of method for the date/time classes*

```
System.out.println("First landing on the Moon:");
LocalDate moonLandingDate = LocalDate.of(1969, Month.JULY, 20);
LocalTime moonLandingTime = LocalTime.of(20, 18);
System.out.println("Date: " + moonLandingDate);
System.out.println("Time: " + moonLandingTime);

System.out.println("Neil Armstrong steps onto the surface: ");
LocalTime walkTime = LocalTime.of(20, 2, 56, 150_000_000);
LocalDateTime walk = LocalDateTime.of(moonLandingDate, walkTime);
System.out.println(walk);
```

The output of the demo in Example 8-3 is:

```
First landing on the Moon:
Date: 1969-07-20
Time: 20:18
Neil Armstrong steps onto the surface:
1969-07-20T20:02:56.150
```

The last argument to the `LocalTime.of` method is nanoseconds, so this example used a feature from Java 7 where you can insert an underscore inside a numerical value for readability.

The `Instant` class models a single, instantaneous point along the time line.

The `ZonedDateTime` class combines dates and times with time zone information from the `ZoneId` class. Time zones are expressed relative to UTC.

There are two types of zone IDs:

- Fixed offsets, relative to UTC/Greenwich, like `-05:00`
- Geographical regions, like `America/Chicago`

Technically there's a third type of ID, which is an offset that is assumed to be from Zulu time. It includes a `Z` along with the numerical value.

The rules for offset changes come from the `ZoneRules` class, where the rules are loaded from a `ZoneRulesProvider`. The `ZoneRules` class has methods such as `isDaylightSavings(Instant)`.

You can get the current value of the `ZoneId` from the static `systemDefault` method. The complete list of available region IDs comes from the static `getAvailableZoneIds` method:

```
Set<String> regionNames = ZoneId.getAvailableZoneIds();
System.out.println("There are " + regionNames.size() + " region names");
```

For jdk1.8.0_131, there are 600 region names.[2]

The Date-Time API uses standard prefixes for method names. If you are familiar with the prefixes in Table 8-1, you can usually guess what a method does.[3]

*Table 8-1. Prefixes used on Date-Time methods*

| Method | Type | Use |
|---|---|---|
| `of` | Static factory | Creates an instance |
| `from` | Static factory | Converts input parameters to target class |
| `parse` | Static factory | Parses an input string |
| `format` | Instance | Produces formatted output |
| `get` | Instance | Returns part of an object |
| `is` | Instance | Queries the state of the object |
| `with` | Instance | Creates a new object by changing one element of an existing one |
| `plus`, `minus` | Instance | Creates a new object by adding or subtracting from an existing one |

2 Maybe it's just me, but that seems like a lot.

3 Based on a similar table in the Java Tutorial, *https://docs.oracle.com/javase/tutorial/datetime/overview/naming.html.*

| Method | Type | Use |
|---|---|---|
| `to` | Instance | Converts an object to another type |
| `at` | Instance | Combines this object with another |

The `of` method was shown earlier. The `parse` and `format` methods are discussed in Recipe 8.5. The `with` method is covered in Recipe 8.2, and is the immutable equivalent of a set method. Using `plus` and `minus` and their variations are part of Recipe 8.2 as well.

An example of using the `at` method is to add a time zone to a local date and time, as in Example 8-4.

*Example 8-4. Applying a time zone to a LocalDateTime*

```
LocalDateTime dateTime = LocalDateTime.of(2017, Month.JULY, 4, 13, 20, 10);
ZonedDateTime nyc = dateTime.atZone(ZoneId.of("America/New_York"));
System.out.println(nyc);

ZonedDateTime london = nyc.withZoneSameInstant(ZoneId.of("Europe/London"));
System.out.println(london);
```

This prints:

```
2017-07-04T13:20:10-04:00[America/New_York]
2017-07-04T18:20:10+01:00[Europe/London]
```

As the result shows, the `withZoneSameInstant` method allows you to take one `ZonedDateTime` and find out what it would be in another time zone.

There are two enums in the package: `Month` and `DayOfWeek`. `Month` has constants for each month in the standard calendar (`JANUARY` through `DECEMBER`). `Month` also has many convenient methods, as shown in Example 8-5.

*Example 8-5. Some methods in the Month enum*

```
System.out.println("Days in Feb in a leap year: " +
    Month.FEBRUARY.length(true));              ❶
System.out.println("Day of year for first day of Aug (leap year): " +
    Month.AUGUST.firstDayOfYear(true));  ❶
System.out.println("Month.of(1): " + Month.of(1));
System.out.println("Adding two months: " + Month.JANUARY.plus(2));
System.out.println("Subtracting a month: " + Month.MARCH.minus(1));
```

❶ Argument is `boolean leapYear`

The output of Example 8-5 is:

```
Days in Feb in a leap year: 29
Day of year for first day of Aug (leap year): 214
Month.of(1): JANUARY
Adding two months: MARCH
Subtracting a month: FEBRUARY
```

The last two examples, which use the `plus` and `minus` methods, create new instances.

Because the `java.time` classes are immutable, any instance method that seems to modify one, like `plus`, `minus`, or `with`, produces a new instance.

The `DayOfWeek` enum has constants representing the seven weekdays, from `MONDAY` through `SUNDAY`. Again the int value for each follows the ISO standard, so that `MONDAY` is 1 and `SUNDAY` is 7.

## See Also

Parsing and formatting methods are discussed in Recipe 8.5. Converting existing dates and times to new ones is covered in Recipe 8.2. The `Duration` and `Period` classes are discussed in Recipe 8.8.

# 8.2 Creating Dates and Times from Existing Instances

## Problem

You want to modify an existing instance of one of the Date-Time classes.

## Solution

If you need a simple addition or subtraction, use one of the `plus` or `minus` methods. Otherwise use the `with` method.

## Discussion

One of the features of the new Date-Time API is that all of the instances are immutable. Once you've created a `LocalDate`, `LocalTime`, `LocalDateTime`, or `ZonedDateTime`, it can no longer be changed. This has the great advantage of making them thread safe, but what if you want to make a new instance based on the existing one?

The `LocalDate` class has several methods for adding and subtracting values from dates. Specifically, there are:

- `LocalDate plusDays(long daysToAdd)`
- `LocalDate plusWeeks(long weeksToAdd)`
- `LocalDate plusMonths(long monthsToAdd)`
- `LocalDate plusYears(long yearsToAdd)`

Each method returns a new `LocalDate`, which is a copy of the current date with the specified value added to it.

The `LocalTime` class has similar methods:

- `LocalTime plusNanos(long nanosToAdd)`
- `LocalTime plusSeconds(long secondsToAdd)`
- `LocalTime plusMinutes(long minutesToAdd)`
- `LocalTime plusHours(long hoursToAdd)`

Again, each returns a new instance, which is a copy of the original with the added amount. `LocalDateTime` has all the methods for both `LocalDate` and `LocalTime`. For instance, the various `plus` methods for `LocalDate` and `LocalTime` are shown in Example 8-6.

*Example 8-6. Using plus methods on LocalDate and LocalTime*

```
@Test
public void localDatePlus() throws Exception {
    DateTimeFormatter formatter = DateTimeFormatter.ofPattern("yyyy-MM-dd");
    LocalDate start = LocalDate.of(2017, Month.FEBRUARY, 2);

    LocalDate end = start.plusDays(3);
    assertEquals("2017-02-05", end.format(formatter));

    end = start.plusWeeks(5);
    assertEquals("2017-03-09", end.format(formatter));

    end = start.plusMonths(7);
    assertEquals("2017-09-02", end.format(formatter));

    end = start.plusYears(2);
    assertEquals("2019-02-02", end.format(formatter));
}

@Test
public void localTimePlus() throws Exception {
    DateTimeFormatter formatter = DateTimeFormatter.ISO_LOCAL_TIME;

    LocalTime start = LocalTime.of(11, 30, 0, 0);
```

```
    LocalTime end = start.plusNanos(1_000_000);
    assertEquals("11:30:00.001", end.format(formatter));

    end = start.plusSeconds(20);
    assertEquals("11:30:20", end.format(formatter));

    end = start.plusMinutes(45);
    assertEquals("12:15:00", end.format(formatter));

    end = start.plusHours(5);
    assertEquals("16:30:00", end.format(formatter));
}
```

The classes also have two additional `plus` and `minus` methods. Here are the signatures for those methods in `LocalDateTime`:

```
LocalDateTime plus(long amountToAdd, TemporalUnit unit)
LocalDateTime plus(TemporalAmount amountToAdd)

LocalDateTime minus(long amountToSubtract, TemporalUnit unit)
LocalDateTime minus(TemporalAmount amountToSubtract)
```

The corresponding methods in `LocalDate` and `LocalTime` are the same, with the corresponding return types. Interestingly enough, the `minus` versions just call the `plus` versions with the amounts negated.

For the methods that take a `TemporalAmount`, the argument is usually a `Period` or a `Duration`, but may be any type implementing the `TemporalAmount` interface. That interface has methods called `addTo` and `subtractFrom`:

```
Temporal addTo(Temporal temporal)
Temporal subtractFrom(Temporal temporal)
```

If you follow the call stack, invoking `minus` delegates to `plus` with a negated argument, which delegates to `TemporalAmount.addTo(Temporal)`, which calls back to `plus(long, TemporalUnit)`, which actually does the work.[4]

Some examples with the `plus` and `minus` methods are shown in Example 8-7.

*Example 8-7. The plus and minus methods*

```
@Test
public void plus_minus() throws Exception {
    Period period = Period.of(2, 3, 4); // 2 years, 3 months, 4 days
    LocalDateTime start = LocalDateTime.of(2017, Month.FEBRUARY, 2, 11, 30);
    LocalDateTime end = start.plus(period);
```

4 Holy Layers of Indirection, Batman!

```
    assertEquals("2019-05-06T11:30:00",
        end.format(DateTimeFormatter.ISO_LOCAL_DATE_TIME));

    end = start.plus(3, ChronoUnit.HALF_DAYS);
    assertEquals("2017-02-03T23:30:00",
        end.format(DateTimeFormatter.ISO_LOCAL_DATE_TIME));

    end = start.minus(period);
    assertEquals("2014-10-29T11:30:00",
        end.format(DateTimeFormatter.ISO_LOCAL_DATE_TIME));

    end = start.minus(2, ChronoUnit.CENTURIES);
    assertEquals("1817-02-02T11:30:00",
        end.format(DateTimeFormatter.ISO_LOCAL_DATE_TIME));

    end = start.plus(3, ChronoUnit.MILLENNIA);
    assertEquals("5017-02-02T11:30:00",
        end.format(DateTimeFormatter.ISO_LOCAL_DATE_TIME));
}
```

When the API calls for `TemporalUnit`, remember that the provided implementation class is `ChronoUnit`, which has many convenient constants.

Finally, there are a series of `with` methods on each class that can be used to change one field at a time.

The signatures range from `withNano` to `withYear`, with a few interesting ones thrown in. Here is the set from `LocalDateTime`:

```
LocalDateTime withNano(int nanoOfSecond)
LocalDateTime withSecond(int second)
LocalDateTime withMinute(int minute)
LocalDateTime withHour(int hour)
LocalDateTime withDayOfMonth(int dayOfMonth)
LocalDateTime withDayOfYear(int dayOfYear)
LocalDateTime withMonth(int month)
LocalDateTime withYear(int year)
```

The code in Example 8-8 puts these methods through their paces.

*Example 8-8. Using with methods on LocalDateTime*

```
@Test
public void with() throws Exception {
    LocalDateTime start = LocalDateTime.of(2017, Month.FEBRUARY, 2, 11, 30);
    LocalDateTime end = start.withMinute(45);
    assertEquals("2017-02-02T11:45:00",
        end.format(DateTimeFormatter.ISO_LOCAL_DATE_TIME));
```

```
        end = start.withHour(16);
        assertEquals("2017-02-02T16:30:00",
            end.format(DateTimeFormatter.ISO_LOCAL_DATE_TIME));

        end = start.withDayOfMonth(28);
        assertEquals("2017-02-28T11:30:00",
            end.format(DateTimeFormatter.ISO_LOCAL_DATE_TIME));

        end = start.withDayOfYear(300);
        assertEquals("2017-10-27T11:30:00",
            end.format(DateTimeFormatter.ISO_LOCAL_DATE_TIME));

        end = start.withYear(2020);
        assertEquals("2020-02-02T11:30:00",
            end.format(DateTimeFormatter.ISO_LOCAL_DATE_TIME));
    }

    @Test(expected = DateTimeException.class)
    public void withInvalidDate() throws Exception {
        LocalDateTime start = LocalDateTime.of(2017, Month.FEBRUARY, 2, 11, 30);
        start.withDayOfMonth(29);
    }
```

Since 2017 is not a leap year, you can't set the date to February 29. The result is a `DateTimeException`, as the last test shows.

There are also `with` methods that take a `TemporalAdjuster` or a `TemporalField`:

```
LocalDateTime with(TemporalAdjuster adjuster)
LocalDateTime with(TemporalField field, long newValue)
```

The version with `TemporalField` lets the field resolve the date to make it valid. For instance, Example 8-9 takes the last day of January and tries to change the month to February. According to the Javadocs, the system chooses the previous valid date, which in this case is the last day of February.

*Example 8-9. Adjusting the month to an invalid value*

```
@Test
public void temporalField() throws Exception {
    LocalDateTime start = LocalDateTime.of(2017, Month.JANUARY, 31, 11, 30);
    LocalDateTime end = start.with(ChronoField.MONTH_OF_YEAR, 2);
    assertEquals("2017-02-28T11:30:00",
        end.format(DateTimeFormatter.ISO_LOCAL_DATE_TIME));
}
```

As you might imagine, there are some fairly complicated rules involved, but they're well documented in the Javadocs.

The `with` method taking a `TemporalAdjuster` is discussed in Recipe 8.3.

## See Also

See Recipe 8.3 for information about `TemporalAdjuster` and `TemporalQuery`.

# 8.3 Adjusters and Queries

## Problem

Given a temporal value, you want to adjust it to a new one based on your own logic, or you want to retrieve information about it.

## Solution

Create a `TemporalAdjuster` or formulate a `TemporalQuery`.

## Discussion

The `TemporalAdjuster` and `TemporalQuery` classes provide interesting ways to work with the Date-Time classes. They provide useful built-in methods and ways to implement your own. This recipe will illustrate both possibilities.

### Using TemporalAdjuster

The `TemporalAdjuster` interface provides methods that take a `Temporal` value and return an adjusted one. The `TemporalAdjusters` class contains a set of adjusters as static methods you might find convenient.

You use a `TemporalAdjuster` via the `with` method on a temporal object, as in this version from `LocalDateTime`:

```
LocalDateTime with(TemporalAdjuster adjuster)
```

The `TemporalAdjuster` class has an `adjustInto` method that also works, but the one listed here is preferred.

Looking first at the `TemporalAdjusters` class methods, there are many convenience methods:

```
static TemporalAdjuster firstDayOfNextMonth()
static TemporalAdjuster firstDayOfNextYear()
static TemporalAdjuster firstDayOfYear()

static TemporalAdjuster firstInMonth(DayOfWeek dayOfWeek)
static TemporalAdjuster lastDayOfMonth()
static TemporalAdjuster lastDayOfYear()
static TemporalAdjuster lastInMonth(DayOfWeek dayOfWeek)

static TemporalAdjuster next(DayOfWeek dayOfWeek)
```

```
static TemporalAdjuster nextOrSame(DayOfWeek dayOfWeek)
static TemporalAdjuster previous(DayOfWeek dayOfWeek)
static TemporalAdjuster previousOrSame(DayOfWeek dayOfWeek)
```

The test case in Example 8-10 shows a couple of those methods in action.

*Example 8-10. Using static methods in TemporalAdjusters*

```
@Test
public void adjusters() throws Exception {
    LocalDateTime start = LocalDateTime.of(2017, Month.FEBRUARY, 2, 11, 30);
    LocalDateTime end = start.with(TemporalAdjusters.firstDayOfNextMonth());
    assertEquals("2017-03-01T11:30", end.toString());

    end = start.with(TemporalAdjusters.next(DayOfWeek.THURSDAY));
    assertEquals("2017-02-09T11:30", end.toString());

    end = start.with(TemporalAdjusters.previousOrSame(DayOfWeek.THURSDAY));
    assertEquals("2017-02-02T11:30", end.toString());
}
```

The fun comes when you write your own adjuster. `TemporalAdjuster` is a functional interface, whose single abstract method is:

```
Temporal adjustInto(Temporal temporal)
```

For example, the Java Tutorial for the Date-Time package has an example of a `PaydayAdjuster`, which assumes that an employee is being paid twice a month. The rules are that payment occurs on the 15th of the month and again on the last day of the month, but if either occurs on a weekend, the previous Friday is used.

The code from the online example is reproduced in Example 8-11 for reference. Note that in this case, the method has been added to a class that implements `TemporalAdjuster`.

*Example 8-11. PaydayAdjuster (from the Java Tutorial)*

```
import java.time.DayOfWeek;
import java.time.LocalDate;
import java.time.temporal.Temporal;
import java.time.temporal.TemporalAdjuster;
import java.time.temporal.TemporalAdjusters;

public class PaydayAdjuster implements TemporalAdjuster {
    public Temporal adjustInto(Temporal input) {
        LocalDate date = LocalDate.from(input);  ❶
        int day;
        if (date.getDayOfMonth() < 15) {
            day = 15;
        } else {
```

```
            day = date.with(TemporalAdjusters.lastDayOfMonth())
                    .getDayOfMonth();
        }
        date = date.withDayOfMonth(day);
        if (date.getDayOfWeek() == DayOfWeek.SATURDAY ||
                date.getDayOfWeek() == DayOfWeek.SUNDAY) {
            date = date.with(TemporalAdjusters.previous(DayOfWeek.FRIDAY));
        }

        return input.with(date);
    }
}
```

❶ Useful way to convert any `Temporal` to a `LocalDate`

In July 2017, the 15th occured on a Saturday and the 31st was on a Monday. The test in Example 8-12 shows that it works correctly for July 2017.

*Example 8-12. Testing the adjuster for July 2017*

```
@Test
public void payDay() throws Exception {
  TemporalAdjuster adjuster = new PaydayAdjuster();
  IntStream.rangeClosed(1, 14)
           .mapToObj(day -> LocalDate.of(2017, Month.JULY, day))
           .forEach(date ->
               assertEquals(14, date.with(adjuster).getDayOfMonth()));

  IntStream.rangeClosed(15, 31)
           .mapToObj(day -> LocalDate.of(2017, Month.JULY, day))
           .forEach(date ->
               assertEquals(31, date.with(adjuster).getDayOfMonth()));
}
```

This works, but there are a couple of minor irritations. First of all, as of Java 8, you can't create a stream of dates without going through another mechanism, like counting days as shown. That changes in Java 9, which includes a method that return a stream of dates. See Recipe 10.7 for details.

The other issue with the preceding code is that a class was created to implement the interface. Because `TemporalAdjuster` is a functional interface, you can provide a lambda expression or a method reference as an implementation instead.

You can now make a utility class called `Adjusters` that has static methods for whatever you want to do, as in Example 8-13.

*Example 8-13. Utility class with adjusters*

```
public class Adjusters {                                      ❶
    public static Temporal adjustInto(Temporal input) {    ❷
        LocalDate date = LocalDate.from(input);
        // ... implementation as before ...
        return input.with(date);
    }
}
```

❶ Does not implement `TemporalAdjuster`

❷ Static method, so no instantiation required

Now the comparable test is shown in Example 8-14.

*Example 8-14. Using a method reference for the temporal adjuster*

```
@Test
public void payDayWithMethodRef() throws Exception {
    IntStream.rangeClosed(1, 14)
        .mapToObj(day -> LocalDate.of(2017, Month.JULY, day))
        .forEach(date ->
              assertEquals(14,
                  date.with(Adjusters::adjustInto).getDayOfMonth()));  ❶

    IntStream.rangeClosed(15, 31)
        .mapToObj(day -> LocalDate.of(2017, Month.JULY, day))
        .forEach(date ->
              assertEquals(31,
                  date.with(Adjusters::adjustInto).getDayOfMonth()));
}
```

❶ Method reference to `adjustInto`

You may find this approach more versatile if you have multiple temporal adjusters in mind.

## Using TemporalQuery

The `TemporalQuery` interface is used as the argument to the `query` method on temporal objects. For example, on `LocalDate`, the signature of the `query` method is:

```
<R> R query(TemporalQuery<R> query)
```

This method invokes `TemporalQuery.queryFrom(TemporalAccessor)` with `this` as an argument and returns whatever the query is designed to do. All the methods on `TemporalAccessor` are available for performing the calculation.

The API includes a class called `TemporalQueries`, which includes constants defining many common queries:

```
static TemporalQuery<Chronology>   chronology()
static TemporalQuery<LocalDate>    localDate()
static TemporalQuery<LocalTime>    localTime()
static TemporalQuery<ZoneOffset>   offset()
static TemporalQuery<TemporalUnit> precision()
static TemporalQuery<ZoneId>       zone()
static TemporalQuery<ZoneId>       zoneId()
```

A simple test to show how some work is given in Example 8-15.

*Example 8-15. Using the methods from TemporalQueries*

```
@Test
public void queries() throws Exception {
    assertEquals(ChronoUnit.DAYS,
        LocalDate.now().query(TemporalQueries.precision()));
    assertEquals(ChronoUnit.NANOS,
        LocalTime.now().query(TemporalQueries.precision()));
    assertEquals(ZoneId.systemDefault(),
        ZonedDateTime.now().query(TemporalQueries.zone()));
    assertEquals(ZoneId.systemDefault(),
        ZonedDateTime.now().query(TemporalQueries.zoneId()));
}
```

Like with `TemporalAdjuster`, however, the interesting part comes when you write your own. The `TemporalQuery` interface has only a single abstract method:

```
R queryFrom(TemporalAccessor temporal)
```

Say we have a method that, given a `TemporalAccessor`, computes the number of days between the argument and International Talk Like A Pirate Day, September 19.[5] Such a method is shown in Example 8-16.

*Example 8-16. Method to calculate days until Talk Like A Pirate Day*

```
private long daysUntilPirateDay(TemporalAccessor temporal) {
    int day = temporal.get(ChronoField.DAY_OF_MONTH);
    int month = temporal.get(ChronoField.MONTH_OF_YEAR);
    int year = temporal.get(ChronoField.YEAR);
    LocalDate date = LocalDate.of(year, month, day);
    LocalDate tlapd = LocalDate.of(year, Month.SEPTEMBER, 19);
    if (date.isAfter(tlapd)) {
        tlapd = tlapd.plusYears(1);
    }
```

5 For example, "Ahoy, matey, I'd like t' add ye t' me professional network on LinkedIn."

```
    return ChronoUnit.DAYS.between(date, tlapd);
}
```

Since that method has a signature that is compatible with the single abstract method in the `TemporalQuery` interface, you can use a method reference to invoke it, as in Example 8-17.

*Example 8-17. Using a TemporalQuery via a method reference*

```
@Test
public void pirateDay() throws Exception {
    IntStream.range(10, 19)
             .mapToObj(n -> LocalDate.of(2017, Month.SEPTEMBER, n))
             .forEach(date ->
                assertTrue(date.query(this::daysUntilPirateDay) <= 9));
    IntStream.rangeClosed(20, 30)
             .mapToObj(n -> LocalDate.of(2017, Month.SEPTEMBER, n))
             .forEach(date -> {
                Long days = date.query(this::daysUntilPirateDay);
                assertTrue(days >= 354 && days < 365);
            });
}
```

You can use this approach to define your own custom queries.

# 8.4 Convert from java.util.Date to java.time.LocalDate

## Problem

You want to convert from `java.util.Date` or `java.util.Calendar` to the new classes in the `java.time` package.

## Solution

Use the `Instant` class as a bridge, or use `java.sql.Date` and `java.sql.Timestamp` methods, or even strings or integers for the conversion.

## Discussion

When looking at the new classes in `java.time`, you may be surprised to find that there aren't a lot of built-in mechanisms for converting from the standard date and time classes in `java.util` to the new preferred classes.

One approach to convert a `java.util.Date` to a `java.time.LocalDate` is to invoke the `toInstant` method to create an `Instant`. Then you can apply the default `ZoneId` and extract a `LocalDate` from the resulting `ZonedDateTime`, as in Example 8-18.

*Example 8-18. Converting java.util.Date to java.time.LocalDate via Instant*

```
public LocalDate convertFromUtilDateUsingInstant(Date date) {
    return date.toInstant().atZone(ZoneId.systemDefault()).toLocalDate();
}
```

Since `java.util.Date` includes date and time information but no time zone,[6] it represents an `Instant` in the new API. Applying the `atZone` method on the system default time zone reapplies the time zone. Then you can extract the `LocalDate` from the resulting `ZonedDateTime`.

Another approach to changing from util dates to Date-Time dates is to notice that there are convenient conversion methods in `java.sql.Date` (see Example 8-19) and `java.sql.Timestamp` (see Example 8-20).

*Example 8-19. Conversion methods in java.sql.Date*

```
LocalDate   toLocalDate()
static Date valueOf(LocalDate date)
```

*Example 8-20. Conversion methods in java.sql.Timestamp*

```
LocalDateTime    toLocalDateTime()
static Timestamp valueOf(LocalDateTime dateTime)
```

Creating a class to do the conversion is easy enough, as in Example 8-21.

*Example 8-21. Converting java.util classes to java.time classes (more to come)*

```
package datetime;

import java.sql.Timestamp;
import java.time.LocalDate;
import java.time.LocalDateTime;
import java.util.Date;

public class ConvertDate {
    public LocalDate convertFromSqlDatetoLD(java.sql.Date sqlDate) {
        return sqlDate.toLocalDate();
    }

    public java.sql.Date convertToSqlDateFromLD(LocalDate localDate) {
        return java.sql.Date.valueOf(localDate);
    }
```

6 When you print a `java.util.Date`, it uses Java's default time zone to format the string.

```
    public LocalDateTime convertFromTimestampToLDT(Timestamp timestamp) {
        return timestamp.toLocalDateTime();
    }

    public Timestamp convertToTimestampFromLDT(LocalDateTime localDateTime) {
        return Timestamp.valueOf(localDateTime);
    }
}
```

Since the methods you need are based on `java.sql.Date`, the question then becomes, how do you convert from `java.util.Date` (which most developers use) and `java.sql.Date`? One way is to use the constructor from SQL date that takes a `long` representing the milliseconds elapsed in the current epoch.

### The Epoch and Java

On Unix-based operating systems, the *epoch* is defined as the number of seconds elapsed since 00:00:00 UTC on Thursday, January 1, 1970 (not counting leap seconds). The system clocks on current computers are based on this value.

Note that the number of seconds since the beginning of the epoch overflows a signed, 32-bit integer at 3:14:07 UTC on January 19, 2038, at which point every 32-bit operating system in the world will suddenly think it's December 13, 1901. This is known as the "Year 2038 Problem,"[7] and while virtually all systems should be on 64-bit operating systems by then, embedded systems rarely, if ever, get updated.[8]

In Java, the elapsed time is measured in milliseconds, which would seem to make the problem worse, but stored in a `long` rather than an integer, giving us several thousand years before the overflow issue arises.

The `java.util.Date` class has a method called `getTime` that returns the `long` value, and the `java.sql.Date` class has a constructor that takes this `long` as an argument.[9]

This means another way to convert from a `java.util.Date` instance to a `java.time.LocalDate` is to go through the `java.sql.Date` class, as in Example 8-22.

7 See *https://en.wikipedia.org/wiki/Year_2038_problem* for details.

8 While I expect to be safely retired by that point, I can imagine being on a respirator somewhere when the failover occurs.

9 In fact, this is the only nondeprecated constructor in the `java.sql.Date` class, though you can also use the `setTime` method to adjust the value of an existing `java.sql.Date`.

*Example 8-22. Converting a java.util.Date to a java.time.LocalDate*

```
public LocalDate convertUtilDateToLocalDate(java.util.Date date) {
    return new java.sql.Date(date.getTime()).toLocalDate()
}
```

Way back in Java 1.1, virtually the entire `java.util.Date` class was deprecated in favor of `java.util.Calendar`. Converting between calendar instances and the new `java.time` package can be done with the `toInstant` method, adjusting for the time zone (Example 8-23).

*Example 8-23. Converting from java.util.Calendar to java.time.ZonedDateTime*

```
public ZonedDateTime convertFromCalendar(Calendar cal) {
    return ZonedDateTime.ofInstant(cal.toInstant(), cal.getTimeZone().toZoneId());
}
```

This method uses the `ZonedDateTime` class. The `LocalDateTime` class also has an `ofInstant` method, but for some reason it also takes a `ZoneId` second argument. This is strange because a `LocalDateTime` doesn't contain time zone information. It seems more intuitive, therefore, to use the method from `ZonedDateTime` instead.

You can also use the various getter methods on `Calendar` explicitly and go directly to `LocalDateTime` (Example 8-24), if you want to bypass the time zone information entirely.

*Example 8-24. Using getter methods from Calendar to LocalDateTime*

```
public LocalDateTime convertFromCalendarUsingGetters(Calendar cal) {
    return LocalDateTime.of(cal.get(Calendar.YEAR),
        cal.get(Calendar.MONTH),
        cal.get(Calendar.DAY_OF_MONTH),
        cal.get(Calendar.HOUR),
        cal.get(Calendar.MINUTE),
        cal.get(Calendar.SECOND));
}
```

Another mechanism is to generate a formatted string from the calendar, which can then be parsed into the new class (Example 8-25).

*Example 8-25. Generating and parsing a timestamp string*

```
public LocalDateTime convertFromUtilDateToLDUsingString(Date date) {
    DateFormat df = new SimpleDateFormat("yyyy-MM-dd'T'HH:mm:ss");
    return LocalDateTime.parse(df.format(date),
        DateTimeFormatter.ISO_LOCAL_DATE_TIME);
}
```

That's not really an advantage, but it's nice to know you can do it. Finally, although `Calendar` doesn't have a direct conversion method, it turns out `GregorianCalendar` does (Example 8-26).

*Example 8-26. Converting a GregorianCalendar to a ZonedDateTime*

```
public ZonedDateTime convertFromGregorianCalendar(Calendar cal) {
    return ((GregorianCalendar) cal).toZonedDateTime();
}
```

That works, but it does assume you're using a Gregorian calendar. Since that's the only `Calendar` implementation in the standard library, it's probably true, but not necessarily so.

Finally, Java 9 added the `ofInstant` method to `LocalDate`, making the conversion simpler, as in Example 8-27.

*Example 8-27. Converting java.util.Dat to java.time.LocalDate (JAVA 9 ONLY)*

```
public LocalDate convertFromUtilDateJava9(Date date) {
    return LocalDate.ofInstant(date.toInstant(), ZoneId.systemDefault());
}
```

That approach is more direct, but is restricted to Java 9.

# 8.5 Parsing and Formatting

## Problem

You want to parse and/or format the new date-time classes.

## Solution

The `DateTimeFormatter` class creates date-time formats, which can be used for both parsing and formatting.

## Discussion

The `DateTimeFormatter` class has a wide variety of options, from constants like `ISO_LOCAL_DATE` to pattern letters like `uuuu-MMM-dd` to localized styles for any given `Locale`.

Fortunately, the process of parsing and formatting is almost trivially easy. All the main date-time classes have a `format` and a `parse` method. Example 8-28 shows the signatures for `LocalDate`:

*Example 8-28. Methods to parse and format LocalDate instances*

```
static LocalDate parse(CharSequence text) ❶
static LocalDate parse(CharSequence text, DateTimeFormatter formatter)
       String    format(DateTimeFormatter formatter)
```

❶ Uses `ISO_LOCAL_DATE`

Parsing and formatting are shown in Example 8-29.

*Example 8-29. Parsing and formatting a LocalDate*

```
LocalDateTime now = LocalDateTime.now();
String text = now.format(DateTimeFormatter.ISO_DATE_TIME);  ❶
LocalDateTime dateTime = LocalDateTime.parse(text);         ❷
```

❶ Format from `LocalDateTime` to string

❷ Parse from string to `LocalDateTime`

With that in mind, the real fun comes from playing with various date-time formats, locales, and so on. The code in Example 8-30 shows some examples.

*Example 8-30. Formatting dates*

```
LocalDate date = LocalDate.of(2017, Month.MARCH, 13);

System.out.println("Full   : " +
    date.format(DateTimeFormatter.ofLocalizedDate(FormatStyle.FULL)));
System.out.println("Long   : " +
    date.format(DateTimeFormatter.ofLocalizedDate(FormatStyle.LONG)));
System.out.println("Medium : " +
    date.format(DateTimeFormatter.ofLocalizedDate(FormatStyle.MEDIUM)));
System.out.println("Short  : " +
    date.format(DateTimeFormatter.ofLocalizedDate(FormatStyle.SHORT)));

System.out.println("France : " +
    date.format(DateTimeFormatter.ofLocalizedDate(FormatStyle.FULL)
        .withLocale(Locale.FRANCE)));
System.out.println("India  : " +
    date.format(DateTimeFormatter.ofLocalizedDate(FormatStyle.FULL)
        .withLocale(new Locale("hin", "IN"))));
System.out.println("Brazil : " +
    date.format(DateTimeFormatter.ofLocalizedDate(FormatStyle.FULL)
        .withLocale(new Locale("pt", "BR"))));
System.out.println("Japan  : " +
    date.format(DateTimeFormatter.ofLocalizedDate(FormatStyle.FULL)
        .withLocale(Locale.JAPAN)));

Locale loc = new Locale.Builder()
```

```
        .setLanguage("sr")
        .setScript("Latn")
        .setRegion("RS")
        .build();
System.out.println("Serbian: " +
    date.format(DateTimeFormatter.ofLocalizedDate(FormatStyle.FULL)
        .withLocale(loc)));
```

The output looks something like:[10]

```
    Full   : Monday, March 13, 2017
    Long   : March 13, 2017
    Medium : Mar 13, 2017
    Short  : 3/13/17

    France : lundi 13 mars 2017
    India  : Monday, March 13, 2017
    Brazil : Segunda-feira, 13 de Março de 2017
    Japan  : 2017 年 3 月 13 日
    Serbian: ponedeljak, 13. mart 2017.
```

The `parse` and `format` methods throw a `DateTimeParseException` and `DateTimeException`, respectively, so you might want to consider catching them in your own code.

If you have your own format in mind, use the `ofPattern` method to create it. All the legal values are described in detail in the Javadocs. As an example of what's possible, see Example 8-31.

*Example 8-31. Defining your own format pattern*

```
ZonedDateTime moonLanding = ZonedDateTime.of(
        LocalDate.of(1969, Month.JULY, 20),
        LocalTime.of(20, 18),
        ZoneId.of("UTC")
);
System.out.println(moonLanding.format(DateTimeFormatter.ISO_ZONED_DATE_TIME));

DateTimeFormatter formatter =
    DateTimeFormatter.ofPattern("uuuu/MMMM/dd hh:mm:ss a zzz GG");
System.out.println(moonLanding.format(formatter));

formatter = DateTimeFormatter.ofPattern("uuuu/MMMM/dd hh:mm:ss a VV xxxxx");
System.out.println(moonLanding.format(formatter));
```

These produce:

10 There's no truth to the rumor that I deliberately chose unusual languages and output formats just to challenge O'Reilly Media's ability to print the results correctly, at least as far as you know.

```
1969-07-20T20:18:00Z[UTC]
1969/July/20 08:18:00 PM UTC AD
1969/July/20 08:18:00 PM UTC +00:00
```

Again, to see what's possible and what all the different formatting letters mean, see the Javadocs for `DateTimeFormatter`. The process is always as simple as shown.

To show an example of a localized date-time formatter, consider the daylight savings time issue. In the United States, daylight savings moves the clocks forward at 2 A.M. on March 11, 2018, in the Eastern time zone. What happens when you ask for a zoned date time at 2:30 A.M. on that day? See Example 8-32.

*Example 8-32. Move the clocks forward*

```
ZonedDateTime zdt = ZonedDateTime.of(2018, 3, 11, 2, 30, 0, 0,
    ZoneId.of("America/New_York"));
System.out.println(
    zdt.format(DateTimeFormatter.ofLocalizedDateTime(FormatStyle.FULL)));
```

This uses an overload of the `of` method that takes the year, month, `dayOfMonth`, hours, minutes, seconds, `nanoOfSecond`, and `ZoneId`. Note that all the fields (other than the `ZoneId`) are of type `int`, which means you can't use the `Month` enum.

The output of this code is:

```
Sunday, March 11, 2018 3:30:00 AM EDT
```

So the method correctly changed the time from 2:30 A.M. (which doesn't exist) to 3:30 A.M.

# 8.6 Finding Time Zones with Unusual Offsets

## Problem

You want to find all the time zones with non-integral hour offsets.

## Solution

Get the time zone offset for each time zone and determine its remainder when dividing the total seconds by 3,600.

## Discussion

Most time zones are offset from UTC by an integral number of hours. For example, what we normally called Eastern Time is `UTC-05:00` and metropolitan France (CET) is `UTC+01:00`. There are time zones, however, that are offset by the half-hour, like Indian Standard Time (IST), which is `UTC+05:30`, or even 45 minutes, like the Chatham Islands in New Zealand, which is UTC+12:45. This recipe demonstrates how you can use the java.time package to find all the time zones that are off by nonintegral amounts.

Example 8-33 demonstrates how to find the ZoneOffset for each regional zone ID, and compare its total seconds to the number of seconds in an hour.

*Example 8-33. Finding the offset seconds for each zone ID*

```
public class FunnyOffsets {
    public static void main(String[] args) {
        Instant instant = Instant.now();
        ZonedDateTime current = instant.atZone(ZoneId.systemDefault());
        System.out.printf("Current time is %s%n%n", current);

        System.out.printf("%10s %20s %13s%n", "Offset", "ZoneId", "Time");
        ZoneId.getAvailableZoneIds().stream()
                .map(ZoneId::of)  ❶
                .filter(zoneId -> {
                    ZoneOffset offset = instant.atZone(zoneId).getOffset(); ❷
                    return offset.getTotalSeconds() % (60 * 60) != 0; ❸
                })
                .sorted(comparingInt(zoneId ->
                        instant.atZone(zoneId).getOffset().getTotalSeconds()))
                .forEach(zoneId -> {
                    ZonedDateTime zdt = current.withZoneSameInstant(zoneId);
                    System.out.printf("%10s %25s %10s%n",
                        zdt.getOffset(), zoneId,
                        zdt.format(DateTimeFormatter.ofLocalizedTime(
                            FormatStyle.SHORT)));
                });
    }
}
```

❶ Map the string region IDs to zone IDs

❷ Calculate the offset

❸ Only use zone IDs whose offsets are not divisible by 3,600

The static ZoneId.getAvailableZoneIds method returns a Set<String> representing all the region IDs in the world. Using the ZoneId.of method, the resulting stream of strings is transformed into a stream of ZoneId instances.

The lambda expression in the filter first applies the atZone method to an Instant in order to create a ZonedDateTime, which then has a getOffset method. Finally, the ZoneOffset class provides a getTotalSeconds method. The Javadocs for that method describe it as "the primary way to access the offset amount. It returns the total of the hours, minutes and seconds fields as a single offset that can be added to a time." The `Predicate` in the filter then returns true only for those total seconds amounts that aren't evenly divisible by 3,600 (`60 sec/min * 60 min/hour`).

Before printing, the resulting `ZoneId` instances are sorted. The `sorted` method takes a `Comparator`. Here, the static `Comparator.comparingInt` method is used, which generates a `Comparator` that will sort by a given integer key. In this case, the same calculation is used to determine the total seconds in the offsets. The result is that the `ZoneId` instances are sorted by the offset amounts.

Then, to print the results, the current `ZonedDateTime` in the default time zone is evaluated for each `ZoneId` using the `withZoneSameInstant` method. The printed string then shows the offset, the regional zone ID, and a formatted, localized version of the local time in that zone.

The result is shown in Example 8-34.

*Example 8-34. Time zones offset by non-hour amounts*

```
Current time is 2016-08-08T23:12:44.264-04:00[America/New_York]

    Offset                ZoneId         Time
    -09:30       Pacific/Marquesas    5:42 PM
    -04:30         America/Caracas   10:42 PM
    -02:30        America/St_Johns   12:42 AM
    -02:30     Canada/Newfoundland   12:42 AM
    +04:30                    Iran    7:42 AM
    +04:30             Asia/Tehran    7:42 AM
    +04:30              Asia/Kabul    7:42 AM
    +05:30            Asia/Kolkata    8:42 AM
    +05:30            Asia/Colombo    8:42 AM
    +05:30           Asia/Calcutta    8:42 AM
    +05:45          Asia/Kathmandu    8:57 AM
    +05:45           Asia/Katmandu    8:57 AM
    +06:30            Asia/Rangoon    9:42 AM
    +06:30            Indian/Cocos    9:42 AM
    +08:45         Australia/Eucla   11:57 AM
    +09:30         Australia/North   12:42 PM
    +09:30    Australia/Yancowinna   12:42 PM
    +09:30      Australia/Adelaide   12:42 PM
    +09:30   Australia/Broken_Hill   12:42 PM
    +09:30         Australia/South   12:42 PM
    +09:30        Australia/Darwin   12:42 PM
    +10:30     Australia/Lord_Howe    1:42 PM
    +10:30           Australia/LHI    1:42 PM
    +11:30         Pacific/Norfolk    2:42 PM
    +12:45                 NZ-CHAT    3:57 PM
    +12:45         Pacific/Chatham    3:57 PM
```

This example shows how several of the classes in `java.time` can be combined to solve an interesting problem.

# 8.7 Finding Region Names from Offsets

## Problem

You want to know the ISO 8601 region name given an offset from UTC.

## Solution

Filter all the available zone IDs by the given offset.

## Discussion

While time zone names like "Eastern Daylight Time" or "Indian Standard Time" are well-known, they are unofficial and their abbreviations like EDT and IST are sometimes not even unique. The ISO 8601 specification defines time zone IDs two ways:

- By region name, like "America/Chicago"
- By offset from UTC in hours and minutes, like "+05:30"

Say you want to know what the region name is for a given offset from UTC. Many regions share the same UTC offset at any given time, but you can calculate a `List` of region names that have a given offset easily.

The `ZoneOffset` class specifies a time zone offset from Greenwich/UTC time. If you already have a value for the offset, you can filter the complete list of region names using it, as in Example 8-35.

*Example 8-35. Getting region names given an offset*

```
public static List<String> getRegionNamesForOffset(ZoneOffset offset) {
    LocalDateTime now = LocalDateTime.now();
    return ZoneId.getAvailableZoneIds().stream()
            .map(ZoneId::of)
            .filter(zoneId -> now.atZone(zoneId).getOffset().equals(offset))
            .map(ZoneId::toString)
            .sorted()
            .collect(Collectors.toList());
}
```

The `ZoneId.getAvailableZoneIds` method returns a `List` of strings. Each one can be mapped to a `ZoneId` using the static `ZoneId.of` method. Then, after determining the corresponding `ZonedDateTime` for that `ZoneId` using the `atZone` method in `Local`

`DateTime`, you can get the `ZoneOffset` for each and filter the set by only those that match it. The result is then mapped to strings, which are sorted and collected into a `List`.

How do you get a `ZoneOffset`? One way is to use a given `ZoneId`, as shown in Example 8-36.

*Example 8-36. Get region names for a given offset*

```
public static List<String> getRegionNamesForZoneId(ZoneId zoneId) {
    LocalDateTime now = LocalDateTime.now();
    ZonedDateTime zdt = now.atZone(zoneId);
    ZoneOffset offset = zdt.getOffset();

    return getRegionNamesForOffset(offset);
}
```

This works for any given `ZoneId`.

For example, if you want to determine the list of region names that correspond to your current location, use the code in Example 8-37.

*Example 8-37. Getting the current region names*

```
@Test
public void getRegionNamesForSystemDefault() throws Exception {
    ZonedDateTime now = ZonedDateTime.now();
    ZoneId zoneId = now.getZone();
    List<String> names = getRegionNamesForZoneId(zoneId);

    assertTrue(names.contains(zoneId.getId()));
}
```

If you don't know a region name but you do know the hours and minutes it is offset from GMT, the `ZoneOffset` class has a convenient method called `ofHoursMinutes` for that as well. The overload in Example 8-38 shows how to do that.

*Example 8-38. Getting region names given an hour and minute offset*

```
public static List<String> getRegionNamesForOffset(int hours, int minutes) {
    ZoneOffset offset = ZoneOffset.ofHoursMinutes(hours, minutes);
    return getRegionNamesForOffset(offset);
}
```

The tests in Example 8-39 demonstrate how the given code works.

*Example 8-39. Testing region names for a given offset*

```
@Test
public void getRegionNamesForGMT() throws Exception {
    List<String> names = getRegionNamesForOffset(0, 0);

    assertTrue(names.contains("GMT"));
    assertTrue(names.contains("Etc/GMT"));
    assertTrue(names.contains("Etc/UTC"));
    assertTrue(names.contains("UTC"));
    assertTrue(names.contains("Etc/Zulu"));
}

@Test
public void getRegionNamesForNepal() throws Exception {
    List<String> names = getRegionNamesForOffset(5, 45);

    assertTrue(names.contains("Asia/Kathmandu"));
    assertTrue(names.contains("Asia/Katmandu"));
}

@Test
public void getRegionNamesForChicago() throws Exception {
    ZoneId chicago = ZoneId.of("America/Chicago");
    List<String> names = RegionIdsByOffset.getRegionNamesForZoneId(chicago);

    assertTrue(names.contains("America/Chicago"));
    assertTrue(names.contains("US/Central"));
    assertTrue(names.contains("Canada/Central"));
    assertTrue(names.contains("Etc/GMT+5") || names.contains("Etc/GMT+6"));
}
```

A complete list of region names can be found in Wikipedia at *https://en.wikipedia.org/wiki/List_of_tz_database_time_zones*.

# 8.8 Time Between Events

## Problem

You need to know the amount of time between two events.

## Solution

If you want times readable by people, use the `between` or `until` methods on the temporal classes or `between` method on `Period` to generate a `Period` object. Otherwise use the `Duration` class for seconds and nanoseconds on the timeline.

## Discussion

The Date-Time API includes the interface `java.time.temporal.TemporalUnit`, which is implemented by the enum `ChronoUnit` in the same package. The `between` method on that interface takes two `TemporalUnit` instances and returns a `long`:

```
long between(Temporal temporal1Inclusive,
             Temporal temporal2Exclusive)
```

The start and end times must be of compatible types. The implementation converts the second argument to be an instance of the first type before calculating the amount. The result is negative if the second argument occurs before the first argument.

The return value is the number of "units" between the arguments. This becomes convenient when using the constants in the `ChronoUnit` enum.

For example, say you want to know how many days you need to wait until a particular date. Since you're interested in days, use the `ChronoUnit.DAYS` constant from the enum, as in Example 8-40.

*Example 8-40. Days to Election Day*

```
LocalDate electionDay = LocalDate.of(2020, Month.NOVEMBER, 3);
LocalDate today = LocalDate.now();

System.out.printf("%d day(s) to go...%n",
    ChronoUnit.DAYS.between(today, electionDay));
```

Since the `between` method is invoked on the `DAYS` enum value, this will return the number of days. Other constants in `ChronoUnit` include `HOURS`, `WEEKS`, `MONTHS`, `YEARS`, `DECADES`, `CENTURIES`, and more.[11]

### Using the Period class

If you're interested in a breakdown into years, months, and days, use the `Period` class. The `until` method in many of the basic classes has an overload that returns a `Period`:

```
// In java.time.LocalDate
Period until(ChronoLocalDate endDateExclusive)
```

This example can be rewritten as in Example 8-41.

11 Including, believe it or not, `FOREVER`. If you ever need that value, please send me a message. I'd love to know what the use case was.

*Example 8-41. Using Period to get days, months, and years*

```
LocalDate electionDay = LocalDate.of(2020, Month.NOVEMBER, 3);
LocalDate today = LocalDate.now();

Period until = today.until(electionDay); ❶

years  = until.getYears();
months = until.getMonths();
days   = until.getDays();
System.out.printf("%d year(s), %d month(s), and %d day(s)%n",
        years, months, days);
```

❶ Equivalent to `Period.between(today, electionDay)`

As the comment states, the `Period` class also has a `static` method called `between` that works the same way. The recommendation is to use whichever style makes the code more readable.

The `Period` class is used when you need to deal with human-readable times, like days, months, and years.

### Using the Duration class

The `Duration` class represents an amount of time in terms of seconds and nanoseconds, which makes it suitable for working with `Instant`. The result can be converted to many other types. The class stores a `long` representing seconds and an `int` representing nanoseconds, and can be negative if the end point comes before the starting point.

A primitive timing mechanism using `Duration` is shown in Example 8-42.

*Example 8-42. Timing a method*

```
public static double getTiming(Instant start, Instant end) {
    return Duration.between(start, end).toMillis() / 1000.0;
}

Instant start = Instant.now();
// ... call method to be timed ...
Instant end = Instant.now();
System.out.println(getTiming(start, end) + " seconds");
```

This is a "poor developer's" approach to timing a method, but it is easy.

The `Duration` class has conversion methods: `toDays`, `toHours`, `toMillis`, `toMinutes`, and `toNanos`, which is why the `getTiming` method in Example 8-42 used `toMillis` and divided by 1,000.

CHAPTER 9

# Parallelism and Concurrency

This chapter confronts the issues of parallelization and concurrency in Java 8. Some of the concepts extend back to language additions from much earlier versions of the language (especially the `java.util.concurrent` package added in Java 5), but Java 8 specifically added several capabilities to the language to help you operate at a higher level of abstraction.

One hazard of parallelization and concurrency is that when you try to talk about them, someone will care a lot—very vocally—about the distinction between the two words. Let's get that out of the way right now:

- *Concurrency* is when multiple tasks can run in overlapping time periods
- *Parallelism* is when multiple tasks run at literally the same time

You design for concurrency—the ability to decompose your problem into independent operations that can run simultaneously, even if they aren't doing so at the moment. A concurrent application is composed of independently executing processes. You can then implement the concurrent tasks in parallel, which may or may not improve performance, assuming you have multiple processing units.[1]

Why wouldn't parallelization help performance? There are many reasons, but parallelization in Java by default splits work into multiple sections, assigning each to the common fork-join pool, executing them, and joining the results together. All of that work introduces overhead. A lot of expected performance improvements will be decided by how well your problem maps to that algorithm. One of the recipes in this

1 An excellent, (relatively) short discussion of these concepts can be found in "Concurrency Is Not Parallelism," by Rob Pike, creator of the Go programming language. See *https://www.youtube.com/watch?v=cN_DpYBzKso* for a video.

chapter gives some guidelines on how to make the decision on whether or not to parallelize.

Java 8 makes it easy to try out parallelism. There is a classic presentation by Rich Hickey (the creator of the Clojure programming language) called "Simple Made Easy."[2] One of the basic concepts in his talk is that the words *simple* and *easy* imply different concepts. In short, something that is simple is conceptually clear, while something that is *easy* might be elementary to do but might hide massive complexity under the hood. For example, some sorting algorithms are simple and some are not, but calling the `sorted` method on a `Stream` is always easy.[3]

Parallel and concurrent processing is a complex topic, and difficult to get right. From the beginning, Java included low-level mechanisms to support multithreaded access, with methods like `wait`, `notify`, and `notifyAll` in `Object`, as well as the `synchronized` keyword. Getting concurrency right with such primitives is extremely difficult, so later the language added the `java.util.concurrent` package, which allowed developers to work with concurrency at a higher level of abstraction using classes like `ExecutorService`, `ReentrantLock`, and `BlockingQueue`. Still, managing concurrency is hard, especially in the presence of the dreaded "shared mutable state" monster.

With Java 8, asking for parallel streams is easy because it involves a single method call. That's unquestionably easy. The problem is, improving performance is hardly simple. All the problems from before are still there; they're just hidden under the surface.

The recipes in this section are not a complete discussion of concurrency and parallelization. Those topics can and do span entire books.[4] Here the goal is to show you what the available mechanisms are and how they are intended to be used. You can then apply the concepts to your code and make your own measurements and decisions.

# 9.1 Converting from Sequential to Parallel Streams

## Problem

You want to make a stream either `sequential` or `parallel`, regardless of the default.

2 Video: *http://www.infoq.com/presentations/Simple-Made-Easy*, Transcript: *http://bit.ly/hickey-simplemadeeasy*

3 Another great example of simple versus easy is found in a story told about Patrick Stewart while he was playing Captain Picard in *Star Trek: The Next Generation*. A writer tried to describe to him all the detailed steps necessary to enter orbit around a planet. "Nonsense," Stewart replied. "You just say, 'Standard orbit, Ensign.'"

4 Of particular note are *Java Concurrency in Practice* by Brian Goetz (Addison-Wesley Professional) and *Programming Concurrency on the JVM* by Venkat Subramaniam (Pragmatic Bookshelf).

## Solution

Use the `stream` or `parallelStream` methods on `Collection`, or the `sequential` or `parallel` methods on `Stream`.

## Discussion

By default, when you create a stream in Java the result is sequential. In `BaseStream` (the superclass of the `Stream` interface), you can use the method `isParallel` to determine whether the stream is operating sequentially or in parallel.

Example 9-1 shows how all the standard mechanisms used to create streams are sequential by default.

*Example 9-1. Creating sequential streams (parts of a JUnit test)*

```
@Test
public void sequentialStreamOf() throws Exception {
    assertFalse(Stream.of(3, 1, 4, 1, 5, 9).isParallel());
}

@Test
public void sequentialIterateStream() throws Exception {
    assertFalse(Stream.iterate(1, n -> n + 1).isParallel());
}

@Test
public void sequentialGenerateStream() throws Exception {
    assertFalse(Stream.generate(Math::random).isParallel());
}

@Test
public void sequentialCollectionStream() throws Exception {
    List<Integer> numbers = Arrays.asList(3, 1, 4, 1, 5, 9);
    assertFalse(numbers.stream().isParallel());
}
```

If the source was a collection, you can use the `parallelStream` method to yield a (possibly) parallel stream, as in Example 9-2.

*Example 9-2. Using the parallelStream method*

```
@Test
public void parallelStreamMethodOnCollection() throws Exception {
    List<Integer> numbers = Arrays.asList(3, 1, 4, 1, 5, 9);
    assertTrue(numbers.parallelStream().isParallel());
}
```

The reason for the "possibly" qualification is that it is allowable for this method to return a sequential stream, but by default the stream will be parallel. The Javadocs imply that the sequential case will only occur if you create your own `spliterator`, which is pretty unusual.[5]

The other way to create a parallel stream is to use the method `parallel` on an existing stream, as in Example 9-3.

*Example 9-3. Using the parallel method on a stream*

```
@Test
public void parallelMethodOnStream() throws Exception {
    assertTrue(Stream.of(3, 1, 4, 1, 5, 9)
            .parallel()
            .isParallel());
}
```

Interestingly enough, there is also a `sequential` method, which returns a sequential stream, as in Example 9-4.

*Example 9-4. Converting a parallel stream to sequential*

```
@Test
public void parallelStreamThenSequential() throws Exception {
    List<Integer> numbers = Arrays.asList(3, 1, 4, 1, 5, 9);
    assertFalse(numbers.parallelStream()
            .sequential()
            .isParallel());
}
```

Be careful, though. There's a trap here. Say you plan a pipeline where part of the processing can reasonably be done in parallel, but other parts should be done sequentially. You might be tempted to try the code in Example 9-5.

*Example 9-5. Switching from parallel to sequential (NOT WHAT YOU MIGHT EXPECT)*

```
List<Integer> numbers = Arrays.asList(3, 1, 4, 1, 5, 9);
List<Integer> nums = numbers.parallelStream()  ❶
      .map(n -> n * 2)
      .peek(n -> System.out.printf("%s processing %d%n",
              Thread.currentThread().getName(), n))
      .sequential()                            ❷
      .sorted()
      .collect(Collectors.toList());
```

5 An interesting topic, to be sure, but ultimately beyond the scope of this book.

❶ Ask for a parallel stream

❷ Before sorting, switch to sequential

The idea here is that you want to double all the numbers, and then sort them. Since the doubling function is stateless and associative, there's no reason not to do it parallel. Sorting, however, is inherently sequential.[6]

The `peek` method is used to show the name of the thread doing the processing, and in the example `peek` is invoked after the call to `parallelStream` but before the call to `sequential`. The output is:

```
main processing 6
main processing 2
main processing 8
main processing 2
main processing 10
main processing 18
```

The `main` thread did all the processing. In other words, the stream is sequential, despite the call to `parallelStream`. Why is that? Remember that with streams, no processing is done until the terminal expression is reached, so it's at that moment that the state of the stream is evaluated. Since the last `parallel` or `sequential` call before the `collect` method was to `sequential`, the stream is sequential and the elements are processed accordingly.

When executing, a stream can be either parallel or sequential. The `parallel` or `sequential` methods effectively set or unset a boolean, which is checked when the terminal expression is reached.

If you really have your heart set on processing part of a stream in parallel and part sequentially, use two separate streams. It's an awkward solution, but there aren't any better alternatives.

# 9.2 When Parallel Helps

## Problem

You want to see a benefit from using parallel streams.

6 Think of it this way: sorting using a parallel stream would mean dividing up the range into equal parts and sorting each of them individually, then trying to combine the resulting sorted ranges. The output wouldn't be sorted overall.

## Solution

Use parallel streams under the right conditions.

## Discussion

The stream API was designed to make it easy to switch from sequential to parallel streams, but that may or may not help your performance. Keep in mind that moving to parallel streams is an optimization. Make sure you have working code first. Then try to decide whether or not using parallel streams is worth it. Those decisions are best made with actual data.

By default, Java 8 parallel streams use a common fork-join pool to distribute the work. The size of that pool is equal to the number of processors, which you can determine via `Runtime.getRuntime().availableProcessors()`.[7] Managing the fork-join pool requires overhead, both in dividing the work into individual segments and in combining the individual results back into a final answer.

For the additional overhead to be worthwhile, you need:

- A large amount of data, or
- A time-consuming process for each element, and
- A source of data that is easy to divide, and
- Operations that are stateless and associative

The first two requirements are often combined. If `N` is the number of data elements and `Q` is the amount of computational time required for each element, then in general you need `N * Q` to exceed some threshold.[8] The next requirement means that you need to have a data structure that is easy to divide into segments, like an array. Finally, doing anything stateful or where order matters is clearly going to cause problems when going parallel.

Here is an example that is about the simplest demonstration of a computation where parallel streams help. The stream code in Example 9-6 adds a very small number of integers.

*Example 9-6. Adding integers in a sequential stream*

```
public static int doubleIt(int n) {
    try {
```

7 Technically the pool size is processors minus one, but the main thread is still used as well.

8 Frequently you'll see this expressed as `N * Q > 10,000`, but nobody ever seems to put dimensions on `Q`, so that's difficult to interpret.

```
        Thread.sleep(100);                  ❶
    } catch (InterruptedException ignore) {
    }
    return n * 2;
}

// in main...
Instant before = Instant.now();             ❷
total = IntStream.of(3, 1, 4, 1, 5, 9)
        .map(ParallelDemo::doubleIt)
        .sum();
Instant after = Instant.now();              ❷
Duration duration = Duration.between(start, end);
System.out.println("Total of doubles = " + total);
System.out.println("time = " + duration.toMillis() + " ms");
```

❶ Artificial delay

❷ Measure time before and after

Since adding numbers is blazingly fast, going parallel isn't likely to show much improvement unless an artificial delay is introduced. Here `N` is very small, so `Q` is inflated by introducing a 100-millisecond `sleep`.

By default, streams are sequential. Since the doubling of each element is delayed by 100 milliseconds and there are six elements, the overall process should take just over 0.6 seconds, and that's what happens:

```
Total of doubles = 46
time = 621 ms
```

Now change the stream code to use a `parallel` stream instead. The `Stream` interface has a method called `parallel` for this purpose, shown in Example 9-7.

*Example 9-7. Using a parallel stream*

```
total = IntStream.of(3, 1, 4, 1, 5, 9)
    .parallel()                         ❶
    .map(ParallelDemo::doubleIt)
    .sum();
```

❶ Use a parallel stream

On a machine with eight cores, the instantiated fork-join pool will be of size eight.[9] That means each element in the stream can have its own core (assuming nothing else

[9] The size will actually be seven, but there will be eight separate threads involved including the main thread.

is going on—a point to be addressed later), so all the doubling operations can happen essentially simultaneously.

The result now is:

```
Total of doubles = 46
time = 112 ms
```

Since each doubling operation is delayed by 100 milliseconds and there are enough threads for every number to be handled individually, the overall computation only took just over 100 milliseconds.

### Timing using JMH

Performance measurements are notoriously difficult to get right, because they are dependent on many different issues like caching, JVM startup times, and more. The demonstration shown here is quite crude. One mechanism that can be used for more rigorous testing is the micro-benchmarking framework JMH (Java Micro-benchmark Harness, available at *http://openjdk.java.net/projects/code-tools/jmh/*).

JMH lets you use annotations to specify the timing mode, scope, JVM arguments, and more. Refactoring the example from this section to use JMH is shown in Example 9-8.

*Example 9-8. Timing the doubling operation using JMH*

```
import org.openjdk.jmh.annotations.*;

import java.util.concurrent.TimeUnit;
import java.util.stream.IntStream;

@BenchmarkMode(Mode.AverageTime)
@OutputTimeUnit(TimeUnit.MILLISECONDS)
@State(Scope.Thread)
@Fork(value = 2, jvmArgs = {"-Xms4G", "-Xmx4G"})
public class DoublingDemo {
    public int doubleIt(int n) {
        try {
            Thread.sleep(100);
        } catch (InterruptedException ignored) {
        }
        return n * 2;
    }

    @Benchmark
    public int doubleAndSumSequential() {
        return IntStream.of(3, 1, 4, 1, 5, 9)
                .map(this::doubleIt)
                .sum();
    }
```

```
    @Benchmark
    public int doubleAndSumParallel() {
        return IntStream.of(3, 1, 4, 1, 5, 9)
                .parallel()
                .map(this::doubleIt)
                .sum();
    }
}
```

The default settings are to run 20 iterations in two separate threads, after a series of warmup iterations. The results in a typical run are:

```
Benchmark                             Mode  Cnt    Score   Error  Units
DoublingDemo.doubleAndSumParallel     avgt   40  103.523 ± 0.247  ms/op
DoublingDemo.doubleAndSumSequential   avgt   40  620.242 ± 1.656  ms/op
```

The values are essentially the same as the crude estimate—that is, the sequential processing averaged about 620 ms while the parallel case averaged about 103. Running in parallel on a system that can assign an individual thread to each of six numbers is about six times faster than doing each computation consecutively, as long as there are enough processors to go around.

### Summing primitives

The previous example artificially inflated `Q` for a small `N` in order to show the effectiveness of using parallel streams. This section will make `N` large enough to draw some conclusions, and compare both parallel and sequential for both generic streams and primitive streams, as well as straight iteration.

The example in this section is basic, but it is based on a similar demo in the excellent book *Java 8 and 9 in Action*.[10]

The iterative approach is shown in Example 9-9.

*Example 9-9. Iteratively summing numbers in a loop*

```
public long iterativeSum() {
    long result = 0;
    for (long i = 1L; i <= N; i++) {
        result += i;
    }
```

10 *Java 8 and 9 in Action*, Urma, Fusco, and Mycroft (Manning Publishers, 2017)

```
    return result;
}
```

Next, Example 9-10 shows both sequential and iterative approaches to summing a `Stream<Long>`.

*Example 9-10. Summing generic streams*

```
public long sequentialStreamSum() {
    return Stream.iterate(1L, i -> i + 1)
            .limit(N)
            .reduce(0L, Long::sum);
}

public long parallelStreamSum() {
    return Stream.iterate(1L, i -> i + 1)
            .limit(N)
            .parallel()
            .reduce(0L, Long::sum);
}
```

The `parallelStreamSum` method is working with the worst situation possible, in that the computation is using `Stream<Long>` instead of `LongStream` and working with a collection of data produced by the `iterate` method. The system does not know how to divide the resulting work easily.

By contrast, Example 9-11 both uses the `LongStream` class (which has a `sum` method) and works with `rangeClosed`, which Java knows how to partition.

*Example 9-11. Using LongStream*

```
public long sequentialLongStreamSum() {
    return LongStream.rangeClosed(1, N)
            .sum();
}

public long parallelLongStreamSum() {
    return LongStream.rangeClosed(1, N)
            .parallel()
            .sum();
}
```

Sample results using JMH for `N = 10,000,000` elements are:

```
Benchmark                Mode  Cnt   Score   Error  Units
iterativeSum             avgt   40   6.441 ± 0.019  ms/op
sequentialStreamSum      avgt   40  90.468 ± 0.613  ms/op
parallelStreamSum        avgt   40  99.148 ± 3.065  ms/op
sequentialLongStreamSum  avgt   40   6.191 ± 0.248  ms/op
parallelLongStreamSum    avgt   40   6.571 ± 2.756  ms/op
```

See how much all the boxing and unboxing costs? The approaches that use `Stream<Long>` instead of `LongStream` are much slower, especially combined with the fact that using a fork-join pool with `iterate` is not easy to divide. Using `LongStream` with a `rangeClosed` method is so fast that there is very little difference between sequential and parallel performance at all.

## 9.3 Changing the Pool Size

### Problem

You want to use a different number of threads in the common pool than the default.

### Solution

Change the proper system parameter, or submit the tasks to your own instance of `ForkJoinPool`.

### Discussion

The Javadocs for the `java.util.concurrent.ForkJoinPool` class state that you can control the construction of the common pool using three system properties:

- `java.util.concurrent.ForkJoinPool.common.parallelism`
- `java.util.concurrent.ForkJoinPool.common.threadFactory`
- `java.util.concurrent.ForkJoinPool.common.exceptionHandler`

By default, the size of the common thread pool equals the number of processors on your machine, computed from `Runtime.getRuntime().availableProcessors()`. Setting the `parallelism` flag to a nonnegative integer lets you specify the parallelism level.

The flag can be specified either programmatically or on the command line. For instance, Example 9-12 shows how to use `System.setProperty` to create the desired degree of parallelism.

*Example 9-12. Specifying the common pool size programmatically*

```
System.setProperty(
    "java.util.concurrent.ForkJoinPool.common.parallelism", "20");
long total = LongStream.rangeClosed(1, 3_000_000)
    .parallel()
    .sum();
```

```
int poolSize = ForkJoinPool.commonPool().getPoolSize();
System.out.println("Pool size: " + poolSize); ❶
```

❶ Prints `Pool size: 20`

Setting the pool size to a number greater than the number of available cores is not likely to improve performance.

On the command line, you can use the `-D` flag as with any system property. Note that the programmatic setting overrides the command-line setting, as shown in Example 9-13:

*Example 9-13. Setting the common pool size using a system parameter*

```
$ java -cp build/classes/main concurrency.CommonPoolSize
Pool size: 20

// ...comment out the System.setProperty("...parallelism,20") line...
$ java -cp build/classes/main concurrency.CommonPoolSize
Pool size: 7

$ java -cp build/classes/main                                  \
    -Djava.util.concurrent.ForkJoinPool.common.parallelism=10 \
    concurrency.CommonPoolSize
Pool size: 10
```

This example was run on a machine with eight processors. The pool size by default is seven, but that doesn't include the `main` thread, so there are eight active threads by default.

### Using your own ForkJoinPool

The `ForkJoinPool` class has a constructor that takes an integer representing the degree of parallelism. You can therefore create your own pool, separate from the common pool, and submit your jobs to that pool instead.

The code in Example 9-14 uses this mechanism to create its own pool.

*Example 9-14. Creating your own ForkJoinPool*

```
ForkJoinPool pool = new ForkJoinPool(15);          ❶
ForkJoinTask<Long> task = pool.submit(              ❷
    () -> LongStream.rangeClosed(1, 3_000_000)
                    .parallel()
                    .sum());
```

```
try {
    total = task.get();                          ❸
} catch (InterruptedException | ExecutionException e) {
    e.printStackTrace();
} finally {
    pool.shutdown();
}
poolSize = pool.getPoolSize();
System.out.println("Pool size: " + poolSize);  ❹
```

❶ Instantiate a `ForkJoinPool` of size 15

❷ Submit a `Callable<Integer>` as the job

❸ Execute the job and wait for a reply

❹ Prints `Pool size: 15`

The common pool used when invoking `parallel` on a stream performs quite well in most circumstances. If you need to change its size, use the system property. If that still doesn't get you what you want, try creating your own `ForkJoinPool` and submit the jobs to it.

In any case, be sure to collect data on the resulting performance before deciding on a long-term solution.

## See Also

A related way to do parallel computations with your own pool is use `CompletableFuture`, as discussed in Recipe 9.5.

# 9.4 The Future Interface

## Problem

You want to represent the result of an asynchronous computation, check if it is complete, cancel if necessary, and retrieve the result.

## Solution

Use a class that implements the `java.util.concurrent.Future` interface.

## Discussion

This book is about the new features in Java 8 and 9, one of which is the very helpful class `CompletableFuture`. Among its other qualities, a `CompletableFuture` implements the `Future` interface, so it's worth a brief review to see what `Future` can do.

The `java.util.concurrent` package was added to Java 5 to help developers operate at a higher level of abstraction than simple `wait` and `notify` primitives. One of the interfaces in that package is `ExecutorService`, which has a `submit` method that takes a `Callable` and returns a `Future` wrapping the desired object.

For instance, Example 9-15 contains code that submits a job to an `ExecutorService`, prints a string, then retrieves the value from the `Future`.

*Example 9-15. Submitting a Callable and returning the Future*

```
ExecutorService service = Executors.newCachedThreadPool();
Future<String> future = service.submit(new Callable<String>() {
    @Override
    public String call() throws Exception {
        Thread.sleep(100);
        return "Hello, World!";
    }
});
System.out.println("Processing...");
getIfNotCancelled(future);
```

The `getIfNotCancelled` method is shown in Example 9-16.

*Example 9-16. Retrieving a value from a Future*

```
public void getIfNotCancelled(Future<String> future) {
    try {
        if (!future.isCancelled()) {            ❶
            System.out.println(future.get()); ❷
        } else {
            System.out.println("Cancelled");
        }
    } catch (InterruptedException | ExecutionException e) {
        e.printStackTrace();
    }
}
```

❶ Check status of `Future`

❷ Blocking call to retrieve its value

The method `isCancelled` does exactly what it sounds like. Retrieving the value inside the `Future` is done with the `get` method, which is a blocking call that returns the generic type inside it. The method shown uses a try/catch block to deal with the declared exceptions.

The output is:

```
Processing...
Hello, World!
```

Since the submitted call returns the `Future<String>` immediately, the code prints "Processing..." right away. Then the call to `get` blocks until the `Future` completes, and then prints the result.

Of course, this is a book on Java 8, so it's worth noting that the anonymous inner class implementation of the `Callable` interface can be replaced with a lambda expression, as shown in Example 9-17.

*Example 9-17. Using a lambda expression and checking if the Future is done*

```
future = service.submit(() -> {                  ❶
    Thread.sleep(10);
    return "Hello, World!";
});

System.out.println("More processing...");

while (!future.isDone()) {                       ❷
    System.out.println("Waiting...");
}

getIfNotCancelled(future);
```

❶ Lambda expression for the `Callable`

❷ Wait until `Future` is finished

This time, in addition to using the lambda expression, the `isDone` method is invoked in a `while` loop to poll the `Future` until it is finished.

Using `isDone` in a loop is called *busy waiting* and is not generally a good idea because of the potentially millions of calls it generates. The `CompletableFuture` class, discussed in the rest of this chapter, provides a better way to react when a `Future` completes.

This time the output is:

```
More processing...
Waiting...
Waiting...
Waiting...
// ... lots more waiting ...
Waiting...
Waiting...
Hello, World!
```

Clearly a more elegant mechanism is needed to notify the developer when the `Future` is completed, especially if the plan is to use the result of this `Future` as part of another calculation. That's one of the issues addressed by `CompletableFuture`.

Finally, the `Future` interface has a `cancel` method in case you change your mind about it, as shown in Example 9-18.

*Example 9-18. Cancelling the Future*

```
future = service.submit(() -> {
    Thread.sleep(10);
    return "Hello, World!";
});

future.cancel(true);

System.out.println("Even more processing...");

getIfNotCancelled(future);
```

This code prints:

```
Even more processing...
Cancelled
```

Since `CompletableFuture` extends `Future`, all the methods covered in this recipe are available there as well.

## See Also

Completable `Futures` are discussed in Recipes 9.5, 9.6, and 9.7.

# 9.5 Completing a CompletableFuture

## Problem

You want to explicitly complete a `CompletableFuture`, giving it a value or causing it to throw an exception when the `get` method is invoked.

## Solution

Use the completedFuture, complete, or the completeExceptionally methods.

## Discussion

The CompletableFuture class implements the Future interface. The class also implements the CompletionStage interface, whose dozens of methods open up a wide range of possible use cases.

The real benefit of CompletableFuture is that it allows you to coordinate activities without writing nested callbacks. That will be the subject of the next two recipes. Here the question is how to complete a CompletableFuture when you know the value you want to return.

Say your application needs to retrieve a product based on its ID, and that the retrieval process may be expensive because it involves some kind of remote access. The cost could be a network call to a RESTful web service, or a database call, or any other relatively time-consuming mechanism.

You therefore decide to create a cache of products locally in the form of a Map. That way, when a product is requested, the system can check the map first, and if it returns null, then undergo the more expensive operation. The code in Example 9-19 represents both local and remote ways of fetching a product.

*Example 9-19. Retrieving a product*

```
private Map<Integer, Product> cache = new HashMap<>();
private Logger logger = Logger.getLogger(this.getClass().getName());

private Product getLocal(int id) {
    return cache.get(id);                                 ❶
}

private Product getRemote(int id) {
    try {
        Thread.sleep(100);                                ❷
        if (id == 666) {
            throw new RuntimeException("Evil request");   ❸
        }
    } catch (InterruptedException ignored) {
    }
    return new Product(id, "name");
}
```

❶ Returns right away, but might be null

❷ Simulate a delay followed by a retrieval

❸ Simulate a network, database, or other kind of error

The idea now is to create a `getProduct` method that takes an ID for an argument and returns a product. If you make the return type `CompletableFuture<Product>`, however, the method can return immediately and you can do other work while the retrieval actually happens.

To make this work, you need a way to complete a `CompletableFuture`. There are three methods relevant here:

```
            boolean               complete(T value)
static <U> CompletableFuture<U> completedFuture(U value)
            boolean               completeExceptionally(Throwable ex)
```

The `complete` method is used when you already have a `CompletableFuture` and you want to give it a specific value. The `completedFuture` method is a factory method that creates a `CompletableFuture` with an already-computed value. The `completeExceptionally` method completes the `Future` with a given exception.

Using them together produces the code in Example 9-20. The code assumes that you already have a legacy mechanism for returning a product from a remote system, which you want to use to complete the `Future`.

*Example 9-20. Completing a CompletableFuture*

```
public CompletableFuture<Product> getProduct(int id) {
    try {
        Product product = getLocal(id);
        if (product != null) {
            return CompletableFuture.completedFuture(product);  ❶
        } else {
            CompletableFuture<Product> future = new CompletableFuture<>();
            Product p = getRemote(id);                          ❷
            cache.put(id, p);
            future.complete(p);                                 ❸
            return future;
        }
    } catch (Exception e) {
        CompletableFuture<Product> future = new CompletableFuture<>();
        future.completeExceptionally(e);                        ❹
        return future;
    }
}
```

❶ Complete with the product from the cache if available

❷ Legacy retrieval

❸ Complete after legacy retrieval (for async, see next example)

❹ Complete with an exception if something goes wrong

The method first tries to retrieve a product from the cache. If the map returns a non-null value, then the factory method `CompletableFuture.completedFuture` is used to return it.

If the cache returns null, then remote access is necessary. The code simulates a synchronous approach (more about that later) that would presumably be the legacy code. A `CompletableFuture` is instantiated, and the `complete` method is used to populate it with the generated value.

Finally, if something goes horribly wrong (simulated here with an ID of 666), then a `RuntimeException` is thrown. The `completeExceptionally` method takes that exception as an argument and completes the `Future` with it.

The way the exception handling works is shown in the test cases in Example 9-21.

*Example 9-21. Using completeExceptionally on a CompletableFuture*

```
@Test(expected = ExecutionException.class)
public void testException() throws Exception {
    demo.getProduct(666).get();
}

@Test
public void testExceptionWithCause() throws Exception {
    try {
        demo.getProduct(666).get();
        fail("Houston, we have a problem...");
    } catch (ExecutionException e) {
        assertEquals(ExecutionException.class, e.getClass());
        assertEquals(RuntimeException.class, e.getCause().getClass());
    }
}
```

Both of these tests pass. When `completeExceptionally` is called on a `CompletableFuture`, the `get` method throws an `ExecutionException` whose cause is the exception that triggered the problem in the first place. Here that's a `RuntimeException`.

The `get` method declares an `ExecutionException`, which is a checked exception. The `join` method is the same as `get` except that it throws an unchecked `CompletionException` if completed exceptionally, again with the underlying exception as its cause.

The part of the example code most likely to be replaced is the synchronous retrieval of the product. For that, you can use `supplyAsync`, one of the other static factory methods available in `CompletableFuture`. The complete list is given by:

```
static     CompletableFuture<Void> runAsync(Runnable runnable)
static     CompletableFuture<Void> runAsync(Runnable runnable,
                                            Executor executor)

static <U> CompletableFuture<U>    supplyAsync(Supplier<U> supplier)
static <U> CompletableFuture<U>    supplyAsync(Supplier<U> supplier,
                                               Executor executor)
```

The `runAsync` methods are useful if you don't need to return anything. The `supplyAsync` methods return an object using the given `Supplier`. The single-argument methods use the default common fork-join pool, while the two-argument overloads use the executor given as the second argument.

The asynchronous version is shown in Example 9-22.

*Example 9-22. Using supplyAsync to retrieve a product*

```
public CompletableFuture<Product> getProductAsync(int id) {
    try {
        Product product = getLocal(id);
        if (product != null) {
            logger.info("getLocal with id=" + id);
            return CompletableFuture.completedFuture(product);
        } else {
            logger.info("getRemote with id=" + id);

            return CompletableFuture.supplyAsync(() -> {  ❶
                Product p = getRemote(id);
                cache.put(id, p);
                return p;
            });
        }
    } catch (Exception e) {
        logger.info("exception thrown");
        CompletableFuture<Product> future = new CompletableFuture<>();
        future.completeExceptionally(e);
        return future;
    }
}
```

❶ Same operation as before, but returns the product asynchronously

In this case, the product is retrieved in the lambda expression shown that implements `Supplier<Product>`. You could always extract that as a separate method and reduce the code here to a method reference.

The challenge is how to invoke another operation after the `CompletableFuture` has finished. Coordinating multiple `CompletableFuture` instances is the subject of the next recipe.

### See Also

The example in this recipe is based on a similar one in a blog post by Kenneth Jørgensen (*http://kennethjorgensen.com/blog/2016/introduction-to-completablefutures*).

## 9.6 Coordinating CompletableFutures, Part 1

### Problem

You want the completion of one `Future` to trigger another action.

### Solution

Use the various instance methods in `CompletableFuture` that coordinate actions, like `thenApply`, `thenCompose`, `thenRun`, and more.

### Discussion

The best part about the `CompletableFuture` class is that it makes it easy to chain `Futures` together. You can create multiple futures representing the various tasks you need to perform, and then coordinate them by having the completion of one `Future` trigger the execution of another.

As a trivial example, consider the following process:

- Ask a `Supplier` for a string holding a number
- Parse the number into an integer
- Double the number
- Print it

The code in Example 9-23 shows how simple that can be.

*Example 9-23. Coordinating tasks using a CompletableFuture*

```
private String sleepThenReturnString() {
    try {
        Thread.sleep(100);                        ❶
    } catch (InterruptedException ignored) {
    }
    return "42";
```

```
}

CompletableFuture.supplyAsync(() -> this::sleepThenReturnString)
        .thenApply(Integer::parseInt)          ❷
        .thenApply(x -> 2 * x)                 ❷
        .thenAccept(System.out::println)       ❸
        .join();                               ❹
System.out.println("Running...");
```

❶ Introduce an artificial delay

❷ Apply a function when previous stage is finished

❸ Apply a consumer when previous stage is finished

❹ Retrieve the finished result

The output is "Running..." followed by 84. The `supplyAsync` method takes a `Supplier` (in this case of type `String`). The `thenApply` method takes a `Function`, whose input argument is the result of the previous `CompletionStage`. The function in the first `thenApply` converts the string into an integer, then the function in the second `thenApply` doubles the integer. Finally, the `thenAccept` method takes a `Consumer`, which it executes when the previous stage completes.

There are many different coordination methods in `CompletableFuture`. The complete list (other than overloads, discussed following the table) is shown in Table 9-1.

*Table 9-1. Coordinating methods for CompletableFuture*

| Modifier(s) | Return type | Method name | Arguments |
| --- | --- | --- | --- |
| | `CompletableFuture<Void>` | `acceptEither` | `CompletionStage<? extends T> other, Consumer<? super T> action` |
| `static` | `CompletableFuture<Void>` | `allOf` | `CompletableFuture<?>... cfs` |
| `static` | `CompletableFuture<Object>` | `anyOf` | `CompletableFuture<?>... cfs` |
| `<U>` | `CompletableFuture<U>` | `applyToEither` | `CompletionStage<? extends T> other, Function<? super T, U> fn` |
| | `CompletableFuture<Void>` | `runAfterBoth` | `CompletionStage<?> other, Runnable action` |
| | `CompletableFuture<Void>` | `runAfterEither` | `CompletionStage<?> other, Runnable action` |
| | `CompletableFuture<Void>` | `thenAccept` | `Consumer<? super T> action` |
| `<U>` | `CompletableFuture<U>` | `thenApply` | `Function<? super T> action, ? extends U> fn` |

| Modifier(s) | Return type | Method name | Arguments |
|---|---|---|---|
| <U,V> | CompletableFuture<V> | thenCombine | CompletionStage<? extends U> other, BiFunction<? super T, ? super U, ? extends V> fn |
| <U> | CompletableFuture<U> | thenCompose | Function<? super T, ? extends CompletionStage<U>> fn |
| | Completable Future<Void> | thenRun | Runnable action |
| | CompletableFuture<T> | whenComplete | BiConsumer<? super T, ? super Throwa ble> action |

All of the methods shown in the table use the common ForkJoinPool of worker threads, whose size is equal to the total number of processors. We have already discussed the runAsync and supplyAsync methods. They are factory methods that let you specify a Runnable or a Supplier and return a CompletableFuture. As the table shows, you can then chain additional methods like thenApply or thenCompose to add tasks that will start when the previous one completes.

The table omits a set of similar patterns for each method—two for each that end in the word Async: one with an Executor and one without. For example, looking at thenAccept, the variations are:

```
CompletableFuture<Void> thenAccept(Consumer<? super T> action)
CompletableFuture<Void> thenAcceptAsync(Consumer<? super T> action)
CompletableFuture<Void> thenAcceptAsync(
  Consumer<? super T> action, Executor executor)
```

The thenAccept method executes its Consumer argument in the same thread as the original task, while the second version submits it to the pool again. The third version supplies an Executor, which is used to run the task instead of the common fork-join pool.

Choosing whether or not to use the Async versions of the methods is a trade-off. You may get faster individual task execution with asynchronous tasks, but they also add overhead, so the overall completion speed may not improve.

If you want to use your own Executor instead of the common pool, remember that the ExecutorService implements the Executor interface. The code in Example 9-24 shows a variation using a separate pool.

*Example 9-24. Running CompletableFuture tasks on a separate thread pool*

```
ExecutorService service = Executors.newFixedThreadPool(4);
```

```
CompletableFuture.supplyAsync(() -> this::sleepThenReturnString, service) ❶
        .thenApply(Integer::parseInt)
        .thenApply(x -> 2 * x)
        .thenAccept(System.out::println)
        .join();
System.out.println("Running...");
```

❶ Supply the separate pool as an argument

The subsequent `thenApply` and `thenAccept` methods use the same thread as the `supplyAsync` method. If you use `thenApplyAsync`, the task will be submitted to the pool, unless you add yet another pool as an additional argument.

### Waiting to Finish in the Common ForkJoinPool

By default, a `CompletableFuture` uses the so-called "common" fork-join pool, which is an optimized thread pool that performs *work stealing*, meaning all threads in the pool "attempt to find and execute tasks submitted to the pool and/or created by other active tasks," according to the Javadocs. One important point to note is that all the worker threads are *daemon* threads, meaning if the program exits before the threads are finished, they will be terminated.

This means that if you execute the code in Example 9-23 without the call to `join()`, you'll see only "Running..." but not the result of the `Future`. The system will terminate before the task completes.

There are two ways to fix that. One is to invoke either `get` or `join` as shown, which blocks until the result is retrieved. The other is to tell the program to wait until all threads are completed, by giving the common pool a time-out period:

```
ForkJoinPool.commonPool().awaitQuiesence(long timeout, TimeUnit unit)
```

If you give the pool a sufficiently long waiting period, the `Futures` will complete. The `awaitQuiescence` method tells the system to wait until all the worker threads are idle, or until the given time period elapses, whichever comes first.

For those `CompletableFuture` instances that return a value, you can retrieve the value using either the `get` or `join` methods. Both block until the `Future` completes or throws an exception. The difference between the two is that `get` throws a (checked) `ExecutionException`, while `join` throws an (unchecked) `CompletionException`. This means that `join` is easier to use in lambda expressions.

You can also cancel a `CompletableFuture` using the `cancel` method, which takes a boolean:

```
boolean cancel(boolean mayInterruptIfRunning)
```

If the `Future` has not already completed, this method will complete it by using a `CancellationException`. Any dependent `Futures` will also complete exceptionally with a `CompletionException` caused by the `CancellationException`. As it happens, the boolean argument does nothing.[11]

The code in Example 9-23 demonstrated the `thenApply` and `thenAccept` methods. `thenCompose` is an instance method that allows you to chain another `Future` to the original, with the added benefit that the result of the first is available in the second. The code in Example 9-25 is probably the world's most complicated way of adding two numbers.

*Example 9-25. Composing two Futures together*

```
@Test
public void compose() throws Exception {
    int x = 2;
    int y = 3;
    CompletableFuture<Integer> completableFuture =
        CompletableFuture.supplyAsync(() -> x)
            .thenCompose(n -> CompletableFuture.supplyAsync(() -> n + y));

    assertTrue(5 == completableFuture.get());
}
```

The argument to `thenCompose` is a function, which takes the result of the first `Future` and transforms it into the output of the second. If you would rather that the `Futures` be independent, you can use `thenCombine` instead, as in Example 9-26.[12]

*Example 9-26. Combining two Futures*

```
@Test
public void combine() throws Exception {
    int x = 2;
    int y = 3;
    CompletableFuture<Integer> completableFuture =
        CompletableFuture.supplyAsync(() -> x)
            .thenCombine(CompletableFuture.supplyAsync(() -> y),
                         (n1, n2) -> n1 + n2);

    assertTrue(5 == completableFuture.get());
}
```

11 Interestingly enough, according to the Javadocs the boolean parameter "has no effect because interrupts are not used to control processing."

12 OK, *this* is probably the most complicated way of adding two numbers ever.

The thenCombine method takes a Future and a BiFunction as arguments, where the results of both Futures are available in the function when computing the result.

One other special method is of note. The handle method has the signature:

```
<U> CompletableFuture<U> handle(BiFunction<? super T, Throwable, ? extends U> fn)
```

The two input arguments to the BiFunction are the result of the Future if it completes normally and the thrown exception if not. Your code decides what to return. There are also handleAsyc methods that take either a BiFunction or a BiFunction and an Executor. See Example 9-27.

*Example 9-27. Using the handle method*

```
private CompletableFuture<Integer> getIntegerCompletableFuture(String num) {
    return CompletableFuture.supplyAsync(() -> Integer.parseInt(num))
        .handle((val, exc) -> val != null ? val : 0);
}

@Test
public void handleWithException() throws Exception {
    String num = "abc";
    CompletableFuture<Integer> value = getIntegerCompletableFuture(num);
    assertTrue(value.get() == 0);
}

@Test
public void handleWithoutException() throws Exception {
    String num = "42";
    CompletableFuture<Integer> value = getIntegerCompletableFuture(num);
    assertTrue(value.get() == 42);
}
```

The example simply parses a string, looking for an integer. If the parse is successful, the integer is returned. Otherwise a ParseException is thrown and the handle method returns zero. The two tests show that the operation works in either case.

As you can see, there are a wide variety of ways you can combine tasks, both synchronously and asynchronously, on the common pool or your own executors. The next recipe gives a larger example of how they can be used.

## See Also

A more complex example is given in Recipe 9.7.

# 9.7 Coordinating CompletableFutures, Part 2

## Problem

You want to see a larger example of coordinating `CompletableFuture` instances.

## Solution

Access a set of web pages for each date in baseball season, each of which contains links to the games played on that day. Download the box score information for each game and transform it into a Java class. Then asynchronously save the data, compute the results for each game, find the game with the highest total score, and print the max score and the game in which it occurred.

## Discussion

This recipe demonstrates a more complex example than the simple demonstrations shown in the rest of this book. Hopefully it will give you an idea of what is possible, and how you might combine `CompletableFuture` tasks to accomplish your own goals.

The application relies on the fact that Major League Baseball maintains a set of web pages with the box scores of each game played on a given date.[13] Figure 9-1 shows the web page for all the games played on June 14, 2017.

13 For this example, all you need to know about baseball is that two teams play, each scores runs until one team wins, and that the collection of statistics for a game is called a box score.

← → C ⌂ ⓘ gd2.mlb.com/components/game/mlb/year_2017/month_06/day_14/

**Index of /components/game/mlb/year_2017/month_06/day_14**

- Parent Directory
- batters/
- epg.xml
- gid_2017_06_14_arimlb_detmlb_1/
- gid_2017_06_14_atlmlb_wasmlb_1/
- gid_2017_06_14_balmlb_chamlb_1/
- gid_2017_06_14_bosmlb_phimlb_1/
- gid_2017_06_14_chnmlb_nynmlb_1/
- gid_2017_06_14_cinmlb_sdnmlb_1/
- gid_2017_06_14_colmlb_pitmlb_1/
- gid_2017_06_14_kcamlb_sfnmlb_1/
- gid_2017_06_14_lanmlb_clemlb_1/
- gid_2017_06_14_milmlb_slnmlb_1/
- gid_2017_06_14_nyamlb_anamlb_1/
- gid_2017_06_14_oakmlb_miamlb_1/
- gid_2017_06_14_seamlb_minmlb_1/
- gid_2017_06_14_tbamlb_tormlb_1/
- gid_2017_06_14_texmlb_houmlb_1/
- grid.json
- grid.xml
- grid_ce.json

*Figure 9-1. Games played on June 14, 2017*

On that page, each of the links to a game begins with the letters "gid", followed by the year, month, and day, then by the code for the away team and the code for the home team. If you follow each link, the resulting site has a list of files, one of which is called *boxscore.json*.

The design of this application is to:

1. Access the site that contains the games for a range of dates.
2. Determine the game links on each page.
3. Download the *boxscore.json* file for each game.
4. Convert the JSON file for each game to a Java object.
5. Save the downloaded result into local files.
6. Determine the scores of each game.
7. Determine the game with the biggest total score.
8. Print the individual scores along with the maximum game and score.

Many of these tasks can be arranged to execute concurrently, and many can be run in parallel.

The complete code for this example is too large to fit in this book, but is available on the companion website (*https://github.com/kousen/cfboxscores*). This recipe will illustrate the uses of parallel streams and completable `Future`s.

The first challenge is to find the game links for each date in a given range. The `GamePageLinksSupplier` class in Example 9-28 implements the `Supplier` interface to produce a list of strings representing the game links.

*Example 9-28. Get the game links for a range of dates*

```
public class GamePageLinksSupplier implements Supplier<List<String>> {
    private static final String BASE =
        "http://gd2.mlb.com/components/game/mlb/";
    private LocalDate startDate;
    private int days;

    public GamePageLinksSupplier(LocalDate startDate, int days) {
        this.startDate = startDate;
        this.days = days;
    }

    public List<String> getGamePageLinks(LocalDate localDate) {
        // Use the JSoup library to parse the HTML web page and
        // extract the links that start with "gid"
    }

    @Override
    public List<String> get() {        ❶
        return Stream.iterate(startDate, d -> d.plusDays(1))
            .limit(days)
            .map(this::getGamePageLinks)
            .flatMap(list -> list.isEmpty() ? Stream.empty() : list.stream())
            .collect(Collectors.toList());
    }
}
```

❶ Required method for `Supplier<List<String>>`

The `get` method iterates over a range of dates by using the `iterate` method on `Stream`. It starts with the given date and adds days up to the limit.

The `datesUntil` method added in Java 9 to `LocalDate` produces a `Stream<LocalDate>`. See Recipe 10.7 for details.

Each `LocalDate` becomes the argument to the `getGamePageLinks` method, which uses the JSoup library (*http://jsoup.org*) to parse the HTML page, find all the links that start with "gid", and return them as strings.

The next step is to access the *boxscore.json* file at each game link. That is done using the `BoxscoreRetriever` class, which implements `Function<List<String>, List<Result>>` and is shown in Example 9-29.

*Example 9-29. Retrieving the list of box scores from the list of game links*

```
public class BoxscoreRetriever implements Function<List<String>, List<Result>> {
    private static final String BASE =
        "http://gd2.mlb.com/components/game/mlb/";

    private OkHttpClient client = new OkHttpClient();
    private Gson gson = new Gson();

    @SuppressWarnings("ConstantConditions")
    public Optional<Result> gamePattern2Result(String pattern) {
        // ... code omitted ...
        String boxscoreUrl = BASE + dateUrl + pattern + "boxscore.json";

        // .. set up OkHttp to make the network call ...
        try {
            // ... get the response ...
            if (!response.isSuccessful()) {
                System.out.println("Box score not found for " + boxscoreUrl);
                return Optional.empty();        ❶
            }

            return Optional.ofNullable(
                gson.fromJson(response.body().charStream(), Result.class)); ❷
        } catch (IOException e) {
            e.printStackTrace();
            return Optional.empty();            ❶
        }
    }

    @Override
    public List<Result> apply(List<String> strings) {
        return strings.parallelStream()
                .map(this::gamePattern2Result)
                .filter(Optional::isPresent)
                .map(Optional::get)
                .collect(Collectors.toList());
    }
}
```

❶ If no box score is found (due to rain or other problem), return an empty `Optional`

❷ Use Gson to convert the JSON into a `Result`

This class relies on the OkHttp library (*http://square.github.io/okhttp/*) and the Gson JSON parsing library (*https://github.com/google/gson*) to download the box score in JSON form and convert it into an object of type `Result`. The class implements the `Function` interface, so it implements the `apply` method to convert the list of strings into a list of results. A box score for a given game may not exist if the game is rained out or if some other network error occurs, so the `game Pattern2Result` method returns an `Optional<Result>`, which is empty in those cases.

The `apply` method streams over the game links, converting each one into an `Optional<Result>`. Next it filters the stream, passing only the `Optional` instances that are not empty, and then invokes the `get` method on each one. Finally it collects them into a list of results.

Java 9 also adds a `stream` method to `Optional`, which would simplify the `filter(Optional::isPresent)` followed by `map(Optional::get)` process. See Recipe 10.6 for details.

Once the box scores are retrieved, they can be saved locally. This can be done in the methods shown in Example 9-30.

*Example 9-30. Save each box score to a file*

```
private void saveResultList(List<Result> results) {
    results.parallelStream().forEach(this::saveResultToFile);
}

public void saveResultToFile(Result result) {
    // ... determine a file name based on the date and team names ...
    try {
        File file = new File(dir + "/" + fileName);
        Files.write(file.toPath().toAbsolutePath(),      ❶
                    gson.toJson(result).getBytes());
    } catch (IOException e) {
        e.printStackTrace();
    }
}
```

❶ Create or overwrite file, then close it

The `Files.write` method with its default options creates a file if it doesn't exist or overwrites it if it does, then closes it.

Two other postprocessing methods are used. One, called `getMaxScore`, determines the maximum total score from a given game. The other, called `getMaxGame`, returns the game with the max score. Both are shown in Example 9-31.

*Example 9-31. Getting the maximum total score and the game where it occurred*

```
private int getTotalScore(Result result) {
    // ... sum the scores of both teams ...
}

public OptionalInt getMaxScore(List<Result> results) {
    return results.stream()
            .mapToInt(this::getTotalScore)
            .max();
}

public Optional<Result> getMaxGame(List<Result> results) {
    return results.stream()
            .max(Comparator.comparingInt(this::getTotalScore));
}
```

Now, at last, all of the preceding methods and classes can be combined with completable `Futures`. See Example 9-32 for the main application code.

*Example 9-32. Main application code*

```
public void printGames(LocalDate startDate, int days) {
    CompletableFuture<List<Result>> future =
        CompletableFuture.supplyAsync(
            new GamePageLinksSupplier(startDate, days))
                .thenApply(new BoxscoreRetriever());           ❶

    CompletableFuture<Void> futureWrite =
        future.thenAcceptAsync(this::saveResultList)           ❷
            .exceptionally(ex -> {
                System.err.println(ex.getMessage());
                return null;
            });

    CompletableFuture<OptionalInt> futureMaxScore =
        future.thenApplyAsync(this::getMaxScore);
    CompletableFuture<Optional<Result>> futureMaxGame =
        future.thenApplyAsync(this::getMaxGame);
    CompletableFuture<String> futureMax =
        futureMaxScore.thenCombineAsync(futureMaxGame,         ❸
            (score, result) ->
                String.format("Highest score: %d, Max Game: %s",
                              score.orElse(0), result.orElse(null)));

    CompletableFuture.allOf(futureWrite, futureMax).join(); ❹

    future.join().forEach(System.out::println);
    System.out.println(futureMax.join());
}
```

❶ Coordinated tasks to retrieve the box scores

❷ Save to files, completing exceptionally if problems occur

❸ Combine the two max tasks

❹ Complete everything

Several `CompletableFuture` instances are created. The first uses the `GamePageLinksSupplier` to retrieve all the game page links for the desired dates, then applies the `BoxscoreRetriever` to convert them into results. The second sets up writing each one to disk, completing exceptionally if something goes wrong. Then the post-processing steps of finding the maximum total score and the game in which it occurred are set up.[14] The `allOf` method is used to complete all of the tasks, then the results are printed.

Note the use of `thenApplyAsync`, which isn't strictly necessary, but allows for the tasks to run asynchronously.

If you run the program for May 5, 2017, for three days, you get:

```
GamePageParser parser = new GamePageParser();
parser.printGames(LocalDate.of(2017, Month.MAY, 5), 3);
```

The output results are:

```
Box score not found for Los Angeles at San Diego on May 5, 2017
May 5, 2017: Arizona Diamondbacks 6, Colorado Rockies 3
May 5, 2017: Boston Red Sox 3, Minnesota Twins 4
May 5, 2017: Chicago White Sox 2, Baltimore Orioles 4
// ... more scores ...
May 7, 2017: Toronto Blue Jays 2, Tampa Bay Rays 1
May 7, 2017: Washington Nationals 5, Philadelphia Phillies 6
Highest score: 23, Max Game: May 7, 2017: Boston Red Sox 17, Minnesota Twins 6
```

Hopefully this will give you a sense of how you can combine many features discussed throughout this book, from future tasks using `CompletableFuture` to functional interfaces like `Supplier` and `Function` to classes like `Optional`, `Stream`, and `LocalDate`, and even methods like `map`, `filter`, and `flatMap`, to accomplish an interesting problem.

## See Also

The coordination methods for completable `Futures` are discussed in Recipe 9.6.

14 Clearly this could be done together, but it makes for a nice `thenCombine` example.

CHAPTER 10

# Java 9 Additions

At the time of this writing, Java SDK 9 is considered feature complete, but not yet released. The new feature garnering the most press coverage is Project Jigsaw, which introduces a new modularization mechanism into the language.

This chapter contains recipes involving the new additions, like private methods in interfaces, factory methods for immutable collections, and the new methods for streams, `Optional`, and `Collectors`. Each of the recipes has been tested with Java SE 9 Early Access build 174.

FYI, the new features in Java 9 *not* covered in this chapter are:

- The `jshell` interactive console
- The modified `try-with-resources` block
- The relaxed syntax for the diamond operator
- The new deprecation warnings
- The reactive streams classes
- The stack-walking API
- The revised `Process` class

Several are relatively minor (like the diamond operator changes, `try-with-resources` requirements, and deprecation warnings). Some are specialty topics (like the stack-walking API and the changes to the Process API). The new shell is covered heavily in the documentation, along with a tutorial.

Finally, the reactive streams additions are fascinating, but the open source community already provides APIs like Reactive Streams (*http://www.reactive-streams.org/*),

RxJava, and more, and it might be a good idea to wait to see how the community decides to support the new Java 9 API.

The recipes in this chapter hopefully cover the most common use cases. Should that turn out not to be the case, more recipes will be added in the next edition of this book.[1]

The recipes in this chapter also have a different feel to them from the rest of the book. This book has been use-case driven, in that each recipe is supposed to solve a particular type of problem. In this chapter, some of the recipes are just placeholders for discussions about new features in the API.

## 10.1 Modules in Jigsaw

### Problem

You want to access Java modules from the standard library, and encapsulate your own code in modules.

### Solution

Learn the basics of Jigsaw modules and learn how to use the modularized JDK. Then wait for the final release of Java 9 to make any upgrade-related decisions.

### Discussion

JSR 376, the Java Platform Module System, is both the biggest change coming in Java 9 and the most controversial one. Attempts have been made to modularize Java for nearly ten years,[2] with varying degrees of success and adoption, culminating in JPMS.

While the goal of "strong" encapsulation enforced by a module system has benefits for maintenance, no new feature comes without a cost. In this case, making such a fundamental change to a language with twenty years of backward compatibility to maintain is bound to be difficult.

For example, the concept of *modules* changes the nature of `public` and `private`. If a module does not export a particular package, you can't access classes inside it even if they are made `public`. Likewise, you can no longer use reflection to access non-public members of a class that isn't in an exported package. This affects reflection-based libraries and frameworks (including popular ones like Spring and Hibernate), as well as virtually every non-Java language on the JVM. As a concession, the team

1 They may even have the details of Jigsaw worked out by then. Here's hoping. :)

2 The Jigsaw project itself was created in 2008.

has proposed that a command-line flag called `--illegal-access=permit` will be the default in Java 9 and disallowed in a future release (*http://bit.ly/javanews-may-2017*).

At the time of this writing (late June 2017), the inclusion of the JPMS specification in Java 9 has been rejected once, but is under revision in preparation for another vote.[3] In addition, the release date of Java 9 has been pushed back to late September 2017.

Still, it is likely that some form of Jigsaw will be included in Java 9, and its basic capabilities are well established. The purpose of this recipe is to give you the necessary background on those basics, so that if and when the JPMS system is adopted, you'll be ready to take advantage of it.

The first thing to know is that you do not have to modularize your own code. The Java libraries have been modularized, and other dependency libraries are the process of doing so, but you can wait to do the same for your own code until the system stabilizes.

### Modules

The new system defines modules, which have a name (except for the so-called *unnamed* module) and express their dependencies and export packages via a file called *module-info.java*. A module includes a compiled *module-info.class* inside its deliverable JAR. The *module-info.java* file is known as a *module descriptor*.

The contents of *module-info.java* start with the word `module` and then use a combination of `requires` and `exports` keywords to describe what the module does. To demonstrate this, following is a trivial "Hello, World!" example that will use two modules and the JVM.

The example modules are `com.oreilly.suppliers` and `com.kousenit.clients`.

The "reversed URL" pattern is currently the recommended naming convention for modules.

The former supplies a `Stream` of strings representing names. The latter prints each name to the console with a welcome message.

For the `Supplier` module, the source code for the `NamesSupplier` class is shown in Example 10-1.

3 In the second vote, which ended June 26, the JPMS specification was unanimously approved (with one abstention). See *https://jcp.org/en/jsr/results?id=6016* for the detailed results.

*Example 10-1. Supplying a stream of names*

```
package com.oreilly.suppliers;

// imports ...

public class NamesSupplier implements Supplier<Stream<String>> {
    private Path namesPath = Paths.get("server/src/main/resources/names.txt");

    @Override
    public Stream<String> get() {
        try {
            return Files.lines(namesPath);
        } catch (IOException e) {
            e.printStackTrace();
            return null;
        }
    }
}
```

(The module is stored in an IntelliJ module—unfortunately IntelliJ IDEA also uses the word "module" for a different concept—called "server," which is why that name is in the path for the text file.)

The contents of *names.txt* are:[4]

```
Londo
Vir
G'Kar
Na'Toth
Delenn
Lennier
Kosh
```

In the client module, the source code for the `Main` class is in Example 10-2.

*Example 10-2. Printing the names*

```
package com.kousenit.clients;

// imports ...

public class Main {
    public static void main(String[] args) throws IOException {
        NamesSupplier supplier = new NamesSupplier();

        try (Stream<String> lines = supplier.get()) { ❶
```

4 It's about time there was a *Babylon 5* reference in this book. Presumably the space station was built out of modules, too (sorry).

```
            lines.forEach(line -> System.out.printf("Hello, %s!%n", line));
        }
    }
}
```

❶ `try-with-resources` auto-closes stream

The *module-info.java* file for the `Supplier` code is shown in Example 10-3.

*Example 10-3. Defining the Supplier module*

```
module com.oreilly.suppliers {      ❶
    exports com.oreilly.suppliers;  ❷
}
```

❶ Module name

❷ Make module available to others

The *module-info.java* file for the client module is shown in Example 10-4.

*Example 10-4. Defining the client module*

```
module com.kousenit.clients {       ❶
    requires com.oreilly.suppliers; ❷
}
```

❶ Module name

❷ Needs `Supplier` module

When this program is executed, the output is:

```
Hello, Vir!
Hello, G'Kar!
Hello, Na'Toth!
Hello, Delenn!
Hello, Lennier!
Hello, Kosh!
```

The `exports` clause is necessary in the `Supplier` module for the `NamesSupplier` class to be visible to the client. The `requires` clause in the client module tells the system that this module needs classes from the `Supplier` module.

If you would like to log accesses to the server in that module, you can add a `Logger` from the `java.util.logging` package in the JVM, as in Example 10-5.

*Example 10-5. Add logging to Supplier module*

```
public class NamesSupplier implements Supplier<Stream<String>> {
    private Path namesPath = Paths.get("server/src/main/resources/names.txt");
    private Logger logger = Logger.getLogger(this.getClass().getName()); ❶

    @Override
    public Stream<String> get() {
        logger.info("Request for names on " + Instant.now());          ❷
        try {
            return Files.lines(namesPath);
        } catch (IOException e) {
            e.printStackTrace();
            return null;
        }
    }
}
```

❶ Create a Java util logger

❷ Log accesses with a timestamp

This code will not compile. The JVM has been modularized as part of Java 9, and the `java.util.logging` package is not part of `java.base`, which is the only module provided by the JVM by default. In order to use the `Logger` class, you need to update the *module-info.java* file to match that in Example 10-6.

*Example 10-6. Updated module-info.java file*

```
module com.oreilly.suppliers {
    requires java.logging;          ❶
    exports com.oreilly.suppliers;
}
```

❶ Require a module from the JVM other than `java.base`

The JVM modules are each documented with their own *module-info.java* files. For instance, Example 10-7 shows the *module-info.java* file from the `java.logging` module.

*Example 10-7. The module-info.java file for the Java Logging API*

```
module java.logging {
    exports java.util.logging;
    provides jdk.internal.logger.DefaultLoggerFinder with
        sun.util.logging.internal.LoggingProviderImpl;
}
```

This file does not only exports the module. It also provides an internal implementation of a Service Provider Interface (SPI) `DefaultLoggerFinder` in the form of the `LoggingProviderImpl` class when a logger is requested by a client.

Jigsaw also establishes mechanisms for working with service locators and providers. See the documentation for details.

Hopefully this gives you a sense of how modules are defined and how they work together. Expect to hear much more about this in the coming months.

There are many more issues related to modules that will be resolved before the specification is approved. Many of them involve porting legacy code. Terms like the unnamed module and automatic modules involve code that is not in any module but on the "module path," and modules formed by existing legacy JAR files. Much of the debate about JPMS is about how to handle those cases.

## See Also

The development of Jigsaw is part of the Open JDK project. See the quick-start guide at *http://openjdk.java.net/projects/jigsaw/quick-start*. The current documentation is at *http://openjdk.java.net/projects/jigsaw/spec/sotms/* (entitled "State of the Module System").

# 10.2 Private Methods in Interfaces

## Problem

You want to add private methods to interfaces that can be called by other methods in the interface.

## Solution

Java SE 9 now supports using the `private` keyword on interface methods.

## Discussion

In Java SE 8, for the first time developers could add implementations to interface methods, labeling them as `default` or `static`. The next logical step was to add `private` methods as well.

Private methods use the keyword `private` and must have an implementation. Like private methods in classes, they cannot be overridden. Even more, they can only be invoked from within the same source file.

Example 10-8 is somewhat contrived, but still illustrative.

*Example 10-8. Private method in an interface*

```
import java.util.function.IntPredicate;
import java.util.stream.IntStream;

public interface SumNumbers {
    default int addEvens(int... nums) {
        return add(n -> n % 2 == 0, nums);
    }

    default int addOdds(int... nums) {
        return add(n -> n % 2 != 0, nums);
    }

    private int add(IntPredicate predicate, int... nums) { ❶
        return IntStream.of(nums)
                .filter(predicate)
                .sum();
    }
}
```

❶ Private method

The `addEvens` and `addOdds` methods are both `public` (because the default access in an interface is public) and take a variable argument list of integers as an argument. The provided `default` implementation for each delegates to the `add` method, which also takes an `IntPredicate` as an argument. By making `add` private, it is not accessible to any client, even through a class that implements the interface.

Example 10-9 shows how the method is used.

*Example 10-9. Testing the private interface method*

```
class PrivateDemo implements SumNumbers {} ❶

import org.junit.Test;
import static org.junit.Assert.*;

public class SumNumbersTest {
    private SumNumbers demo = new PrivateDemo();

    @Test
    public void addEvens() throws Exception {
```

```
        assertEquals(2 + 4 + 6, demo.addEvens(1, 2, 3, 4, 5, 6)); ❷
    }

    @Test
    public void addOdds() throws Exception {
        assertEquals(1 + 3 + 5, demo.addOdds(1, 2, 3, 4, 5, 6)); ❷
    }
}
```

❶ Class that implements the interface

❷ Invoking public methods that delegate to the private method

You can only instantiate a class, so an empty class called `PrivateDemo` is created that implements the `SumNumbers` interface. That class is instantiated, and its public interface methods can be invoked.

# 10.3 Creating Immutable Collections

## Problem

You want to create immutable lists, sets, or maps in Java 9.

## Solution

Use the static factory methods `List.of`, `Set.of`, and `Map.of` available in Java 9.

## Discussion

The Javadocs on Java 9 state that the `List.of()` static factory methods provide a convenient way to create immutable lists. The `List` instances created by these methods have the following characteristics:

- They are structurally immutable. Elements cannot be added, removed, or replaced. Calling any mutator method will always cause `UnsupportedOperationException` to be thrown. However, if the contained elements are themselves mutable, this may cause the List's contents to appear to change.
- They disallow null elements. Attempts to create them with null elements result in `NullPointerException`.
- They are serializable if all elements are serializable.
- The order of elements in the list is the same as the order of the provided arguments, or of the elements in the provided array.
- They are serialized as specified on the Serialized Form page.

The available overloads of the `of` method for `List` are shown in Example 10-10.

*Example 10-10. Static factory methods for creating immutable lists*

```
static <E> List<E>      of()
static <E> List<E>      of(E e1)
static <E> List<E>      of(E e1, E e2)
static <E> List<E>      of(E e1, E e2, E e3)
static <E> List<E>      of(E e1, E e2, E e3, E e4)
static <E> List<E>      of(E e1, E e2, E e3, E e4, E e5)
static <E> List<E>      of(E e1, E e2, E e3, E e4, E e5, E e6)
static <E> List<E>      of(E e1, E e2, E e3, E e4, E e5, E e6, E e7)
static <E> List<E>      of(E e1, E e2, E e3, E e4, E e5, E e6, E e7, E e8)
static <E> List<E>      of(E e1, E e2, E e3, E e4, E e5, E e6, E e7, E e8, E e9)
static <E> List<E>      of(E e1, E e2, E e3, E e4, E e5, E e6, E e7, E e8, E e9,
    E e10)
static <E> List<E>      of(E... elements)
```

The resulting lists are, as the docs say, *structurally* immutable, so none of the normal mutator methods on `List` can be invoked: `add`, `addAll`, `clear`, `remove`, `removeAll`, `replaceAll`, and `set` all throw `UnsupportedOperationException`. A couple of test cases[5] are shown in Example 10-11.

*Example 10-11. Demonstrating immutability*

```
@Test(expected = UnsupportedOperationException.class)
public void showImmutabilityAdd() throws Exception {
    List<Integer> intList = List.of(1, 2, 3);
    intList.add(99);
}

@Test(expected = UnsupportedOperationException.class)
public void showImmutabilityClear() throws Exception {
    List<Integer> intList = List.of(1, 2, 3);
    intList.clear();
}

@Test(expected = UnsupportedOperationException.class)
public void showImmutabilityRemove() throws Exception {
    List<Integer> intList = List.of(1, 2, 3);
    intList.remove(0);
}

@Test(expected = UnsupportedOperationException.class)
public void showImmutabilityReplace() throws Exception {
    List<Integer> intList = List.of(1, 2, 3);
```

5 The complete set of tests is in the source code for the book.

```
    intList.replaceAll(n -> -n);
}

@Test(expected = UnsupportedOperationException.class)
public void showImmutabilitySet() throws Exception {
    List<Integer> intList = List.of(1, 2, 3);
    intList.set(0, 99);
}
```

If the contained objects are themselves mutable, however, a list of them can appear to change. Say you have a simple class that holds a mutable value, an in Example 10-12.

*Example 10-12. A trivial class that holds a mutable value*

```
public class Holder {
    private int x;

    public Holder(int x) { this.x = x; }

    public void setX(int x) {
        this.x = x;
    }

    public int getX() {
        return x;
    }
}
```

If you create an immutable list of holders, the values in the holders can change, which makes the list appear to change, as in Example 10-13.

*Example 10-13. Changing the wrapped integer*

```
@Test
public void areWeImmutableOrArentWe() throws Exception {
    List<Holder> holders = List.of(new Holder(1), new Holder(2)); ❶
    assertEquals(1, holders.get(0).getX());

    holders.get(0).setX(4);                                      ❷
    assertEquals(4, holders.get(0).getX());
}
```

❶ Immutable list of `Holder` instances

❷ Change the contained value inside a `Holder`

This works, but it violates the spirit of the law, if not the letter. In other words, if you're going to make an immutable list, try to have it contain immutable objects.

For sets (again from the Javadocs):

- They reject duplicate elements at creation time. Duplicate elements passed to a static factory method result in `IllegalArgumentException`.
- The iteration order of set elements is unspecified and is subject to change.

All of the `of` methods have the same signature as the corresponding `List` methods, except that they return `Set<E>`.

Maps are the same way, but the signatures of the `of` methods take alternating keys and values as arguments, as in Example 10-14.

*Example 10-14. Static factory methods for creating immutable maps*

```
static <K,V> Map<K,V>   of()
static <K,V> Map<K,V>   of(K k1, V v1)
static <K,V> Map<K,V>   of(K k1, V v1, K k2, V v2)
static <K,V> Map<K,V>   of(K k1, V v1, K k2, V v2, K k3, V v3)
static <K,V> Map<K,V>   of(K k1, V v1, K k2, V v2, K k3, V v3,
    K k4, V v4)
static <K,V> Map<K,V>   of(K k1, V v1, K k2, V v2, K k3, V v3,
    K k4, V v4, K k5, V v5)
static <K,V> Map<K,V>   of(K k1, V v1, K k2, V v2, K k3, V v3,
    K k4, V v4, K k5, V v5, K k6, V v6)
static <K,V> Map<K,V>   of(K k1, V v1, K k2, V v2, K k3, V v3,
    K k4, V v4, K k5, V v5, K k6, V v6, K k7, V v7)
static <K,V> Map<K,V>   of(K k1, V v1, K k2, V v2, K k3, V v3,
    K k4, V v4, K k5, V v5, K k6, V v6, K k7, V v7, K k8, V v8)
static <K,V> Map<K,V>   of(K k1, V v1, K k2, V v2, K k3, V v3,
    K k4, V v4, K k5, V v5, K k6, V v6, K k7, V v7, K k8, V v8,
    K k9, V v9)
static <K,V> Map<K,V>   of(K k1, V v1, K k2, V v2, K k3, V v3,
    K k4, V v4, K k5, V v5, K k6, V v6, K k7, V v7, K k8, V v8,
    K k9, V v9, K k10, V v10)
static <K,V> Map<K,V>   ofEntries(Map.Entry<? extends K,? extends V>... entries)
```

For creating maps of up to 10 entries, use the associated `of` methods that alternate the keys and the values. That can be awkward, so the interface also provides the `ofEntries` method and a static `entry` method for creating them:

```
static <K,V> Map<K,V> ofEntries(Map.Entry<? extends K,? extends V>... entries)
static <K,V> Map.Entry<K,V>     entry(K k, V v)
```

The code in Example 10-15 shows how to use those methods to create an immutable map.

*Example 10-15. Immutable map from entries*

```
@Test
public void immutableMapFromEntries() throws Exception {
    Map<String, String> jvmLanguages = Map.ofEntries(                ❶
        Map.entry("Java", "http://www.oracle.com/technetwork/java/index.html"),
        Map.entry("Groovy", "http://groovy-lang.org/"),
        Map.entry("Scala", "http://www.scala-lang.org/"),
        Map.entry("Clojure", "https://clojure.org/"),
        Map.entry("Kotlin", "http://kotlinlang.org/"));

    Set<String> names = Set.of("Java", "Scala", "Groovy", "Clojure", "Kotlin");
    List<String> urls = List.of("http://www.oracle.com/technetwork/java/index.html",
            "http://groovy-lang.org/",
            "http://www.scala-lang.org/",
            "https://clojure.org/",
            "http://kotlinlang.org/");

    Set<String> keys = jvmLanguages.keySet();
    Collection<String> values = jvmLanguages.values();

    names.forEach(name -> assertTrue(keys.contains(name)));
    urls.forEach(url -> assertTrue(values.contains(url)));

    Map<String, String> javaMap = Map.of("Java",                     ❷
            "http://www.oracle.com/technetwork/java/index.html",
            "Groovy",
            "http://groovy-lang.org/",
            "Scala",
            "http://www.scala-lang.org/",
            "Clojure",
            "https://clojure.org/",
            "Kotlin",
            "http://kotlinlang.org/");
    javaMap.forEach((name, url) -> assertTrue(
            jvmLanguages.keySet().contains(name) && \
              jvmLanguages.values().contains(url)));
}
```

❶ Using `Map.ofEntries`

❷ Using `Map.of`

The combination of the `ofEntries` and `entry` methods is a nice simplification.

## See Also

Recipe 4.8 discusses how to create immutable collections using Java 8 or earlier.

# 10.4 Stream: ofNullable, iterate, takeWhile, and dropWhile

## Problem

You want to use the new functionality added to streams in Java 9.

## Solution

Use the new `Stream` methods `ofNullable`, `iterate`, `takeWhile`, and `dropWhile`.

## Discussion

A few new methods have been added to the `Stream` interface in Java 9. This recipe will show how to use `ofNullable`, `iterate`, `takeWhile`, and `dropWhile`.

### The ofNullable method

In Java 8, the `Stream` interface has an overloaded static factory method called `of`, which takes either a single value or a variable argument list. Either way, you can't use a null argument.

In Java 9, the `ofNullable` method lets you create a single-element stream that wraps a value if not null, or is an empty stream otherwise. See the test case in Example 10-16 for details.

*Example 10-16. Using Stream.ofNullable(arg)*

```
@Test
public void ofNullable() throws Exception {
    Stream<String> stream = Stream.ofNullable("abc");  ❶
    assertEquals(1, stream.count());

    stream = Stream.ofNullable(null);                   ❷
    assertEquals(0, stream.count());
}
```

❶ Stream with one element

❷ Returns `Stream.empty()`

The `count` method returns the number of nonempty elements in a stream. You can now use the `ofNullable` method on any argument without checking whether or not it's null first.

### Using iterate with a Predicate

The next interesting method is a new overload for `iterate`. The `iterate` method in Java 8 has the signature:

```
static<T> Stream<T> iterate(final T seed, final UnaryOperator<T> f)
```

So creating a stream starts with a single element (the seed), and subsequent elements are produced by successively applying the unary operator. The result is an infinite stream, so using it normally requires a `limit` or some other short-circuiting function, like `findFirst` or `findAny`.

The new overloaded version of `iterate` takes a `Predicate` as the second argument:

```
static<T> Stream<T> iterate(T seed, Predicate<? super T> hasNext,
    UnaryOperator<T> next)
```

The values are produced by starting with the seed and then applying the unary operator as long as the values satisfy the `hasNext` predicate.

For instance, see Example 10-17.

*Example 10-17. Iterate with a Predicate*

```
@Test
public void iterate() throws Exception {
    List<BigDecimal> bigDecimals =                   ❶
            Stream.iterate(BigDecimal.ZERO, bd -> bd.add(BigDecimal.ONE))
            .limit(10)
            .collect(Collectors.toList());

    assertEquals(10, bigDecimals.size());

    bigDecimals = Stream.iterate(BigDecimal.ZERO,    ❷
            bd -> bd.longValue() < 10L,
            bd -> bd.add(BigDecimal.ONE))
            .collect(Collectors.toList());

    assertEquals(10, bigDecimals.size());
}
```

❶ Java 8 way to create a stream of big decimals

❷ Java 9 way

The first stream is the Java 8 way of using `iterate` with a `limit`. The second one uses a `Predicate` as the second argument. The result looks more like a traditional `for` loop.

### takeWhile and dropWhile

The new methods `takeWhile` and `dropWhile` allow you to get portions of a stream based on a predicate. According to the Javadocs, on an ordered stream, `takeWhile` returns "the longest prefix of elements taken from this stream that match the given predicate," starting at the beginning of the stream.

The `dropWhile` method does the opposite—it returns the remaining elements of the stream after dropping the longest prefix of elements that satisfy the predicate.

The code in Example 10-18 shows how they work on an ordered stream.

*Example 10-18. Taking and dropping from a stream*

```
@Test
public void takeWhile() throws Exception {
    List<String> strings = Stream.of("this is a list of strings".split(" "))
            .takeWhile(s -> !s.equals("of"))  ❶
            .collect(Collectors.toList());
    List<String> correct = Arrays.asList("this", "is", "a", "list");
    assertEquals(correct, strings);
}

@Test
public void dropWhile() throws Exception {
    List<String> strings = Stream.of("this is a list of strings".split(" "))
            .dropWhile(s -> !s.equals("of"))  ❷
            .collect(Collectors.toList());
    List<String> correct = Arrays.asList("of", "strings");
    assertEquals(correct, strings);
}
```

❶ Return stream up to where predicate fails

❷ Return stream after predicate fails

Each method splits the stream at the same place, but `takeWhile` returns the elements before the split and `dropWhile` returns the elements after it.

The real advantage to `takeWhile` is that it is a short-circuiting operation. If you have a huge collection of sorted elements, you can stop evaluating once you hit the condition you care about.

For example, say you had a collection of orders from a client, sorted by value in descending order. Using `takeWhile`, you can get just the orders above a certain threshold, without having to apply a filter on every element.

The code in Example 10-19 simulates this situation by generating 50 random integers between 0 and 50, sorting them in descending order, and returning only those whose value is greater than 70.

*Example 10-19. Taking ints above 70*

```
Random random = new Random();
List<Integer> nums = random.ints(50, 0, 100) ❶
        .boxed()                             ❷
        .sorted(Comparator.reverseOrder())
        .takeWhile(n -> n > 90)              ❸
        .collect(Collectors.toList());
```

❶ Generate 50 random ints between 0 and 100

❷ Box them so they can be sorted with a `Comparator` and collected

❸ Split the stream and return the values greater than 70

This particular example is perhaps more intuitive (though not necessarily more efficient) using `dropWhile` instead, as in Example 10-20.

*Example 10-20. Using dropWhile on the integer stream*

```
Random random = new Random();
List<Integer> nums = random.ints(50, 0, 100)
        .sorted()                ❶
        .dropWhile(n -> n < 90)  ❷
        .boxed()
        .collect(Collectors.toList());
```

❶ Sorted in ascending order

❷ Split after the last value less than 90

Methods like `takeWhile` and `dropWhile` have existed in other languages for years. In Java 9 they're available to Java as well.

# 10.5 Downstream Collectors: filtering and flatMapping

## Problem

You want to filter elements as part of a downstream collector, or flatten a generated collection of collections.

## Solution

Java 9 introduces the `filtering` and `flatMapping` methods in `Collectors` for those purposes.

## Discussion

Java 8 introduced a `groupingBy` operation in `Collectors`, so that you can group objects by a particular property. Grouping operations produce a map of keys to lists of values. Java 8 also allows you to use *downstream* collectors, so that instead of generating lists, you can postprocess the lists to get their sizes, or map them to something else, and so on.

Java 9 introduced two new downstream collectors: `filtering` and `flatMapping`.

### The filtering method

Say you have a class called `Task` that has attributes for a budget and a list of developers working on it, which are represented by instances of a `Developer` class. Both classes are shown in Example 10-21.

*Example 10-21. Tasks and Developers*

```
public class Task {
    private String name;
    private long budget;
    private List<Developer> developers = new ArrayList<>();

    // ... constructors, getters and setters, etc. ...
}

public class Developer {
    private String name;

    // ... constructors, getters and setters, etc. ...
}
```

First, say you want to group the tasks by budget. A simple `Collectors.groupingBy` operation is shown in Example 10-22.

*Example 10-22. Grouping tasks by budget*

```
Developer venkat = new Developer("Venkat");
Developer daniel = new Developer("Daniel");
Developer brian = new Developer("Brian");
Developer matt = new Developer("Matt");
Developer nate = new Developer("Nate");
Developer craig = new Developer("Craig");
```

```
Developer ken = new Developer("Ken");

Task java = new Task("Java stuff", 100);
Task altJvm = new Task("Groovy/Kotlin/Scala/Clojure", 50);
Task javaScript = new Task("JavaScript (sorry)", 100);
Task spring = new Task("Spring", 50);
Task jpa = new Task("JPA/Hibernate", 20);

java.addDevelopers(venkat, daniel, brian, ken);
javaScript.addDevelopers(venkat, nate);
spring.addDevelopers(craig, matt, nate, ken);
altJvm.addDevelopers(venkat, daniel, ken);

List<Task> tasks = Arrays.asList(java, altJvm, javaScript, spring, jpa);

Map<Long, List<Task>> taskMap = tasks.stream()
        .collect(groupingBy(Task::getBudget));
```

This results in a `Map` of budget amounts to lists of tasks with that budget:

```
 50: [Groovy/Kotlin/Scala/Clojure, Spring]
 20: [JPA/Hibernate]
100: [Java stuff, JavaScript (sorry)]
```

Now, if you only want tasks that have a budget that exceeds some threshold, you can add a `filter` operation, as in Example 10-23.

*Example 10-23. Grouping with a filter*

```
taskMap = tasks.stream()
        .filter(task -> task.getBudget() >= THRESHOLD)
        .collect(groupingBy(Task::getBudget));
```

The output for a threshold of 50 is:

```
 50: [Groovy/Kotlin/Scala/Clojure, Spring]
100: [Java stuff, JavaScript (sorry)]
```

Tasks with budgets below the threshold will not appear in the output map at all. If you want to see them anyway, you now have an alternative. In Java 9, the `Collectors` class now has an additional static method called `filtering`, similar to `filter`, but applied to the downstream list of tasks. The code in Example 10-24 shows how to use it.

*Example 10-24. Grouping with a downstream filter*

```
taskMap = tasks.stream()
    .collect(groupingBy(Task::getBudget,
          filtering(task -> task.getBudget() >= 50, toList())));
```

Now all the budget values will appear as keys, but the tasks whose budgets fall below the threshold will not appear in the list values:

```
 50: [Groovy/Kotlin/Scala/Clojure, Spring]
 20: []
100: [Java stuff, JavaScript (sorry)]
```

The `filtering` operation is thus a downstream collector, operating on the list generated by the grouping operation.

### The flatMapping method

This time, say you want to get a list of developers on each task. The basic grouping operation produces a group of task names to lists of tasks, as in Example 10-25.

*Example 10-25. Grouping tasks by names*

```
Map<String, List<Task>> tasksByName = tasks.stream()
        .collect(groupingBy(Task::getName));
```

The (formatted) output is:

```
                 Java stuff: [Java stuff]
Groovy/Kotlin/Scala/Clojure: [Groovy/Kotlin/Scala/Clojure]
         JavaScript (sorry): [JavaScript (sorry)]
                     Spring: [Spring]
               JPA/Hibenate: [JPA/Hibernate]
```

To get the associated lists of developers, you can use the `mappingBy` downstream collector, as in Example 10-26.

*Example 10-26. Lists of developers for each task*

```
Map<String, Set<List<Developer>>> map = tasks.stream()
        .collect(groupingBy(Task::getName,
              Collectors.mapping(Task::getDevelopers, toSet())));
```

As the return type shows, the problem is that it returns a `Set<List<Developer>>`. What's needed here is a downstream `flatMap` operation to flatten the collection of collections. That's now possible using the `flatMapping` method on `Collectors`, as in Example 10-27.

*Example 10-27. Using flatMapping to get just a set of developers*

```
Map<String, Set<Developer>> task2setdevs = tasks.stream()
        .collect(groupingBy(Task::getName,
                Collectors.flatMapping(task -> task.getDevelopers().stream(),
                toSet())));
```

Now the result is what you want:

```
                  Java stuff: [Daniel, Brian, Ken, Venkat]
   Groovy/Kotlin/Scala/Clojure: [Daniel, Ken, Venkat]
           JavaScript (sorry): [Nate, Venkat]
                     Spring: [Craig, Ken, Matt, Nate]
              JPA/Hibernate: []
```

The `flatMapping` method is just like the `flatMap` method on `Stream`. Note that the first argument `flatMapping` needs to be a stream, which can be empty or not depending on the source.

## See Also

Downstream collectors are discussed in Recipe 4.6. The `flatMap` operation is in Recipe 3.11.

# 10.6 Optional: stream, or, ifPresentOrElse

## Problem

You want to flat map `Optionals` into a stream of contained elements, or you want to choose from several possibilities, or you want to do something if an element is present and return a default otherwise.

## Solution

Use the new `stream`, `or`, or `ifPresentOrElse` methods in `Optional`.

## Discussion

The `Optional` class, introduced in Java 8, provides a way to indicate to a client that a returned value may legitimately be null. Rather than returning null, you return an empty `Optional`. That makes `Optional` a good wrapper for methods that may or may not return a value.

### The stream method

Consider a finder method to look up customers by ID, as in Example 10-28.

*Example 10-28. Find a customer by ID*

```
public Optional<Customer> findById(int id) {
    return Optional.ofNullable(map.get(id));
}
```

This method assumes that the customers are contained within a `Map` in memory. The `get` method on `Map` returns a value if the key is present or null if not, so making it the argument to `Optional.ofNullable` either wraps a nonnull value inside an `Optional` or returns an empty `Optional`.

Remember that since the `Optional.of` method throws an exception if its argument is null, the `Optional.ofNullable(arg)` is a convenient shortcut. Its implementation is `arg != null ? Optional.of(arg) : Optional.empty()`.

Since `findById` returns an `Optional<Customer>`, trying to return a collection of customers is a bit more complicated. In Java 8, you can write the code in Example 10-29.

*Example 10-29. Using a filter and a Map on Optionals*

```
public Collection<Customer> findAllById(Integer... ids) {
    return Arrays.stream(ids)
            .map(this::findById)            ❶
            .filter(Optional::isPresent)    ❷
            .map(Optional::get)             ❸
            .collect(Collectors.toList());
}
```

❶ Maps to a `Stream<Optional<Customer>>`

❷ Filter out any empty `Optionals`

❸ Call `get`, so maps to a `Stream<Customer>`

This isn't too much of a hardship, but Java 9 has made the process simpler by adding the `stream` method to `Optional`, whose signature is:

```
Stream<T> stream()
```

If a value is present, this method returns a sequential, single element stream containing only that value. Otherwise it returns an empty stream. This method means that a stream of optional customers can be turned into a stream of customers directly, as in Example 10-30.

*Example 10-30. Using flatMap with Optional.stream*

```
public Collection<Customer> findAllById(Integer... ids) {
    return Arrays.stream(ids)
            .map(this::findById)            ❶
            .flatMap(Optional::stream)      ❷
```

```
            .collect(Collectors.toList());
}
```

❶ Map to Stream<Optional<Customer>>

❷ Flat map to Stream<Customer>

This is purely a convenience method, but a useful one.

### The or method

The `orElse` method is used to extract a value from an `Optional`. It takes a default as an argument:

```
Customer customer = findById(id).orElse(Customer.DEFAULT)
```

There is also the `orElseGet` method that uses a `Supplier` to create the default, in the case where doing so is an expensive operation:

```
Customer customer = findById(id).orElseGet(() -> createDefaultCustomer())
```

Both of those return `Customer` instances. The `or` method on `Optional`, added in Java 9, allows you to return an `Optional<Customer>` instead, given a `Supplier` of them, so you can chain alternative ways of finding customers together.

The signature of the `or` method is:

```
Optional<T> or(Supplier<? extends Optional<? extends T>> supplier)
```

If a value is present, this method returns an `Optional` describing it. Otherwise it invokes the `Supplier` and returns the `Optional` it returns.

Therefore, if we have multiple ways to find a customer, you can now write the code in Example 10-31.

*Example 10-31. Using the or method to try alternatives*

```
public Optional<Customer> findById(int id) {
    return findByIdLocal(id)
            .or(() -> findByIdRemote(id))
            .or(() -> Optional.of(Customer.DEFAULT));
```

This method searches for the customer in the local cache and then accesses some remote server. If neither of those finds a nonempty `Optional`, the final clause creates a default, wraps it in an `Optional`, and returns it instead.

### The ifPresentOrElse method

The `ifPresent` method on `Optional` executes a `Consumer` if the `Optional` is not empty, as in Example 10-32.

*Example 10-32. Using ifPresent to only print nonempty customers*

```
public void printCustomer(Integer id) {
    findByIdLocal(id).ifPresent(System.out::println);  ❶
}

public void printCustomers(Integer... ids) {
    Arrays.asList(ids)
            .forEach(this::printCustomer);
}
```

❶ Only prints for nonempty `Optional`s

This works, but you might want to run something else if the returned `Optional` is empty. The new `ifPresentOrElse` method takes a second, `Runnable`, argument that is executed if the `Optional` is empty. Its signature is:

```
void ifPresentOrElse(Consumer<? super T> action, Runnable emptyAction)
```

To use it, simply provide a lambda that takes no arguments and returns void, as in Example 10-33.

*Example 10-33. Printing a customer or a default message*

```
public void printCustomer(Integer id) {
    findByIdLocal(id).ifPresentOrElse(System.out::println,
            () -> System.out.println("Customer with id=" + id + " not found"));
}
```

This version prints the customer if one is found, and prints a default message otherwise.

None of these additions to `Optional` change its behavior in any fundamental way, but they do provide conveniences when applicable.

## See Also

The recipes in Chapter 6 cover the `Optional` class in Java 8.

# 10.7 Date Ranges

## Problem

You want a stream of dates between two given endpoints.

## Solution

Use the new `datesUntil` method in the `LocalDate` class, added in Java 9.

## Discussion

The new Date-Time API added in Java 8 is an enormous improvement over classes like `Date`, `Calendar`, and `TimeStamp` in `java.util`, but one of the additions in Java 9 addresses an annoying hole in the API: there's no easy way to create a stream of dates.

In Java 8, the easiest way to create a stream of dates is to start with an initial date and add an offset. For example, if you want all the days given endpoints a week apart, you can write the code in Example 10-34.

*Example 10-34. Days between two dates (WARNING: BUG!)*

```
public List<LocalDate> getDays_java8(LocalDate start, LocalDate end) {
    Period period = start.until(end);
    return IntStream.range(0, period.getDays())  ❶
            .mapToObj(start:plusDays)
            .collect(Collectors.toList());
}
```

❶ Trap! See next example.

This works by determining the `Period` between the two dates and then creating an `IntStream` of days between them. Looking at days a week apart gives:

```
LocalDate start = LocalDate.of(2017, Month.JUNE, 10);
LocalDate end = LocalDate.of(2017, Month.JUNE, 17);
System.out.println(dateRange.getDays_java8(start, end));

// [2017-06-10, 2017-06-11, 2017-06-12, 2017-06-13,
//  2017-06-14, 2017-06-15, 2017-06-16]
```

This seems to work, but there's actually a trap here. If you change the end date to exactly one month from the start date, the problem is obvious:

```
LocalDate start = LocalDate.of(2017, Month.JUNE, 10);
LocalDate end = LocalDate.of(2017, Month.JULY, 17);
System.out.println(dateRange.getDays_java8(start, end));

// []
```

No values are returned. The problem is that the `getDays` method on `Period` returns the days field from the period, not the number of days total. (The same is true about `getMonths`, `getYears`, and so on.) So if the days are the same, even though the months are different, the result is a range of size zero.

The proper way to handle this problem is to use the `ChronoUnit` enum, which implements the `TemporalUnit` interface and defines constants for `DAYS`, `MONTHS`, etc. The proper implementation for Java 8 is given in Example 10-35.

*Example 10-35. Days between two dates (WORKS)*

```
public List<LocalDate> getDays_java8(LocalDate start, LocalDate end) {
    Period period = start.until(end);
    return LongStream.range(0, ChronoUnit.DAYS.between(start, end)) ❶
            .mapToObj(start:plusDays)
            .collect(Collectors.toList());
}
```

❶ Works

You can also use the `iterate` method, but that requires you to know the number of days, as in Example 10-36.

*Example 10-36. Iterating on LocalDate*

```
public List<LocalDate> getDaysByIterate(LocalDate start, int days) {
    return Stream.iterate(start, date -> date.plusDays(1))
            .limit(days)
            .collect(Collectors.toList());
}
```

Fortunately, Java 9 makes all of this much simpler. Now the `LocalDate` class has a method called `datesUntil`, with an overload that takes a `Period`. The signatures are:

```
Stream<LocalDate> datesUntil(LocalDate endExclusive)
Stream<LocalDate> datesUntil(LocalDate endExclusive, Period step)
```

The version without a `Period` essentially calls the overload with a second argument of one day.

The Java 9 approach to the preceding problem is much simpler, as shown in Example 10-37.

*Example 10-37. Date ranges in Java 9*

```
public List<LocalDate> getDays_java9(LocalDate start, LocalDate end) {
    return start.datesUntil(end)                      ❶
            .collect(Collectors.toList());
}

public List<LocalDate> getMonths_java9(LocalDate start, LocalDate end) {
    return start.datesUntil(end, Period.ofMonths(1)) ❷
            .collect(Collectors.toList());
}
```

❶ Assumes `Period.ofDays(1)`

❷ Counts in months

The `datesUntil` method produces a `Stream`, which can be manipulated with all the normal stream processing techniques.

## See Also

Calculating the days between dates in Java 8 is part of Recipe 8.8.

APPENDIX A

# Generics and Java 8

## Background

Generics capabilities were added in Java way back in version J2SE 1.5, but most Java developers only learned the minimum they needed to know about them to get the job done. With the advent of Java 8, suddenly the Javadocs are filled with method signatures like this one from `java.util.Map.Entry`:

```
static <K extends Comparable<? super K>,V> Comparator<Map.Entry<K,V>>
    comparingByKey()
```

or this one from `java.util.Comparator`:

```
static <T,U extends Comparable<? super U>> Comparator<T> comparing(
    Function<? super T,? extends U> keyExtractor)
```

or even this monster from `java.util.stream.Collectors`:

```
static <T,K,D,A,M extends Map<K, D>> Collector<T,?,M> groupingBy(
    Function<? super T,? extends K> classifier, Supplier<M> mapFactory,
    Collector<? super T,A,D> downstream)
```

Understanding the minimum isn't going to be enough anymore. The purpose of this appendix is to help you break down similar signatures into understandable parts so that you can use the API productively.

## What Everybody Knows

When you want to use a collection like `List` or `Set`, you declare the type of the contained elements by placing their class name in angle brackets:

```
List<String> strings = new ArrayList<String>();
Set<Employee> employees = new HashSet<Employee>();
```

Java 7 made the syntax a bit easier by introducing the *diamond* operator used in the following code samples. Since the reference on the lefthand side declares the collection along with its contained type, like `List<String>` or `List<Integer>`, the instantiation on the same line doesn't have to. You can simply write `new ArrayList<>()` without putting the type inside the angle brackets.

Declaring the data type of the collection accomplishes two goals:

- You can't accidentally place the wrong type inside a collection
- You no longer need to cast a retrieved value to the proper type

For example, if you declare the `strings` variable as shown, then you can only add `String` instances to the collection and you automatically have a `String` when you retrieve an item, as in Example A-1.

*Example A-1. Simple generics demo*

```
List<String> strings = new ArrayList<>();
strings.add("Hello");
strings.add("World");
// strings.add(new Date());    ❶
// Integer i = strings.get(0); ❶

for (String s : strings) {      ❷
    System.out.printf("%s has length %d%n", s, s.length());
}
```

❶ Won't compile

❷ for-each loop knows the contained data type is `String`

Applying type safety to the insertion process is convenient, but developers rarely make that mistake. Being able to deal with the proper type on retrieval without having to cast first, however, saves a lot of code.[1]

The other thing all Java developers know is that you can't add primitive types to generic collections. That means you can't define `List<int>` or `List<double>`.[2] Fortunately, the same version of Java that introduced generics also added auto-boxing and

1 Never once in my entire career did I accidentally add the wrong type to a list. Eliminating the casting on the way out, however, justified even this ugly syntax.

2 Java 10, known as Project Valhalla, has proposed adding primitive types to collections.

unboxing to the language. As a result, when you want to store primitives in a generic type, you declare the type using the wrapper class. See Example A-2.

*Example A-2. Using primitives in generic collections*

```
List<Integer> ints = new ArrayList<>();
ints.add(3); ints.add(1); ints.add(4);
ints.add(1); ints.add(9); ints.add(2);
System.out.println(ints);

for (int i : ints) {
    System.out.println(i);
}
```

Java takes care of wrapping the `int` values inside `Integer` instances on insertion, and extracts them from the `Integer` instances on retrieval. While there may be efficiency concerns regarding boxing and unboxing, the code is easy enough to write.

There's one more aspect of generics that all Java developers know. When you're reading the Javadocs about a class that uses generics, you use a capital letter in brackets for the type itself. For example, the docs for the `List` interface is:

```
public interface List<E> extends Collection<E>
```

Here, `E` is the type parameter. The methods in the interface use the same parameter. Example A-3 shows a sample of those methods.

*Example A-3. Methods declared in the List interface*

```
boolean add(E e)                             ❶
boolean addAll(Collection<? extends E> c)   ❷
void    clear()                              ❸
boolean contains(Object o)                   ❸
boolean containsAll(Collection<?> c)         ❹
E       get(int index)                        ❶
```

❶ Using the type parameter `E` as an argument or return type

❷ A *bounded* wildcard

❸ Methods that do not involve the type itself

❹ An *unknown* type

Some of these methods use the declared generic type, `E`, as either an argument or a return type. Some (specifically, `clear` and `contains`) don't use the type at all. Others involve some kind of wildcard, using a question mark.

As a syntax note, it is legal to declare generic methods even in classes that aren't generic. In that case, the generic parameter or parameters are declared as part of the method signatures. For example, here are some of the static methods from the utility class `java.util.Collections`:

```
static <T>   List<T>    emptyList()
static <K,V> Map<K,V>   emptyMap()
static <T>   boolean    addAll(Collection<? super T> c, T... elements)
static <T extends Object & Comparable<? super T>>
    T min(Collection<? extends T> coll)
```

Three of these methods declare a generic parameter called `T`. The `emptyList` method uses it to specify the contained type in the `List`. The `emptyMap` method uses `K` and `V` for key and value types in a generic map.

The `addAll` method declares the generic type `T`, but then uses a `Collection<? super T>` as the first argument of the method, as well as a variable argument list of type `T`. The syntax `? super T` is a bounded wildcard, which will be the subject of the next section.

The `min` method shows how generic types may provide safety, but can make the documentation much harder to read. This signature is discussed in more detail in a later section, but for the record, `T` is bounded to be both a subclass of `Object` as well as implementing the `Comparable` interface, where `Comparable` is defined for `T` or any of its ancestors. The argument to the method involves any `Collection` of `T` or any of its descendants.

The wildcard is where we transition from syntax everyone knows to the parts with which you may not be comfortable. To prepare for that, consider the strange case when what looks like inheritance turns out not to be inheritance at all.

## What Some Developers Don't Realize

Many developers are surprised to learn that `ArrayList<String>` is not related in any practical way to `ArrayList<Object>`. You can add subclasses of `Object` to an `Object` collection, as in Example A-4.

*Example A-4. Using a List<Object>*

```
List<Object> objects = new ArrayList<Object>();
objects.add("Hello");
objects.add(LocalDate.now());
objects.add(3);
System.out.println(objects);
```

That much is OK. `String` is a subclass of `Object`, so you can assign a `String` to an `Object` reference. You would think that if you declared a list of strings, you could add objects to it. That, as they say, turns out not to be the case. See Example A-5.

*Example A-5. Using a List<String> with objects*

```
List<String> strings = new ArrayList<>();
String s = "abc";
Object o = s;                           ❶
// strings.add(o);                      ❷

// List<Object> moreObjects = strings;  ❸
// moreObjects.add(new Date());
// String s = moreObjects.get(0);       ❹
```

❶ Allowed

❷ Not allowed

❸ Also not allowed, but pretend it was

❹ Corrupted collection

Since `String` is a subclass of `Object`, you can assign a `String` reference to an `Object` reference. You can't, however, add an `Object` reference to a `List<String>`, which feels strange. The problem is that `List<String>` is *not* a subclass of `List<Object>`. When declaring a type, the *only* instances you can add to it are of the declared type. That's it. No sub- or superclass instances allowed. We say that the parameterized type is *invariant*.

The commented out section shows why `List<String>` is not a subclass of `List<Object>`. Say you could assign a `List<String>` to a `List<Object>`. Then, using the list of object references, you could add something that wasn't a string to the list, which would cause a cast exception when you tried to retrieve it using the original reference to the list of strings. The compiler wouldn't know any better.

Still, it seems reasonable that if you defined a list of numbers, you should be able to add integers, floats, and doubles to it. To accomplish that, we need type bounds that involve wildcards.

## Wildcards and PECS

A wildcard is a type argument that uses a question mark, `?`, which may or may not have an upper or lower bound.

## Unbounded Wildcards

Type arguments without bounds are useful, but have limitations. If you declare a `List` of unbounded type, as in Example A-6, you can read from it but not write to it.

*Example A-6. A List with an unbounded wildcard*

```
List<?> stuff = new ArrayList<>();
// stuff.add("abc");            ❶
// stuff.add(new Object());
// stuff.add(3);
int numElements = stuff.size(); ❷
```

❶ No additions allowed

❷ `numElements` is zero

That feels pretty useless, since there's apparently no way to get anything into it. One use for them is that any method that takes a `List<?>` as an argument will accept any list at all when invoked (Example A-7).

*Example A-7. Unbounded List as a method arg*

```
private static void printList(List<?> list) {
    System.out.println(list);
}

public static void main(String[] args) {
    // ... create lists called ints, strings, stuff ...
    printList(ints);
    printList(strings);
    printList(stuff);
}
```

Recall the earlier example, which showed the `containsAll` method from `List<E>`:

```
boolean containsAll(Collection<?> c)
```

That method returns true only if all the elements of the collection appear in the current list. Since the argument uses an unbounded wildcard, the implementation is restricted to only:

- Methods from `Collection` itself that don't need the contained type, or
- Methods from `Object`

In the case of `containsAll`, that's perfectly acceptable. The default implementation (in `AbstractCollection`) in the reference implementation walks through the argument using iterator and invokes the contains method to check that each element in it is also inside the original list. Both iterator and contains are defined in Collection, and equals comes from Object, and the contains implementation delegates to the equals and hashCode methods of Object, which may have been overridden in the contained type. As far as the containsAll method is concerned, all the methods it needs are available. The restrictions on unbounded wildcards are not a problem.

The question mark forms the basis for bounding the types. This is where the fun starts.

## Upper Bounded Wildcards

An upper bounded wildcard uses the extends keyword to set a superclass limit. To define a list of numbers that will allow ints, longs, doubles, and even BigDecimal instances to be added to it, see Example A-8.

The keyword extends is used even if the upper bound is an interface rather than a class, as in List<? extends Comparable>.

*Example A-8. A List with an upper bound*

```
List<? extends Number> numbers = new ArrayList<>();
//        numbers.add(3);                  ❶
//        numbers.add(3.14159);
//        numbers.add(new BigDecimal("3"));
```

❶ Still cannot add values

Well, that seemed like a good idea at the time. Unfortunately, while you can define the list with the upper bounded wildcard, again you can't add to it. The problem is that when you retrieve the value, the compiler has no idea what type it is, only that it extends Number.

Still, you can define a method argument that takes List<? extends Number> and then invoke the method with the different types of lists. See Example A-9.

*Example A-9. Using an upper bound*

```
private static double sumList(List<? extends Number> list) {
    return list.stream()
               .mapToDouble(Number::doubleValue)
               .sum();
}
```

```
public static void main(String[] args) {
    List<Integer> ints = Arrays.asList(1, 2, 3, 4, 5);
    List<Double> doubles = Arrays.asList(1.0, 2.0, 3.0, 4.0, 5.0);
    List<BigDecimal> bigDecimals = Arrays.asList(
        new BigDecimal("1.0"),
        new BigDecimal("2.0"),
        new BigDecimal("3.0"),
        new BigDecimal("4.0"),
        new BigDecimal("5.0")
    );

    System.out.printf("ints sum is         %s%n", sumList(ints));
    System.out.printf("doubles sum is      %s%n", sumList(doubles));
    System.out.printf("big decimals sum is %s%n", sumList(bigDecimals));
}
```

Note that summing `BigDecimal` instances using their corresponding double values cancels the benefit of using big decimals in the first place, but only the primitive streams `IntStream`, `LongStream`, and `DoubleStream` include a `sum` method. This does illustrate the point, however, which is that you can invoke the method with lists of any subtype of `Number`. Since `Number` defines the `doubleValue` method, the code compiles and runs.

When you access an element from the list with an upper bound, the result can definitely be assigned to a reference of upper bound type, as in Example A-10.

*Example A-10. Extracting a value from an upper bound reference*

```
private static double sumList(List<? extends Number> list) {
    Number num = list.get(0);
    // ... from before ...
}
```

When the method is invoked, the elements of the list will be either `Number` or one of its descendants, so a `Number` reference will always be correct.

## Lower Bounded Wildcards

A lower bounded wildcard means any ancestor of your class is acceptable. You use the `super` keyword with the wildcard to specify a lower bound. The implicationn, in the case of a `List<? super Number>`, is that the reference could represent `List<Number>` or `List<Object>`.

With the upper bound, we were specifying the type that the variables must conform to in order for the implementation of the method to work. To add up the numbers, we needed to be sure that the variables had a `doubleValue` method, which is defined in `Number`. All of the `Number` subclasses have that method as well, either directly or through an override. That's why we specified `List<? extends Number>` for the input type.

Here, however, we're taking the items from the list and adding them to a different collection. That destination collection could be a `List<Number>`, but it could also be a `List<Object>` because the individual `Object` references can be assigned to a `Number`.

Here's the classic demonstration of the concept, which isn't really idiomatic Java 8 code for reasons that will be discussed later, but does illustrate the concept.

Consider a method called `numsUpTo` that takes two arguments, an integer and a list to populate with all the numbers up to the first argument, as in Example A-11.

*Example A-11. A method to populate a given list*

```
public void numsUpTo(Integer num, List<? super Integer> output) {
    IntStream.rangeClosed(1, num)
            .forEach(output::add);
}
```

The reason this isn't idiomatic Java 8 is that it's using the supplied list as an output variable. That's essentially a side effect, and therefore frowned upon. Still, by making the second argument of type `List<? super Integer>`, the supplied list can be of type `List<Integer>`, `List<Number>`, or even `List<Object>`, as in Example A-12.

*Example A-12. Using the numsUpTo method*

```
ArrayList<Integer> integerList = new ArrayList<>();
ArrayList<Number>  numberList = new ArrayList<>();
ArrayList<Object>  objectList = new ArrayList<>();

numsUpTo(5, integerList);
numsUpTo(5, numberList);
numsUpTo(5, objectList);
```

The returned lists all contain the numbers 1 through 5. The use of a lower bounded wildcard means we know the list is going to hold integers, but we can use references inside the list of any super type.

With the upper bounded list, we were extracting values and using them. With the lower bounded list, we supplied them. This combination has a traditional name: PECS.

## PECS

The term *PECS* stands for "Producer Extends, Consumer Super," which is an odd acronym coined by Joshua Block in his *Effective Java* book, but provides a mnemonic on what to do. It means that if a parameterized type represents a producer, use `extends`. If it represents a consumer, use `super`. If the parameter is both, don't use wildcards at all—the only type that satisfies both requirements is the explicit type itself.

The advice boils down to:

- Use `extends` when you only *get* values out of a data structure
- Use `super` when you only *put* values into a data structure
- Use an explicit type when you plan to do both

As long as we're on the subject of terminology, there are formal terms for these concepts, which are frequently used in languages like Scala.

The term *covariant* preserves the ordering of types from more specific to more general. In Java, arrays are covariant because `String[]` is a subtype of `Object[]`. As we've seen, collections in Java are not covariant unless we use the `extends` keyword with a wildcard.

The term *contravariant* goes the other direction. In Java, that's where we use the `super` keyword with a wildcard.

An *invariant* means that the type must be exactly as specified. All parameterized types in Java are invariant unless we use `extends` or `super`, meaning that if a method expects a `List<Employee>` then that's what you have to supply. Neither a `List<Object>` nor a `List<Salaried>` will do.

The PECS rule is a restatement of the formal rule that a type constructor is contravariant in the input type and covariant in the output type. The idea is sometimes stated as "be liberal in what you accept and conservative in what you produce."

## Multiple Bounds

One final note before looking at examples from the Java 8 API. A type parameter can have multiple bounds. The bounds are separated by an ampersand when they are defined:

```
T extends Runnable & AutoCloseable
```

You can have as many interface bounds as you like, but only one can be a class. If you have a class as a bound, it must be first in the list.

# Examples from the Java 8 API

With all that in mind, now it's time to review some examples from the Java 8 docs.

## Stream.max

In the `java.util.stream.Stream` interface, consider the `max` method:

```
Optional<T> max(Comparator<? super T> comparator)
```

Note the use of the lower bounded wildcard in the `Comparator`. The `max` method returns the maximum element of a stream by applying the supplied `Comparator` to it. The return type is `Optional<T>`, because there may not be a return value if the stream is empty. The method wraps the minimum in an `Optional` if there is one, and returns an empty `Optional` if not.

To keep things simple, Example A-13 shows an `Employee` POJO.

*Example A-13. A trivial Employee POJO*

```
public class Employee {
    private int id;
    private String name;

    public Employee(int id, String name) {
        this.id = id;
        this.name = name;
    }

    // ... other methods ...
}
```

The code in Example A-14 creates a collection of employees, converts them into a `Stream`, and then uses the `max` method to find the employee with the max `id` and the max `name` (alphabetically[3]). The implementation uses anonymous inner classes to emphasize that the `Comparator` can be of type `Employee` or `Object`.

*Example A-14. Finding the max Employee*

```
List<Employee> employees = Arrays.asList(
    new Employee(1, "Seth Curry"),
    new Employee(2, "Kevin Durant"),
    new Employee(3, "Draymond Green"),
    new Employee(4, "Klay Thompson"));

Employee maxId = employees.stream()
    .max(new Comparator<Employee>() {          ❶
        @Override
        public int compare(Employee e1, Employee e2) {
            return e1.getId() - e2.getId();
```

3 OK, technically it's a lexicographical sort, meaning the capital letters come before the lowercase letters.

```
        }
    }).orElse(Employee.DEFAULT_EMPLOYEE);

Employee maxName = employees.stream()
    .max(new Comparator<Object>() {            ❷
        @Override
        public int compare(Object o1, Object o2) {
            return o1.toString().compareTo(o2.toString());
        }
    }).orElse(Employee.DEFAULT_EMPLOYEE);

System.out.println(maxId);   ❸
System.out.println(maxName); ❹
```

❶ Anonymous inner class implementation of `Comparator<Employee>`

❷ Anonymous inner class implementation of `Comparator<Object>`

❸ Klay Thompson (max ID of 4)

❹ Seth Curry (max name starts with S)

The idea is that the `Comparator` can be written taking advantage of methods in `Employee`, but it's also legal to just use `Object` methods like `toString`. By defining the method in the API using the `super` wildcard, `Comparator<? super T> comparator`), either `Comparator` is allowed.

For the record, nobody would write that code that way any more. The more idiomatic approach is shown in Example A-15.

*Example A-15. Idiomatic approach to finding the max Employee*

```
import static java.util.Comparator.comparing;
import static java.util.Comparator.comparingInt;

// ... create employees ...

Employee maxId = employees.stream()
    .max(comparingInt(Employee::getId))
    .orElse(Employee.DEFAULT_EMPLOYEE);

Employee maxName = employees.stream()
    .max(comparing(Object::toString))
    .orElse(Employee.DEFAULT_EMPLOYEE);

System.out.println(maxId);
System.out.println(maxName);
```

This is certainly cleaner, but it doesn't emphasize the bounded wildcard like the anonymous inner class.

## Stream.map

As another simple example from the same class, consider the `map` method. It takes a `Function` with two arguments, both of which use wildcards:

```
<R> Stream<R> map(Function<? super T,? extends R> mapper)
```

The goal of this method is to apply the `mapper` function to each element of the stream (of type `T`) to transform it into an instance of type `R`.[4] The return type from the `map` function is therefore `Stream<R>`.

Since `Stream` is defined as a generic class with type parameter `T`, the method doesn't also need to define that variable in the signature. The method requires an additional type parameter, `R`, however, so that appears in the signature before the return type. If the class had not been generic, the method would have declared both parameters.

The `java.util.function.Function` interface defines two type parameters, the first (the input argument) is the type *consumed* from the `Stream`, and the second (the output argument) the type of object *produced* by the function. The wildcards imply that when the parameters are specified, the input parameter must be of the same type or above as the `Stream`. The output type can be any child of the returned stream type.

The `Function` example looks confusing because from a PECS perspective, the types are backwards. However, if you keep in mind that `Function<T,R>` consumes a `T` and produces an `R`, it's clearer why `super` goes on `T` and `extends` goes on `R`.

The code in Example A-16 shows how to use the method.

*Example A-16. Mapping a List<Employee> to a List<String>*

```
List<String> names = employees.stream()
    .map(Employee::getName)
    .collect(toList());

List<String> strings = employees.stream()
    .map(Object::toString)
    .collect(toList());
```

4 The Java API uses `T` for a single input variable, or `T` and `U` for two input variables, and so on. It normally uses `R` for return variables. For maps, the API uses `K` for the keys and `V` for the values.

The Function declared two generic variables, one for input and one for output. In the first case, the method reference Employee::getName uses the Employee from the stream as input, and returns a String as output.

The second example shows that the input variable could have been treated as a method from Object rather than Employee, because of the super wildcard. The output type could, in principle, have been a List containing subclasses of String, but String is final so there aren't any.

Next let's look at one of the method signatures that introduced this appendix.

## Comparator.comparing

The example in Example A-15 used the static comparing function from Comparator. The Comparator interface has been around since Java 1.0, so it might surprise developers to see it now has many additional methods. The Java 8 rule is that a *functional interface* is defined as an interface that contains only a single, abstract method (SAM). In the case of Comparator, that method is compare, which takes two arguments, both of generic type T, and returns an int that is negative, zero, or positive depending on whether the first argument is less than, equal to, or greater than, the second.[5]

The signature of comparing is:

```
static <T,U extends Comparable<? super U>> Comparator<T> comparing(
    Function<? super T,? extends U> keyExtractor)
```

Let's start by breaking down the argument to the compare method, whose name is keyExtractor and is of type Function. As before, Function defines two generic types, one for the input and one for the output. In this case, the input is lower bounded by an input type T and the output is upper bounded by an output type U. The name of the argument is the key[6] here: the function uses a method to extract a property to sort by, and the compare method returns a Comparator to do the job.

Because the goal is to use the ordering of a stream by the given property U, that property must implement Comparable. That's why when U is declared, it must extend Comparable. Of course, Comparable itself is a typed interface, whose type would normally be U but is allowed to be any superclass of U.

Ultimately what the method returns is a Comparator<T>, which is then used by other methods in Stream to sort the stream into a new stream of the same type.

The code presented earlier in Example A-15 demonstrates how the method is used.

5 Comparators are covered in Recipe 4.1.

6 Sorry.

## Map.Entry.comparingByKey and Map.Entry.comparingByValue

As a final example, consider adding the employees to a `Map` where the key is the employee ID and the values are the employees themselves. Then the code will sort them by ID or name, and print the results.

The first step, adding the employees to a `Map`, is actually a one-liner when you use the static `toMap` method from `Collectors`:

```
// Add employees to a map using id as key
Map<Integer, Employee> employeeMap = employees.stream()
    .collect(Collectors.toMap(Employee::getId, Function.identity()));
```

The signature of the `Collectors.toMap` method is:

```
static <T, K, U> Collector<T, ?, Map<K, U>> toMap(
    Function<? super T,? extends K> keyMapper,
    Function<? super T,? extends U> valueMapper)
```

`Collectors` is a utility class (i.e., it contains only static methods) that produces implementations of the `Collector` interface.

In this example, the `toMap` method takes two arguments: one function to generate the keys and one function to generate the values in the output map. The return type is a `Collector`, which defines three generic arguments.

The `Collector` interface (from the Javadocs) has the signature:

```
public interface Collector<T,A,R>
```

Where the generic types are defined as:

- `T`, the type of input elements to the reduction operation
- `A`, the mutable accumulation type of the reduction operation (often hidden as an implementation detail)
- `R`, the result of the reduction operation

In this case, we're specifying the `keyMapper`, which is going to the `getId` method of `Employee`. That means here `T` is `Integer`. The result, `R`, is an implementation of the `Map` interface that uses `Integer` for `K` and `Employee` for `U`.

Then comes the fun part—the `A` variable in `Collector` is the actual implementation of the `Map` interface. It's probably a `HashMap`,[7] but we never know because the result is used as the argument to the `toMap` method so we never see it. In the `Collector`, though, the type uses an unbounded wildcard, `?`, which tells us that internally it either

7 In fact, in the reference implementation it is a `HashMap`.

only uses methods from `Object` or it uses methods in `Map` that aren't specific to type. In fact, it only uses the new default `merge` method in `Map`, after calling the `keyMapper` and `valueMapper` functions.

To do the sorting, Java 8 has added static methods `comparingByKey` and `comparingByValue` to `Map.Entry`. Printing the elements sorted by key is shown in Example A-17.

*Example A-17. Sorting Map elements by key and printing*

```
Map<Integer, Employee> employeeMap = employees.stream()
    .collect(Collectors.toMap(Employee::getId, Function.identity())); ❶

System.out.println("Sorted by key:");
employeeMap.entrySet().stream()
    .sorted(Map.Entry.comparingByKey())
    .forEach(entry -> {
        System.out.println(entry.getKey() + ": " + entry.getValue());
    });
```

❶ Add employees to a `Map` using ID as key

❷ Sort employees by ID and print them

The signature of `comparingByKey` is:

```
static <K extends Comparable<? super K>,V>
    Comparator<Map.Entry<K,V>> comparingByKey()
```

The `comparingByKey` method takes no arguments and returns a `Comparator` that compares `Map.Entry` instances. Since we're comparing by the keys, the declared generic type for the key, `K`, must be a subtype of `Comparable` that does the actual comparisons. Of course, the `Comparable` itself defines the generic type `K` or one of its ancestors, meaning that the `compareTo` method could use a property of the `K` class or above.

The result of this sorting is:

```
Sorted by key:
1: Seth Curry
2: Kevin Durant
3: Draymond Green
4: Klay Thompson
```

Sorting by value instead introduces a nice complication, where the error would be hard to understand without knowing something about the generic types involved. First, the signature of the `comparingByValue` method is:

```
static <K,V extends Comparable<? super V>> Comparator<Map.Entry<K,V>>
    comparingByValue()
```

This time it's `V` that needs to be a subtype of `Comparable`.

A naïve implementation of sorting by value would then be:

```
// Sort employees by name and print them (DOES NOT COMPILE)
employeeMap.entrySet().stream()
    .sorted(Map.Entry.comparingByValue())
    .forEach(entry -> {
        System.out.println(entry.getKey() + ": " + entry.getValue());
    });
```

This doesn't compile. The error you get is:

```
Java: incompatible types: inference variable V has incompatible bounds
    equality constraints: generics.Employee
    upper bounds: java.lang.Comparable<? super V>
```

The problem is that the values in the map are instances of `Employee`, and `Employee` doesn't implement `Comparable`. Fortunately, the API defines an overloaded version of `comparingByValue`:

```
static <K,V> Comparator<Map.Entry<K,V>> comparingByValue(
    Comparator<? super V> cmp)
```

This method takes a `Comparator` as an argument and returns a new `Comparator` that compares the `Map.Entry` elements by the argument. The proper way to sort the map values is given in Example A-18.

*Example A-18. Sorting map elements by value and printing*

```
// Sort employees by name and print them
System.out.println("Sorted by name:");
employeeMap.entrySet().stream()
    .sorted(Map.Entry.comparingByValue(Comparator.comparing(Employee::getName)))
    .forEach(entry -> {
        System.out.println(entry.getKey() + ": " + entry.getValue());
    });
```

By providing the `Employee::getName` method reference to the `comparing` method, the employees are sorted by their names in their natural order:

```
Sorted by name:
3: Draymond Green
2: Kevin Durant
4: Klay Thompson
1: Seth Curry
```

Hopefully, these examples give you enough background on how to read and use the API without getting lost in the generics.

## A Note on Type Erasure

One of the challenges of working on a language like Java is that it needs to support years of backward compatibility. When generics were added to the language, the decision was made to remove them during the compilation process. That way no new classes are created for parameterized types, so there is no runtime penalty to using them.

Since all of that is done under the hood, all you really need to know is that at compile time:

- Bounded type parameters are replaced with their bounds
- Unbounded type parameters are replaced with Object
- Type casts are inserted where needed
- Bridge methods are generated to preserve polymorphism

For types, the result is pretty simple. The Map interface defines two generic types: K for the keys and V for the values. When you instantiate a Map<Integer,Employee>, the compiler replaces K with Integer and V with Employee.

In the Map.Entry.comparingByKey example, the keys were declared such that K extends Comparable. Therefore everywhere in the class that uses K will be replaced by Comparable.

the Function interface defines two generic types, T and R, and has a single abstract method:

```
R apply(T t)
```

In Stream, the map method adds the bounds Function<? super T,? extends R>. So when we used that method:

```
List<String> names = employees.stream()
    .map(Employee::getName)
    .collect(Collectors.toList());
```

The Function replaced T with Employee (since the stream was made up of employees) and R with String (since the return type from getName is String).

That's basically it, leaving out some edge cases. See the Java Tutorial for details if you're interested, but type erasure is probably the least complicated part of the whole technology.

# Summary

The generics capabilities originally defined in J2SE 1.5 are still with us, but with the advent of Java 8 the corresponding method signatures have gotten far more complex.

Most of the functional interfaces added to the language use both generic types and bounded wildcards to enforce type safety. Hopefully this appendix will give you the foundation you need to understand what the API is trying to accomplish, and therefore help you use it successfully.

# Index


## Symbols

<> (diamond operator), 268
? (question mark), wildcard type arguments, 271
@FunctionalInterface annotation, 15
@SafeVarargs annotation, 40
_ (underscore) in numerical values, 177

## A

abstract methods
  in functional interfaces, 15
accessors (getters), wrapping result in Optionals, 154
accumulator argument in Collectors, 110
adjusters and queries (for temporal values), 185-190
  TemporalAdjuster class, 185
  TemporalQuery class, 188
  writing your own adjuster, 186
    Adjusters class (example), 187
    PaydayAdjuster (example), 186
  writing your own query, 189
and method (Predicate), 137
andThen method (Consumer), 136
andThen method (Function), 135
anonymous inner classes, 118
  accessing attributes of outer class and local variable, 118
  replacement with lambda expressions, 119
  Runnable implementation, 2
anyMatch, allMatch, and noneMatch methods (Stream), 73-75
  prime number check, 73
  using on empty streams, 75
ArrayList<String> and ArrayList<Object>, 270
arrays
  Arrays.stream method, 40
    creating a stream, 40
  converting IntStream to int array, 45
  creating with Collectors.toArray method, 93
  using constructor references with, 14
Async versions, CompletableFuture coordinating methods, 227
at method, 179
AutoCloseable interface, streams and, 167

## B

BaseStream class, unordered method, 70
BasicFileAttributes object, 172
between method
  Duration class, 204
  Period class, 204
  TemporalUnit interface, 203
BiConsumer interface, 27, 111
  String.collect method taking BiConsumer arguments, 61
BiFunction interface, 37, 48
  CompletableFuture handle method taking, 230
BigInteger class, isProbablyPrime method, 74
binary operators
  identity values, 51
  performing a reduce with, 51
BinaryOperator class, 48, 111
  BinaryOperator as argument to Stream.reduce, 56
  maxBy and minBy methods, 104
  use by Map.merge method, 127

BiPredicate class, 172
boxed streams, 43-45
    using boxed method to convert IntStream to Stream, 44
BufferedReader class, lines method, 166, 168
busy waiting, 219

## C

Calendar class (see java.util.Calendar class)
Callable interface
    anonymous inner class implementation, substituting lambda for, 219
    ExecutorService.submit method taking a Callable, 218
cancel method (CompletableFuture), 228
characteristics function (Collectors), 110
chars and codePoints methods (CharSequence), 60
ChronoUnit class, 183, 203, 263
    constants for time units, 203
class name, instance method invoked via, 8
class-level members, using in interfaces, 21
closure composition, in Consumer interface, 136
closures, 120
collect method (Stream)
    converting stream of characters to a string, 61
    instances of classes implementing Collectors as arguments, 110
    overloaded versions, 91
    with Supplier, accumulator, and combiner, 67
Collection interface, 19
    default methods, 20
    removeIf method, using predicates, 35
collections
    adding a linear collection to a map, 94-96
    Collection.stream method, 42
    Collections class, sort method, 88, 89
    converting a stream to a collection, 91-94
    creating from primitive streams, 43-45
    creating immutable collections in Java 9, 247-251
    generic, 267
        using primitives in, 268
    immutable, creating using Stream API, 107-109
    iterating over, 130-132
    of primitives, 122
    returning a collection and filtering out nulls, 116
    static methods in java.util.Collections, 270
    stream processing versus, 84
Collector interface, 281
    implementing, 109-112
Collectors class, 87
    collectingAndThen method, 107-109
    converting from a stream to a collection, 44
    counting method, 64, 167
    downstream collectors, filtering and flatMapping, 255-259
    groupingBy method, 98, 168
    maxBy method, 106
    methods in Collectors analogous to methods in Stream, 65
    methods using Function, 38
    partitioningBy and groupingBy methods, 100-101
        downstream collectors, 102-104
    partitioningBy method, using predicates, 35
    Stream.collect method taking a Collector, 61
    summarizingDouble method, 67
    toMap method, 281
    using toMap with Function.identity, 94-96
combiners, combiner method in Collectors, 110
Comparable interface, 87, 280
Comparator interface, 17, 167
    BinaryOperator maxBy and minBy methods taking a Comparator, 104
    comparing method, 280
    enhancements in Java 8, 87
    methods using Function, 38
    reverseOrder method, 168
    sorting streams using a Comparator, 87-91
    static methods in, 22
CompletableFuture class, 218, 219, 220-225
    benefit of, 221
    completing, example, 222
    completing, methods for, 222
    coordinating CompletableFutures, 225-237
        combining two Futures, 229
        composing two Futures together, 229
        coordinating tasks, 225
        larger example, 231-237
        methods for, 226
        running CompletableFuture tasks on separate thread pool, 227

using handle method, 230
variations on coordinating methods, 227
runAsync and supplyAsync methods, 224
supplyAsync method, 31
using completeExceptionally on, 223
using supplyAsync to retrieve a product, 224
compose method (Function), 135
composition methods, 135-138
in Consumer interface, 136
in Function interface, 135
in Predicate interface, 137
computeIfAbsent method (Map), 123
computeIfPresent method (Map), 124
concatenating streams, 79-82
creating parallel streams or not, 81
multiple streams, 80
using Stream.concat method, 79
using Stream.flatMap method, 81
using Stream.reduce method, 80
concurrency, 206
(see also parallelism and concurrency)
defined, 205
ConcurrentMap, creating using Collectors.toConcurrentMap method, 94
constructor references, 10-15
copy constructor, 12
using with arrays, 14
varargs constructor, 13
Consumer interface, 130
accept method, 131
consumers, 26-28
additional consumer interfaces in java.util.function, 27
Consumer interface
composition methods, 136
implementing, 26
other uses of, 27
ifPresent method taking a Consumer, 153
Iterable.forEach method taking a Consumer, 120, 130
contravariant, 276
copy constructor, 12
count method (Stream), 63
counting method (Collectors), 64, 103
covariant, 276

## D

daemon threads, 228
Date-Time classes in java.time package, 176-180
adjusters and queries, 185-190
converting java.util.Date or javal.util.Calendar to new classes, 190-194
date ranges, 262-265
in Java 8, 263
in Java 9, using LocalDate.datesUntil, 264
finding region names from UTC offsets, 200-202
finding time zones with non-integral hour offsets, 197-200
getting time between events, 202-204
modifying existing instance, 180-184
parsing and formatting, 194
prefixes on method names, 178
datesUntil method (LocalDate), 264
DateTimeFormatter class, 194
ofPattern method, 196
DayOfWeek enum, 179
constants for seven weekdays, 180
default methods in interfaces, 16, 18-21, 245
conflicts in, 21
conflicts in classes implementing, 127-129
new default methods added to existing interfaces, 20
using, 20
deferred execution, Supplier support for, 29, 134
depth-first traversal of directories, 171
diamond operator (<>), 268
DirectoryStream interface, 169, 171, 173
DoubleConsumer interface, 27
doubles method (Random), 121
DoubleStream interface, 42
max method, 106
summaryStatistics method, 65
DoubleSummaryStatistics class, 66
accept and combine methods, 66
downstream collectors, 64, 255-259
applying Collectors.counting as, 167
filtering method, 256, 256
flatMapping method, 256, 258
from partitioningBy and groupingBy methods in Collectors, 102-104
groupingBy method, 98
partitioningBy method, 101
using Collectors.maxBy method as, 106

using to compute team salaries (example), 67
dropWhile method (Stream), 254
example, using on the integer stream, 255
Duration class, 182, 204
conversion methods for time units, 204
primitive timing mechanism using, 204

## E

easy versus simple, 206
effectively final variables, 119
empty method (Optional), 149
empty streams
using anyMatch, allMatch, and nonMatch methods on, 75
using findFirst method on, 69
using reduce with empty stream and binary operator, 81
encounter order, 69
sets and, 70
epoch, 192
event listeners, 118
exception handling
CompletableFuture.handle method, 230
completeExceptionally method on CompletableFuture, 223
for lambda expressions, using an extracted method for, 138-140
lambda expression throwing checked exception, 141-143
using a generic exception wrapper, 144-145
ExecutionException, 223
Executor interface, 227
CompletableFuture methods using an Executor, 227
handleAsync method, 230
ExecutorService interface, 218, 227
extends keyword, 273
in PECS, 276

## F

Fibonacci numbers, recursive calculation of, 123
file I/O, 165-173
processing text file contents using streams, 166-169
retrieving files as a Stream, 169
searching the filesystem for specified files, 172-173
walking the filesystem, 170-172
FilenameFilter interface, 4
Files class
find method, 172
lines method, 166
list method, 169
methods that return streams, 165
walk method, 170
write method, 235
FileVisitOption enum, 171
filtering method (Collectors), 256
filters
filtering data using predicates, 31-35
using a filter on Optionals, 260
find method (Files), 172
findAny method (Stream), 68
using in parallel after random delay, 70
using on sequential and parallel streams, 72
findFirst method (Stream), 68
finishers, 109
finisher method in Collectors, 110
flatMap method (Optional), 156-159
flatMap method (Stream)
map method versus, 75-79
using to concatenate streams, 81
flatMapping method (Collectors), 258
forEach method (Iterable and Map), 130-132
forEach method (Iterable), taking Consumer as argument, 120
ForkJoinPool class, 227
system properties controlling size of common pool, 215
using your own, 216
waiting to finish in common ForkJoinPool, 228
format method (LocalDate), 194
formatting java.time Date-Time classes
creating your own format, 196
LocalDate class, 195
using DateTimeFormatter, 194
functional interfaces
assigning a lambda to, 4
default methods in, 18-21
defined, 2
java.util.function package, 25-38
static methods in, 21-23
using or writing your own, 15-17
functional programming features in Java 8, 1
functions

Collectors.groupingBy method taking a Function, 101
finishers, 109
Function argument, Stream.map and Stream.flatMap methods, 76
Function interface, 111
composition methods, 135
Function.identity method, using with Collections.toMap, 96
Future interface, 217-220
cancel method, 220
chaining Futures together using CompletableFuture, 225
retrieving a value from a Future, 218
submitting a Callable and returning the Future, 218
using lambda expression and check if Future is done, 219

## G

generics and Java 8, 267-285
declaring generic methods in non-generic types, 270
examples from Java 8, 276-284
Comparator.comparing method, 280
Map.Entry, comparingByKey and comparingByValue methods, 281
Stream.map method, 279
Stream.max method, 277
type erasure, 284
multiple bounds for type parameters, 276
what all Java developers know, 267
what some developers don't know, 270
wildcards and PECS, 271
lower bounded wildcards, 274
PECS, 276
unbounded wildcards, 272
upper bounded wildcards, 273
getAvailableZoneIds method, 178
getOrDefault method (Map), 126
Greenwich/UTC time, time zone offsets from, 200
GregorianCalendar, converting to ZonedDateTime, 194
groupingBy method (Collectors), 101, 168, 256
filtering with, 257
overloaded version taking downstream collector, 103
Gson JSON parsing library, 235

## H

handle method (CompletableFuture), 230

## I

I/O (input/output), 165
(see also file I/O)
identity method (Function), 96
identity method (UnaryOperator), 96
ifPresent method (Optional), 153, 261
ifPresentOrElse method (Optional), 262
immutability
creating an immutable collection, 107-109
creating immutable collections, 247-251
instances of Optional, 148
implementations of interface methods, 245
info method (Logger), using a Supplier, 134
instance method invoked via class name, 8
Instant class
atZone method, 198
now method, 176
using as bridge for java.util.Date conversions, 190
converting Date to LocalDate, 190
working with, using Duration, 204
IntBinaryOperator class, 48
IntConsumer interface, 27
Integer class, min and max methods, 52
intermediate operations on stream pipelines, 57
ints, longs, and doubles static methods (Random), 121
IntStream interface, 42
basic reduce implementations, 48
converting to int array, 45
max method, 106
reduction operations, 46
sum method, 120
summaryStatistics method, 65
invariant, 276
isDone method (Future), 219
isNull method (Objects), 116
ISO 8601 specification, time zone IDs, definitions of, 200
Iterable interface
Consumer as argument in forEach method, 26
forEach method, 130-132
iterate method (Stream), 41, 264
in Java 9, 253

## J

Java 8, changes in, 1
Java 9 additions, 239-265
  date ranges, 262-265
  downstream collectors, filtering and flatMapping, 255-259
  immutable collections, 247-251
  modules in Jigsaw, 240-245
  new features not covered, 239
  Optional type, new methods, 259-262
  private methods in interfaces, 245-247
  streams, new functionality in, 252-255
Java Platform Module System (JPMS), 240
java.base module, 244
java.io.FilenameFilter interface, 4
java.lang.CharSequence, chars and codePoints methods, 60
java.math.BigInteger class, 74
java.nio.file package, 165
java.sql.Date class, 175
  conversion methods in, 191
java.sql.Timestamp class, conversion methods, 191
java.time package, 175
  adjusters and queries, 185-190
  converting java.util.Date or javal.util.Calendar to new classes, 190-194
  finding region names from UTC offsets, 200-202
  finding time zones with non-integral hour offsets, 197-200
  getting time between events, 202-204
  modifying existing Date-Time class instance, 180-184
  parsing and formatting Date-Time classes, 194-197
  using basic Date-Time classes, 176-180
java.util.Calendar class, 175
  converting to java.time.ZonedDateTime, 193
  converting to LocalDateTime
    by generating and parsing timestamp stream, 193
    using Calendar getter methods, 193
java.util.Comparable interface, 87
java.util.concurrent package, 205, 218
java.util.concurrent.ForkJoinPool class, 215
java.util.concurrent.Future interface (see Future interface)
java.util.Date class, 175
  converting to java.sql.Date, 192
  converting to LocalDate, 194
  converting to new classes in java.time package, 190
  deprecation in favor of java.util.Calendar, 193
java.util.function package, 25-38
  Consumer interface, implementing, 26-28
  functions, 35-38
    additional Function interfaces, 36
    other examples from standard library using Functions, 38
  Predicates, 31-35
    Predicate interface, methods, 32
  Suppliers, 28-31
    additional Supplier interfaces, 29
    implementing Supplier interface, 28
    other examples from standard library, 31
java.util.Iterable, Consumer as argument in forEach method, 26
java.util.logging.Logger class, 29, 132
  (see also logging)
java.util.Objects class (see Objects class)
java.util.stream.Collectors (see Collectors class)
Jigsaw, modules in, 240-245
JMH (Java Micro-benchmark Harness), 212
Joda-Time library, 175
JPMS (Java Platform Module System), 240
JSON parsing library (Gson), 235
JSR 376, the Java Platform Module System, 240
JVM, modularization in Java 9, 244

## L

lambda expressions, 1, 2-6
  accessing local variable defined outside of, 117-120
    replacing anonymous inner class, 119
  assigning to a variable, 3
  checked exceptions and, 141-143
    handling exception with extracted method, 143
    handling exception with try/catch block, 141
    using generic exception wrapper, 144-145
  compatibility with method signature, 3
  implementing compare method in Comparator, 89

issues with, 115
method references and, 6-10
replacing Callable anonymous inner class implementation, 219
supplying an IntBinaryOperator, 49
using extracted method for exception handling, 138-140
using in Thread constructor, 3
using to invoke constructor reference, 12
lazy streams, 83-85
lines method (BufferedReader), 168
lines method (Files), 166
list method (Files), 169
List<? extends Number>, 273
List<? super Number>, 274
List<?>, 272
as a method argument, 272
List<String> and List<Object>, 271
lists
creating immutable lists with List.of, 247
overloads for List.of, 248
filtering nulls from generic list, 117
List.of method, 109
sort method on List taking a Comparator, 89
unmodifiable, producing prior to Java 8, 108
unmodifiableList method, Collections, 107
LocalDate class
converting java.util.Date to, 190
datesUntil method, 264
iterating on, 264
methods for adding and subtracting values from dates, 180
now method, 176
of method, 177
ofInstant method, 194
parse and format methods, 194
using plus methods on, 181
LocalDateTime class
applying a time zone using at method, 179
atZone method, 200
converting java.util.Calendar to, by generating and parsing timestamp string, 193
converting java.util.Calendar to, using Calendar getter methods, 193
now method, 176
of method, 177
ofInstant method, 193
plus and minus methods, 182
with methods, 183
using TemporalAdjuster, 185
localized date-time formatter, 197
LocalTime class
methods for adding and subtracting values from time, 181
now method, 176
of method, 177
using plus methods on, 181
Logger class
info method, taking Supplier as argument, 29
overloads for all logging methods taking a Supplier, 31
logging
adding to Supplier module (example), 243
module-info.java file for Java Logging API, 244
using overloaded methods in Logger taking a Supplier, 29, 132-134
LongConsumer interface, 27
longs method (Random), 121
LongStream interface, 42, 214
max method, 106
summaryStatistics method, 65


## M


map method (Optional), 158
map method (Stream), 279
flatMap method versus, 75-79
map-filter-reduce process, 46
Map.computeIfAbsent method, using Function, 38
Map.Entry interface, 97-99, 131
comparingByKey and comparingByValue methods, 168, 281
comparingByKey method, 98
creating an immutable Map from entries, 250
new static methods added in Java 8, 97
maps
adding a linear collection to a Map, 94-96
creating an immutable Map, 109
creating immutable Maps, 250
from entries, 250
creating with Collectors.toMap method, 93
creating with groupingBy collector and sorting, 168
flatMapping downstream collector, 258

- iterating over, using forEach method of Map, 131
- Map.of method, 109
- mapping Optionals using Optional.map, 160-163
- new default methods in Map, 122-127
- sorting, 97-99
- unmodifiableMap method, Collections, 107
- using a Map on Optionals, 260

mapToObject method, using to convert primitives to instances of wrapper class, 44
Math.random method, using as a supplier, 28
max and min values, finding, 104-107
- max method on primitive streams, 106
- minBy method, 107
- using BinaryOperator maxBy and minBy methods, 104
- using Collectors.maxBy method, 106
- using Stream.max method, 106

max method (Stream), 277
merge method (Map), 126
method references, 1, 6-10
- constructor references, 10-15
- issues with, 115
- lambda expression equivalents, 9
- lambda expressions and, 7
- syntax, 8
- using a TemporalQuery via, 190

minus methods, 179, 180
- examples of use, 182
- LocalDateTime class, 182

module descriptor, 241
module-info.java file, 241
- updating for Supplier module (example), 244

modules, 240-245
- client module (example), 242
  - defining the module, 243
- modularization in Java, 240
- Supplier module (example), 241
  - adding logging, 243
  - defining the module, 243
  - updating module-info.java to add logging, 244

Month enum, 179
- methods, 179

Moore's Law, 1
multiple bounds (type parameters), 276
multiple inheritance, 18
multiprocessor environments, 1


## N


negate method (Predicate), 137
new keyword, using in method references, 10
noneMatch method (Stream), 73-75
nonNull method (Objects), 116
now method, 176
nullable attributes, wrapping in Optionals, 154
numsUpTo method, 275


## O


Object class method, in functional interface, 17
objects
- using List<Object>, 270
- using List<String> with objects, 271

Objects class, 115-117
- deepEquals method, 117
- isNull and nonNull methods, 116
  - returning a collection and filtering out nulls, 116
- methods, 115
- requireNonNull method, 31
  - overloaded versions, 116

of method, 92
- Collector.of method, overloaded versions, 112
- for date/time classes, 177
- in List, Set, and Map, 109, 247
- Map.of method, 250
- Optional class, 149, 260
- overloaded version in localied date-time formatter, 197
- Set.of method, 250

ofInstant method, 193, 194
ofNullable method (Optional), 149, 260
ofNullable method (Stream), 252
ofPattern method, 196
Optional type, 147-163, 235
- creating an Optional, 148-150
  - immutability and Optionals, 148
  - of, empty, and ofNullable methods, 149
- filter method, using predicates, 35
- flatMap and map methods, 79
- flatMap versus map method, 156-159
- from reduction operations on IntStream, 47
- Java 9 additions, 259-262
  - ifPresentOrElse method, 262
  - or method, 261

stream method, 259
mapping Optionals with map method, 160-163
orElseGet method, taking Supplier as argument, 29
retrieving values from, 150-154
using get method, 150
using ifPresent method, 153
using orElse method, 151
using orElseGet method, 152
returned by Stream.findAny method, 70
using in accessors and mutators, 154-155
OptionalDouble class, 150
OptionalInt class, 150
OptionalLong class, 150
or method (Optional), 261
or method (Predicate), 137
orElse method, 151
orElseGet method, 152
orElseThrow method, 153


## P


palindrome, checking string for
in Java 7, 61
testing the palindrome checker, 62
using Java 8 streams, 61
parallel method, 208
parallel streams, 70
performance and parallelization, 72
using String.concat or String.flatMap method, 81
parallelism and concurrency, 205
CompletableFuture class, 220-225
converting from sequential to parallel streams, 206-209
coordinating CompletableFutures, 225-237
more complex example, 231-237
definitions of the concepts, 205
using Future interface, 217-220
when parallel helps, 209, 215
adding integers in sequential stream, 210
adding integers using parallel stream, 211
summing primitives, 213
timing using JMH, 212
parallelism flag, 215
parallelStream method, 207
parse method
LocalDate class, 194
LocalDateTime class, 193
parsing java.time Date-Time classes, 194-197
partitioning and grouping, 100-101
downstream collectors produced by Collectors partitioningBy and groupingBy methods, 102-104
grouping strings by length, using Collectors.groupingBy, 101
partitioning strings using Collectors.partitionBy, 100
partitioningBy method (Collectors), 64
PaydayAdjuster class (example), 186
PECS (Producer Extends, Consumer Super), 276
peek method (Stream), debugging streams with, 58
performance measurements, 212
Period class, 182, 203
determining Period between two dates, 263
LocalDate.datesUntil method taking a Period, 264
using to get days, months, and years, 203
plus methods, 179, 180
examples of use, 182
LocalDateTime class, 182
LocalTime class, 181
using on LocalDate and LocalTime, 181
using to modify existing Date-Time class instances, 180
predicates, 31-35
adding constants for common use cases, 33
BiPredicate determining wheter Path should be returned, 172
Collectors.partitioningBy method taking a Predicate, 64, 100
composition methods in Predicate interface, 137
determining if any, all, or no stream elements match a Predicate, 73-75
fashioning composite predicates, 33
finding strings that satisfy an arbitrary predicate, 33
Predicate instance as filter in Objects isNull and nonNull methods, 116
Predicate interface, methods, 32
Stream.iterate method taking a Predicate, 253
use by other methods in standard library, 35
using to find strings of given length, 32

prefixes on Date-Time methods, 178
prime number check, 73
    testing, 74
primitive types, using in generic collections, 268
private methods in interfaces, 245-247
    example, 246
    testing private methods, 246
processors, number of, 210
Producer Extends, Consumer Super (see PECS)
properties, 155
pure functions, 1, 130

## R

Random class, static ints, longs, and doubles methods, 121
random numbers, creating stream of within given bounds, 120-122
range and rangeClosed methods, 42
reduce method (Stream)
    check sorting with, 55-57
        sorting string by length, 56
    concatenating streams with, 80
    taking BinaryOperator as argument, 105
reduction operations using reduce, 46-55
    basic reduce implementations, 48
        summing numbers using reduce, 48
region names, finding from UTC offsets, 200-202
replace method (Map), 126
requireNonNull method (Objects), 116
reverseOrder method (Comparator), 168
runAsync method (CompletableFuture), 224, 227
Runnable interface, anonymous inner class implementation, 2
Runtime.getRuntime.availableProcessors, 210

## S

SAM (single abstract method), 2
SecureRandom class, 122
sequential method, 208
sequential streams, 72
    converting parallel stream to sequential, 208
    methods of creating, 207
    switching from parallel to sequential, problems with, 208
sets
    and encounter order, 70
    creating immutable sets, 250
    Set.of method, 109
    unmodifiable, producing prior to Java 8, 108
    unmodifiableSet method, Collections, 107
short-circuiting operations, 71, 83
side effects, Consumer interface and, 130
simple versus easy, 206
single abstract method (SAM), 2
sorted method, 167
sorting
    sorting a Map, using Map.Entry methods, 97-99
    using a Comparator, 87-91
static methods in interfaces, 16, 21-23, 245
    adding, requirements for, 22
    class-level members, using in interfaces, 21
    key points about, 23
    method references to, 7
Stream interface
    flatMap method, 259
    map method, 279
    max method, 277
    new methods in Java 9, 252
        iterate method, using with a Predicate, 253
        ofNullable method, 252
        takeWhile and dropWhile, 254
stream method (Optional), 163, 259
streams, 1, 7, 39-85
    and AutoCloseable, 167
    check sorting using reduce, 55-57
    concatenating, 79-82
    converting a list to and from a stream, 12
    converting from sequential to parallel streams, 206-209
        creating parallel streams with parallelStream method, 207
        creating sequential streams, 207
        using parallel method on existing stream, 208
    converting stream to IntStream and calling sum, 120
    converting strings to and from, 60-63
    converting to a collection, 91-94
    counting elements in, 63-65
    creating, 39-43
        child interfaces of Stream for working with primitives, 42
        from collections, 42

Stream interface, methods, 40
summary of methods used, 43
using Arrays.stream, 40
using Stream.generate, 41
using Stream.iterate, 41
using Stream.of, 40
creating collection from primitive stream, 43-45
creating immutable collections using Collections.collectingAndThen, 108
creating stream of dates, 187
debugging with peek, 57-60
file I/O and, 165
filtering using predicates, 32
findFirst method on Stream, 30
finding first element, 68-73
flatMap versus map methods, 75-79
invoking instance method via class name in method references, 9
issues with, 115
lazy, 83-85
new functionality added in Java 9, 252-255
of random numbers within given bounds, 120-122
parallel, deciding when to use, 209-215
processing using consumers, 27
reduction operation using reduce, 46-55
retrieving a files as a Stream, 169
sorted method, using with a Comparator, 87-91
Stream methods analogous to Collectors methods, 103
stream processing versus collections, 84
Stream.allMatch method, using predicates, 35
Stream.map method, Function argument in, 36
summary statistics for stream of numerical values, 65-68
using anyMatch, allMatch, and noneMatch methods, 73-75
using to process text file contents, 166-169
strings
collecting using a StringBuilder, 53
concatenating from a stream using reduce, 52
converting to and from streams, 60-63
grouping by length, using Collectors.groupingBy, 101
partitioning, using Collectors.partitioningBy, 100
sorting by length, then equal lengths lexicographically, 89
sorting lexicographically, 88
sorting using sorted method on Stream, 88
sorting using Stream.reduce, 56
sum method, 274
summarizingDouble method (Collectors), 67
summary statistics for a stream, 65-68
limitations of summary statistics classes, 68
super keyword
in PECS, 276
using with default methods, 129
using with lower bounded wildcard, 274
using with method references, 10
suppliers, 28-31
additional Supplier interfaces in java.util.function, 29
Collectors.toCollection method taking a Supplier, 93
implementing Supplier interface, 28
Objects.requireNotNull method taking Supplier as argument, 116
Optional.or method taking a Supplier, 261
orElseGet method, taking Supplier as argument, 152
orElseThrow method taking a Supplier, 153
other examples from standard library using Suppliers, 31
overloaded Logger methods taking a Supplier, 132-134
Stream.collect method taking a Supplier, 61
Supplier interface, 111
supplier method in Collectors, 110
support for deferred execution, 29
supplyAsync method (CompletableFuture), 224, 226, 227
System.setProperty method, setting degree of parallelism, 215

## T

takeWhile method (Stream), 254
example, taking ints above 70, 255
TemporalAccessor class, 188
TemporalAdjuster class, 184, 185
methods, 185
test case using static methods, 186
using, 185

writing your own adjuster, 186
TemporalAmount interface, 182
addTo method, 182
TemporalField class, 184
TemporalQueries class
constants defining common queries, 189
using methods from, 189
TemporalQuery class, 185
queryFrom method, 189
using, 188
using a TemporalQuery via a method reference, 190
TemporalUnit interface, 183, 203, 263
between method, 203
terminal operations, 71, 83
collect method on Stream, 91
thenAccept method (CompletableFuture), 226
variations on, 227
thenApply method (CompletableFuture), 226
thenCombine method (CompletableFuture), 229
thenComparing method (Comparator), 90
thenCompose method (CompletableFuture), 229
this, using with method references, 10
Thread class
Runnable as argument, 2
using lambda expression in constructor, 3
thread pool
changing pool size, 215-217
setting common pool size programmatically, 215
setting common pool size using system parameter, 216
using your own ForkJoinPool, 216
running CompletableFuture tasks on separate pool, 227
size of, 210
waiting to finish in common ForkJoinPool, 228
timing operations using JMH, 212
toArray method (Collectors), 93
toCollection method (Collectors), 93
toConcurrentMap method (Collectors), 94
toInstant method, 193
toMap method (Collectors), 93, 95
using with Function.identity method, 95
try-with-resources block, 98, 167
AutoCloseable and streams, 167
using with Files.find method, 173
using with Files.list method, 169
using with Files.walk method, 171
try/catch block, lambda expression with, 139, 142
type erasure in Java, 284
type parameters (in generics), 269

## U

umodifiable methods in Collections, 107
UnaryOperator class, 37, 41
identity method, 96
unchecked exceptions, 139
lambda expression throwing, 139
Unix-based operating systems, epoch definition, 192
unordered streams, 70
until method, 203
UTC, time zone offsets from, 197, 200
utility classes, 22

## V

varargs constructors, 13

## W

walk method (Files), 170
weakly consistent, 170
wildcards, 271
lower bounded, 274
unbounded type, 272
upper bounded, 273
with methods, 179
LocalDateTime class, 183
using TemporalAdjuster, 185

## Y

Year 2038 problem, 192
Year class, now method, 177
YearMonth class, now method, 177

## Z

ZonedDateTime class, 178, 179, 200
converting GregorianCalendar to, 194
converting java.sql.Calendar to, 193
localized date-time formatter, 197
now method, 176
withZoneSameInstant method, 199
ZoneId class, 200

getAvailableZoneIds method, 178, 198
getting region names by ZoneId, 201
now method, 177
of method, transforming string region IDs
    to zone IDs, 198
    types of zone IDs, 178
ZoneOffset class, 198, 200
    getTotalSeconds method, 198
    ofHoursMinutes method, 201
ZoneRules class, 178

## About the Author

**Ken Kousen** is a technical trainer, software developer, and conference speaker specializing in Java and open source topics, including Android, Spring, Hibernate/JPA, Groovy, Grails, and Gradle. He is the author of the O'Reilly book *Gradle Recipes for Android* and the Manning book *Making Java Groovy*. He also has recorded several video courses for O'Reilly, on topics such as Android, Groovy, Gradle, Grails 3, Advanced Java, and the Spring Framework.

He has delivered talks at technical conferences all over the world, including giving the keynote addresses at DevNexus in Atlanta, and the Gr8conf events in Minneapolis, Copenhagen, and New Delhi. In 2013 and 2016, he received the JavaOne Rockstar award.

His academic background includes BS degrees in mechanical engineering and mathematics from MIT, an MA and PhD in aerospace engineering from Princeton, and an MS in computer science from RPI. He is currently President of Kousen IT, Inc., based in Connecticut.

## Colophon

The animal on the cover of *Modern Java Recipes* is the sambar (*Rusa unicolor*), a species of large deer native to southern Asia that tends to congregate in close proximity to rivers. Adults range in height from 40–63″ at the shoulder, and adults tend to weigh 200–700 pounds, with males being significantly larger than females. The sambar is the third-largest extant cervid species, after the elk and moose.

Sambar are crepuscular or nocturnal, and usually live in small groups, the males living alone for most of the year while females form herds of as few as three individuals. Sambar demonstrate greater bipedal capability than other deer species, allowing them to reach higher foliage and mark territory, as well as to intimidate predators. Sambar are unique among deer species in the proficiency with which females protect their young, preferring to defend themselves in water where they can take advantage of their height and powerful swimming capabilities.

The IUCN Red List assigned Vulnerable status to the sambar in 2008. The decline in global population is due to industrial and agricultural development encroaching on their habitat, as well as overhunting—the males' antlers are highly sought-after for display as trophies and for use in traditional medicine. While its population in Asia is declining, the sambar population in New Zealand and Australia has grown steadily since their introduction in the late 19th century, to an extent that they now presents a threat to endangered native plant species.

Many of the animals on O'Reilly covers are endangered; all of them are important to the world. To learn more about how you can help, go to *animals.oreilly.com*.

The cover image is from Lydekker's *The Royal Natural History*. The cover fonts are URW Typewriter and Guardian Sans. The text font is Adobe Minion Pro; the heading font is Adobe Myriad Condensed; and the code font is Dalton Maag's Ubuntu Mono.

CPSIA information can be obtained
at www.ICGtesting.com
Printed in the USA
BVOW04s0442100817
491489BV00008B/3/P